The Search For ENLIGHTENED LEADERSHIP

VOLUME TWO: MANY-TO-MANY COMMUNICATION

A Breakthrough in Social Science

RICHARD J. SPADY & CECIL H. BELL, JR.

VOLUME TWO IN A TRILOGY: THE CIVILIZATION OF TOMORROW

THE SEARCH FOR

ENLIGHTENED LEADERSHIP

VOLUME TWO: MANY-TO-MANY COMMUNICATION

ISBN: 1-881908-19-4

Library of Congress Number: 98-065943

Published by:

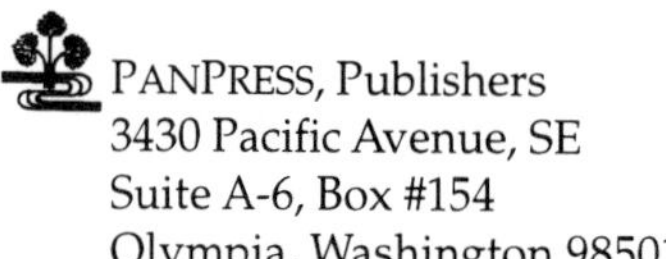
PANPRESS, Publishers
3430 Pacific Avenue, SE
Suite A-6, Box #154
Olympia, Washington 98501

In association with:

Forum Foundation
4426 Second Ave NE
Seattle, Washington 98105-6191
Fax (206) 633-3561
Phone (206) 634-0420

VOLUME TWO IN A TRILOGY: THE CIVILIZATION OF TOMORROW

PRINTED IN THE UNITED STATES OF AMERICA

FRONTISPIECE ONE

SUPERFICIAL ADMINISTRATIVE IDEAS HELD BY MOST LEADERS	ADMINISTRATIVE REALITY
❶ The management process is: Plan, Organize, Motivate, and Control.	❶ The management process is: Diagnose, Theorize, Decide, Accomplish, and Review.
❷ I have the authority here to govern other individuals.	❷ Other individuals here must give me my authority to govern them.
❸ I'm in charge: I have the power	❸ My power is derived from the consent of others.
❹ I can fire anybody, anytime.	❹ Anybody can leave me anytime.
❺ My job is to get the job done.	❺ My job is to help others get the job done.
❻ What we need is knowledge.	❻ What we need is wisdom.
❼ I have to lead everyone— I am the leader.	❼ Everyone is a leader.
❽ I am superior to others.	❽ Others are equal to me.
❾ The basic organizing principle of the human race is A over B over C over D etc. [A>B>C>D...] which is an Authoritarian Hierarchy (Authoritarianism and Totalitarianism); it provides no checks or balances in governance with minimum societal incentives.	❾ The basic organizing principle of the human race is A (Administrators) over B (Bureaucrats) over C (Citizens) over A (Administrators) [A>B>C>A> ...] which is a Participative Heterarchy (Freedom and Democracy); it provides checks and balances in governance with maximum societal incentives.
❿ "Governors" (leaders) have responsibility and authority—ultimately.	❿ "People" (constituents) have responsibility and authority—ultimately.

FRONTISPIECE TWO

SHARING AND BECOMING

A Theological Poem

Ancient man, ancient woman—touching, caressing, thinking, talking.
Ancient family—working, playing, fighting, needing neighbor, clan and
    others.
Ancient community—hungering to talk, to share—
    reaching out to speak and seek the truth. Who am I? Who are we?

On rock walls, in caves, on clay and wood and reed—women, men,
    families, communities
    speaking forth in many ways sharing who they are—seeking more.
And more is happening here in speech and sign and symbol made.
For these are not mere proclamations of our hearts and minds.

Our talk with mate and child and neighbor near and far
    is more than self description and transmittal.
Our speech and sharing in their many forms are invitations to the others—
    humans, creatures, and, yes, The Mighty One!

Our talk is a pleading, an act of faith inviting others—
    the many cosmic bits and pieces—to share with us in word and spirit
    that we might be shaped more fully to the core
    finding order in the midst of trash and dissonance.

So it's been throughout the ages—
    man, woman, child, neighbor, community, nation, nations
    talking, intimate talking, listening, vital hearing—
    sharing symbol, sign, alphabet, words, ideas, dreams, pain, prayer
    and vision.

We who are known as human in every age
have sought to give and receive, to become, to truly be.
It is our nature.
It is our prayer.

This talking, sharing, keeps going on and growing—
stylus, pamphlet, book, telegraph, telephone, cinema, and now computer.
What marvelous means we have today to share who we are,
to receive from others their sensing, dreaming, speaking selves.

My God what potential is in our midst—
screen, keyboard, chip, bit and ram—
means by which we who touch, love, pray, dream and search
can crow aloud our very essence and pick up clearly the speech
and center of the other.

Creator and Shaper of it all, guide us in our speech and sharing,
in our use of symbol, key and screen.
Give us faithfulness in sending and receiving
that the form and shape we become may bear Thy stamp
For Thou Art Word Alive sending, receiving, offering authentic shape,
life and joy!

—THE REV. DR. WILLIAM D. ELLINGTON,
Theologian, The United Methodist Church (Retired),
Co-founder and Board Member, Forum Foundation

Enlightened Leadership:
Depends on an understanding of administrative theory, governance, and human nature.

DEFINITIONS:

THEORY:

"The result of contemplation esp., an analysis of a set of facts in their ideal relations to one another....The general, or abstract principles of any body of facts real or assumed,...science or art."

(Webster's New International Dictionary,
Second Edition, Unabridged)

ADMINISTRATIVE THEORY:

A dynamic which tends to move all organizations, institutions, and societies, universally, toward solving their problems and anticipating or adapting to changes in their internal or external environments.

GOVERNANCE:

The process of governing others.

GOVERNORS:

Persons who govern others, e.g., parents, teachers, principals, superintendents, counselors, ministers, nurses, doctors, CEOs, administrators, managers, supervisors, committee members, board members, military and police officers, bureaucrats, public officials and the like.

Dedication

This book is dedicated to our wives and families.

Dick—

To Lou and our children John, Jim, Walt, Carol and Doug and our grandchildren Alex, Jasmine, Saul, Chad and Danielle; And in memory of my mother Elsie Schmeer;

Cecil—

To Dianne;

And to our former colleague, Dr. Stuart C. Dodd (1900-1975).

This book is also dedicated to those citizens of the world who share a common quest with us to work toward a civilization that we and our posterity can love throughout our future history together on this wonderful planet.

Richard J. Spady & Cecil H. Bell, Jr.

Acknowledgments

This book is based on pure and applied research in both social science and administrative theory that has been conducted since 1970 by the Forum Foundation, a Washington State non-profit educational research corporation, and scholars from the University of Washington in sociology and business administration.

Research in social science and administrative theory requires two things: first, people, and second, organizations. The Forum Foundation conducted the research primarily in the greater Seattle area. School, civic, and religious groups provided the *arena* of people and organizations for the studies. The research is based on collective experiences of (1) over fifty years in leadership positions as a practitioner in small and big organizations, bureaucratic and non-bureaucratic, including military, fraternal, civic, church, and self-employment as a partner in a successful Seattle business firm since 1954 (Richard J. Spady) and (2) scholarship in both the fields of social science (Stuart C. Dodd) and management and organization (Cecil H. Bell, Jr.).

The research has been conducted nearly full-time since 1970 by Richard J. Spady, president of the Forum Foundation, a self-employed Seattle businessman since 1954 (CEO, Dick's Drive-In Restaurants), and a student and practitioner of administrative theory. He was a graduate student in Business Administration concentrating in the field of administrative theory and organizational behavior at the University of Washington from 1968-1970. He studied under the tutelage of Dr. Cecil H. Bell, Jr. and worked with Dr. Stuart C. Dodd, Professor-Emeritus of Sociology at the University of Washington and an acknowledged pioneer in research in social science. He served on the volunteer staff of the Church Council of Greater Seattle, a consortium of over 300 local churches and 17 regional judicatories, with the portfolio of "Futures Research" from 1971 to 1990. We defined "Futures Research" not as forecasting, but rather as the search for ways to influence the sociological and technological future. It was more a process of "forthtelling." Mr. Spady was a co-founder of the Bellevue, Washington Overlake Rotary Club in 1980 and is now a Senior Active (Classification: Futures Research). Mr. Spady received the "Earl Award" as "Religious Futurist of the Year 1993" from the World Network of Religious Futurists.

In 1970 Mr. Spady contracted with the University of Washington Computer Center to write the first Fast Forum® "groupware/socialware" computer program which he designed as a theoretician. It has been updated and revised six times to date at the University of Washington and is currently on the Macintosh and in the process of revision to the PC computer.

Dr. Dodd was 20 years at the American University in Beirut, Lebanon. He was then appointed to the University of Washington in Seattle as a Walker-Ames Professor for a year, but he stayed nearly thirty years including 14 years as head of the Washington State Public Opinion Laboratory at the University. He was a member of the board of directors of the Forum Foundation the last few years before his death in 1975 and did much to focus the foundation's research.

Dr. Bell is an Associate Professor in the Department of Management and Organization in the School of Business Administration at the University of Washington and most recently completed service as chair of the Dept. of Management and Organization. He is co-author with Wendell French of the textbook *Organization Development* and is now on sabbatical to complete the sixth edition with Prentice-Hall, publishers. Dr. Bell was a co-founder and has been vice-president of the Forum Foundation since its start in 1970.

Dr. Arthur W. Combs, whose research contribution in defining the "Helping Professions" we so gratefully acknowledge, is recognized nationally as a pre-eminent educator and perceptual psychologist who has been active in research with the "helping professions" for over thirty years. He has been primarily concerned with the question: What makes a good or poor teacher, counselor, priest and so forth? He was a contributor (with Earl Kelly, Carl Rogers, and Abraham Maslow) and also the editor of the classic and best-selling 1962 yearbook, *Perceiving, Behaving, Becoming* of the Association for Supervision and Curriculum Development, National Education Association.

Nearly all of us can reach back in memory to a teacher who had a profound impact on our own learning. Richard Spady is grateful to and wishes to acknowledge the contribution to this book of the scholarship of Dr. Theodore Barnowe, Professor of Administrative Theory and Organizational Behavior in the Graduate School of Business Administration of the University of Washington in Seattle. He was a gifted teacher who filled his students with his own enthusiasm for the potential of the discipline to make important contributions to the successful functioning of organizations. In an advanced seminar class in management theory in the spring of 1970, he asked his students to write a term paper with the words, "Just take anything in management theory and make it sound rational." It was from this broad challenge in this creative classroom setting together with the enthusiasm and support provided by Dr. Barnowe that the general administrative theories presented in this book were first conceived in a rudimentary fashion.

Thus, the basic general theories of administration advocated here were worked out in a classroom setting in administrative theory and organizational behavior in the spring of 1970 in the Graduate School of Business Administration at the University of Washington by Richard Spady while he was a student. Shortly afterward, they were cross-fertilized with the social theories and insights of Dr. Dodd. We were indeed fortunate to be able to know and work with him. He was a pioneer in sociology and social science and a genius, in our opinion, but more than that he was just a wonderful human being who was warm, friendly, approachable, and who treated everyone with dignity and respect.

The research grants and financial support received by the Forum Foundation since 1970 have been provided essentially from the business partnership interest of Richard Spady. The contribution and support of the many people who have been customers, employees, business associates, and suppliers of Dick's Drive-In Restaurants in Seattle since 1954 are gratefully acknowledged. The underwriting of the studies and research of the Forum Foundation through these many years could never have been accomplished without them. Thank you all!

Thanks is given also to the members of the Forum Foundation board of directors and their spouses who have volunteered their time through many years to interact with our ideas and papers and guide us through the labyrinth of research in social science. Co-founder, Dr. Cecil H. Bell, Jr., Vice-President; The Rev. Dr. William B. Cate (President-Director of the Church Council of Greater Seattle 1970-1990 and now Emeritus and Ph.D. in the field of Social Ethics and a retired United Methodist minister); his wife, Jan Cate (her master's field is in Values Education); Co-founder, The Rev. Dr. William D. Ellington, Ph.D., Theology, a retired United Methodist minister and a former Director of Evangelism Ministries, General Board of Discipleship (1978-82), The United Methodist Church, faculty member of Fuller Theological School and retired Associate Pastor of the large, Central United Protestant Church, Richland, Washington; The Rev. Wallace Bristol, board member emeritus, (past Episcopal Archdeacon of Seattle and currently Associate Pastor, St. Margaret's Episcopal Church, Bellevue, WA); Co-founder, John F. Strickler Jr. (former Director of Administration, Boeing Aerospace Division); Co-founder, Judge Raymond Royal (board member emeritus); Jim Spady (Executive Vice President and attorney) and his wife Fawn (marketing); and John Spady (computer science).

Finally, we wish to acknowledge the invaluable assistance of The Rev. Dr. Richard S. Kirby, Ph. D. Theology, Executive Director, *Stuart C. Dodd Institute for Social Innovation* (organized in May, 1997); International Chair and Director of the Seattle Research Center of the *World Network of Religious Futurists;* Director of Administration, International Mensa, London, 1990-1992. He is currently on the faculty of the University of Washington, School of Business Administration teaching Organization and Environment. Dr. Kirby has served as editor of both Volume One and this Volume Two of the trilogy.

And I, Cecil Bell, wish to acknowledge that this book is Dick Spady's product. The ideas are his; the words are his. His creative genius developed the theories and the Fast Forum® technique. I "went along for the ride" because I was convinced his ideas and their implications were important and sound. When Dick started writing this book in 1985, he asked me to be a co-author even though he would do most of the work. My contributions were primarily those of providing support and discussing his ideas. Again, I "went along for the ride" because journeys with Dick Spady are high adventure. [CHB]

And I, Dick Spady, wish to acknowledge Cecil Bell, who as my teacher first used the word "Zeitgeist" in a lecture in 1968 which, it turns out, subsequently focused my life's study. I also acknowledge him as my advisor and a rigorous scholar who was comfortable and secure enough in his own scholarship that when I asked him for research advice early on in our relationship, he replied, "I think the best thing I can do for you is stay out of your way." The University of Washington and Cecil Bell provided an ideal learning climate for me as a student; I am eternally grateful. [RJS]

RICHARD J. SPADY
CECIL H. BELL, JR.

Table of Contents

3 FRONTISPIECE ONE / *Superficial Ideas Held by Most Leaders*

4 FRONTISPIECE TWO / *Sharing & Becoming, A Theological Poem*

6 DEFINITIONS

7 DEDICATION

9 ACKNOWLEDGMENTS

17 PREFACE

- 18 *The Problem—Lack of Effective Management and Governance*
- 21 *The Achilles' Heel of Democracy*

25 TOWARD THE SOLUTION—POINTERS FROM HISTORY

MANY-TO-MANY COMMUNICATION—*Breakthrough in Social Science*

- 29 *Introduction*
- 34 *The Fast Forum® Technique*
- 35 *Theoretical Foundations*
- 36 *How It Works*
- 41 *Management versus Leadership Forums*

43 PART ONE—
PROPOSED GROUPWARE/SOCIALWARE APPLICATION MODELS

- 45 *1. The Community Forum (For governments and citizens)*
- 57 *2. Psycho-Social Education (About democracy in schools)*
- 67 *3. The Spiritual Forum (For religious organizations)*
- 75 *4. "How to Make Ideas Count" (Proposal for "State of the Union" address and the youth of America)*
- 85 *5. "Time to Talk" (President Clinton's Initiative on Race)*
- 87 *6. Census Forum™ and Time and Talent Survey™ (For churches and organizations)*
- 97 *7. QUEST Forum™ (For organizations)*
- 105 *8. PLAN Forum® (For organizations)*
- 109 *9. The National Debate Opinionnaire® Network (For high school debaters)*
- 111 *10. The Therapeutic Forum*

113 *11. The Fraternal Forum*

12. "Communicate for Peace"

(Rotary International "Idea Bank" proposal)

115 *13. Moving Toward The Future!*

PART TWO—THE FOUR FOUNDATIONS OF THE FAST FORUM® TECHNIQUE

121 *1. Social Resolving Power*

122 *2. The Theory of Learning*

124 *3. Mainstreaming*

125 *4. The Polarization Consensus-Rating*

OTHER FUNDAMENTALS OF THE FAST FORUM® TECHNIQUE

143 *An Opinionnaire®*

144 *Abstention and Objection to the Question*

146 *"Day-in-the-Sun"*

THE FORMAL CLAUSES

147 *The Disclaimer Clause*

148 *The Philosophy Clause*

149 *The Trailer Clause*

149 *The Certification Clause*

151 *Machine Scannable Response Sheet (Form K)*

153 *The Viewspaper®*

153 *Tabulation of Data*

APPENDICES

159 *A. General Administrative Theories (A 19–page Condensation of* The Search for ENLIGHTENED LEADERSHIP, Volume 1: Applying New Administrative Theory, *160 pages, 1996, Spady and Bell)*

178 *B. Letter from Mr. Oleg Yashenko, Principal, Secondary School No 32, Kursk, Russia*

179 *C. A Psycho-Social Proposal For Russia—"New Administrative Theory and Its Meaning for Democracy" a paper presented May 30, 1997, Russia's Open University, Dr. Boris Bim-Bad, President, Russian Academy of Education, Moscow, Russia*

194 *D. Example of Forum Foundation Councilor™ Reproducible Response Sheet and Machine-Scannable Sheet*
196 *E. The Community Forum™ (Letter proposals to Seattle Mayor, Paul Schell)*
202 *F. Example of Viewspaper®—Authority (Oct. 23, 1992) What United Methodists Believe,)*
204 *G. Example of Viewspaper®—Evaluation (Mar. 13, 1994) What United Methodists Believe)*
206 *H. Example of "Everywoman's Delegation" Northwest, Women's International Conf., Beijing, China; Economic Development Opinionnaire, Report, and Viewspaper®*
208 *I. Washington State Senate Resolution 1993-8636*
209 *J. Forum Foundation Fact Sheet and WWW Homepage*
214 *K. Stuart C. Dodd Institute for Social Innovation Fact Sheet*
216 *L. Bibliography*
216 *M. Copyright Information*
217 *N. Instructions to Order Books*
218 *O. Biographies*
220 *P. Endorsements*
221 *Q. Petition to Pacific Northwest Annual Conference, The United Methodist Church, Signed April 12, 1998 (Easter)*
224 *R. Pointers from History (Dodd and Bronowski)*

Preface

This is the continuing story of a quest of the human race. It started in a cave thousands of years ago when man and woman together squinted out at the stars from beneath craggy and furrowed brows and first wondered. It was then that wisps of thought stirred deeply within the God-given soul, distilled from eons of earlier wonder, finally emerged in a swirl of consciousness and burst into history's most violent storm. It is a storm that still rages today. It is the storm within the mind eternal that first asked and has continued to ask in every generation since—Who am I? Where did I come from? Where do I fit in? What is my role in life? Where am I going?

These are spiritual questions that reach far beyond the known into the unknown. Indeed, these questions of an individual's "identity" may be among the most important religious questions of the millennium. From that earliest cave dwelling, man and woman together first organized themselves *naturally* into the basic and most enduring of all human leadership institutions—the family. Instinctively they knew that together, through their "organization," they could achieve more than either could ever do alone, for *organizations are synergistic and can amplify human effort.* It was then that humankind asked not only "Where am I going?" but asked what is perhaps the organizational question of the millennium: "*How* can I get there?" So it all began—*social innovation and civilization building*—the organizational and societal quest of people working together to improve their own future and that of the human race.

It is still so today. People create organizations and institutions to collaborate toward and accomplish their objectives together. Accordingly, every organization is involved in the administrative process. Humankind has learned much about the dynamics of administration in the last few decades just as it has learned much in psychology, sociology, education, and especially the physical sciences where the greatest strides have been made. Unfortunately, most managers of organizations and institutions today, public and private, are still using management theories that are both erroneous and outdated. Leaders often create as many "human" problems through their management styles as they solve in their preoccupation with physical, social, economic, political, and other problems.

In every human heart there lies the hope of finding, or contributing to, true civilization. Yet few people, even academic social scientists and politicians, have tried to define or study civilization. As the 21st century and Third Millennium approach, there is a great need for leaders, and indeed for all citizens, to understand civilization well enough to know its history, to define it, and to share in its creation.

In the three volumes making up this trilogy on the Civilization of Tomorrow, we offer materials for a simple but formal *theory of civilization* and the skills and data of social science required to enable *civilization building* to be accomplished by all. This theory is based on our work in Seattle, Washington where the Forum Foundation has conducted social science research concentrating on Many-To-Many communication since 1970.

The link between the individual person and the building of a civilization is *the life of the citizen.* A person's civic identity is one of the deepest components of human nature. In this trilogy we provide a new set of skills for the persons of tomorrow—*the citizens of the future*—vital energy for the twenty-first century State.

The Problem—Lack of Effective Management and Governance

The problem is lack of effective management and governance, not only in governments at all levels everywhere in the world, but also in private organizations, corporations, churches, civic groups, and parenting.

Harvard Professor Elton Mayo, sometimes called the "father of the human relations movement," wrote in the preface of the classic *Management and the Worker* by Roethlisberger and Dixon in 1939:

> The art of human collaboration seems to have disappeared during two centuries of quite remarkable material progress. The various nations seem to have lost all capacity for interna-

> tional cooperation in the necessary tasks of civilization. The internal condition of the nation is not greatly better; it seems that only a threat from without, an unmistakable emergency, can momentarily quiet the struggle of rival groups....How can humanity's capacity of spontaneous cooperation be restored? It is in this area that leadership is most required, a leadership that has nothing to do with political 'isms' or eloquent speeches. What is wanted is knowledge, *a type of knowledge* that has escaped us in two hundred years of prosperous development. *How* to substitute human responsibility for futile strife and hatreds (emphasis added). [1]

This is a book about the art of human collaboration. Notice that it was not just more "knowledge" for which Mayo was searching, but rather a new type of knowledge that we have somehow missed. It is our belief that this new type of knowledge has been found in the new administrative theories presented in volume one and the new feedback technology of Many-To-Many communications and the Fast Forum® technique presented in this second volume of this trilogy.

Organizations, institutions, and governments have been obsessed with "Life and Liberty" issues for the past two hundred years of the United States' existence and rightly so. Today leaders are beginning to perceive that there is another kind of issue among people everywhere that must be dealt with at some level; this is one that concerns the identity questions of individuals—Who am I? What is my role in life? Where do I fit in? It all has something to do with the feelings, beliefs, attitudes, opinions, and values of people. If organizations, institutions, and governments do not relate to these concerns in a positive manner, those dynamics are reflected back by constituents to their leaders as *alienation*. However, if leaders relate in a positive manner to new cultural dynamics that are emerging everywhere in the world, they are "mirrored back" as *happiness*. And happiness is one of the fundamental reasons we form all governments—for Life, Liberty, and the Pursuit of Happiness.[2] These same imperatives apply to state, county, municipal,

---

[1] *Roethlisberger and Dickson, Management and the Worker, Harvard University Press, 1939.*
[2] *Thomas Jefferson, Declaration of Independence, 1776.*

and to private organizations in society. And as a part of the human rights of all people, they also apply to other governments in the world.

Governments are not charged with providing their citizens with all the amenities of life they feel they need to make them happy. Governments are charged, however, with enabling their citizens to *pursue their own happiness*—primarily through the setting of their own public agenda and pursuing a meaningful citizen dialogue within it that allows every citizen to be responsible. Every citizen must have the opportunity to make a contribution as a "civilization builder" by contributing his or her own thinking, the most precious and distinctive of our human qualities as a race. The opportunity must be available even if the citizen chooses not to take advantage of it.

A major question faced by all organizations, institutions, governments and their leaders today is, *how* can we do it? How can we enable organizational and institutional constituents and citizens to participate meaningfully in the decisions that affect their public and private lives to increase organizational and societal effectiveness? Our culture has evolved to a level that makes it very difficult for the average citizen to participate responsibly. For the most part the individual citizen and organizational member has not been enabled by leaders to participate within the individual's time and energy levels. We need to create new organizational, institutional, and societal contexts and processes in which people can be responsible within their time and energy levels. Citizen participation in the public sector generally has been at the convenience of leaders with the expectation that the primary responsibility of the citizen is to elect representatives periodically. In many private organizations, especially business organizations, enablement by leaders of participation by members in organizational planning and problem-solving is frequently almost nil. In other organizations, such as civic and church groups, it is frequently minimal. This condition exists because of the lack of administrative theories which would encourage new approaches to member participation and, equally important, because of the lack of societal and organizational technological processes actually able to do it.

THE ACHILLES' HEEL OF DEMOCRACY

The essence of more than twenty-five years of research in pure and applied social science in the Forum Foundation is the realization: *Big meetings at often remote distances are the Achilles' heel of the democratic process which undergirds our society, public and private.* Sports events, concerts, shows, and meetings where people are engaged in ritual and ceremony are not a problem. But most big meetings intended for participation of members are a problem. People don't have the time and energy to go to big meetings—especially at remote distances. The logistics at such meetings are such that only a few people can talk and most people can only listen. Emotions rise high often and frequently people and leaders become exhausted just from the cumbersome efforts to communicate to gain consensus. For example, efforts to pass controversial resolutions using Robert's Rules of Order are often highly frustrating experiences. People then drop out of such meetings, and later others remark, "Look at the apathy among the people, they are not coming to our meetings." A popular complaint among leaders nearly everywhere today is, "People are apathetic!"

Our analysis indicates that a better diagnosis is that people simply get exhausted from previous efforts to get their ideas through. They remember their frustration and exhaustion at big meetings in trying to be heard. They reach a point where they say, "Going to these meetings is not worth my time and effort," so they drop out. But that's not apathy. When the issues are critical enough, they will be there, much to the chagrin of leaders who do not understand that kind of behavior.

Freedom of speech, freedom of the press, and the right of the people to peaceably assemble are hollow rights *if people perceive (and perception is reality) that organization, institution, and government processes are such that they cannot be heard.* Good and dedicated people give indications of this every day when they choose to march in the street or otherwise demonstrate to attract attention to a perceived injustice or worthy cause rather than use the normal institutional representative processes. There is a grave danger in the use of such dramatic, confrontational, and "show biz" techniques to access the public agenda if carried to extremes. A backlash and public cry for "law and order" may result in a call for even greater authoritarianism in a society than currently exists. In an extreme case the backlash could lead to the suppression of freedom and human rights through totalitarianism by the state—*the ultimate enemy of democracy and individual freedoms.*

Under dictatorships, private ownership and the free enterprise system are jeopardized as is the genius concept of the "entrepreneur" when economic freedoms (based upon the political freedom of the individual) can be coerced by the sheer power of the state as in communism and fascism. Rather, it is imperative that the entrepreneur makes his or her own economic decisions for his or her own welfare while at the same time improving the welfare of the society of which the individual is a part. The free enterprise system with its unique ability to provide individual incentives, cannot exist to its full potential in any kind of a centralized totalitarian system of control. Free enterprise flourishes best in a democracy. A democracy uniquely decentralizes economic decision-making to the individual at the grassroots level, rather than trying to direct everything through a centralized and often inefficient and cumbersome hierarchical bureaucracy. Therefore, as citizens we must all devote some of our time and energy to helping democratic processes in society function better.

The discovery of new, vital feedback communication techniques applicable in all human groups, communities, organizations, institutions, and societies in the world today holds the key to the release of a fabulous amount of human creativity. This social energy is currently being wasted by most organizations, institutions, and nations because they have adopted inefficient management styles of "control" which often repress rather than encourage human creativity.

The following pages describe a set of ten general administrative theories which we believe are applicable in all human organizations. It has not been done before in quite this way. We have done our best, as practitioners and scholars, to lift up these new theories to help create new organizational and societal contexts for creative leaders and their constituencies. "But we are all babies at creating context—and babies don't always get it right," says scientist Eldon Byrd. "But it is only in getting it wrong that we can ever hope to get it right."[3]

---

[3] *Eldon Byrd, scientist, in an address titled "The Transformation of Societal Institutions" given at a session of the "First Global Conference on the Future" and General Assembly of the World Future Society, Toronto, Canada, July, 1980.*

Up to now, no one has yet provided a comprehensive set of administrative theories able to conceptualize the reality of administering human affairs, in most if not all our contexts, as we navigate individually and corporately through life (see bibliography of readings in the appendix). Perhaps governance will always remain an art and not a science, but we should at least try to identify those principles and dynamics which can be understood and applied by every leader as well as by every individual who is interested and has the capacity and makes the effort to understand. Therefore, as theoreticians, we believe that the administrative theories and concepts published in Volume 1 of this trilogy, *The Civilization of Tomorrow*, met the criteria that we have been guided by in our search. We hope you find them helpful in your similar quest.

We hope also that our collective works will help inform the elusive quest of humanity as it moves from barbarian atrocities and wars of the past and present to a future "civilization." At least that is our intent. Civilization will exist when humankind finally learns how to collaborate through the exercise of individual, societal, economic, religious, and political responsibilities to achieve organizational and institutional objectives in local, regional, state, national, and international arenas, both public and private, governmental and non-governmental.

The way is dimly seen, but the human race is making progress toward a truly spiritual civilization. Perhaps someday others will look back and reflect that a new beginning in social technology started here. We are engaged in the study of a process of civilization building. Our research includes administrative theory and new "groupware" and "socialware" Many-To-Many feedback communication techniques to help govern and administer organizational and societal affairs in the world. New wineskins for new wine: new social technologies *for a new civilization.*

We are hopeful.

TOWARD THE SOLUTION— POINTERS FROM HISTORY

Man is a being in search of meaning.
— Plato.

The minds of men are mirrors to one another....Philosophy is common sense, methodized, and collected....The end of all moral speculations is to teach us our duty.
— David Hume, 18th century Scottish philosopher.

As human systems and organizations grow ever larger, more complex, and more impersonal—in our schools, in our communities, in our churches, in our governments, and in our industries and commerce—the individual shrinks toward facelessness, hopelessness, powerlessness, and frustration.
— Dr. Stuart C. Dodd, Professor-Emeritus Sociology, University of Washington, "Citizen Counselor Proposal," *Seattle Times,* November 10, 1974.

It is not essential that everyone participate....The essence...is that participation should be an available option.
— John W. Gardner, Godkin Lectures, Harvard University, reported in Christian Science Monitor, April 16, 1969.

Science is the world of what is. Ethics is the world of what ought to be....(There are those who are) in love with the aristocracy of the intellect. And that is a belief which can only destroy the civilization that we know. If we are anything, we must be a democracy of the intellect. We must not perish by the distance between people and government, between people and power....
— Dr. Jacob Bronowski, *The Ascent of Man,* p. 435, 1973, Award Winning Book and TV series.

I would urge all of us as futurists...to devote some of our energies to finding new ways to destandardize, deconcentrate, descale, delimit, and democratize *planning.* (emphasis added)

— Alvin Toffler; Closing address, 2nd General Assembly, World Future Society, Washington, DC, June 1975.

No society can function as a society unless it gives the individual member social status *and* function, *and unless the decisive social power is* legitimate *power. "Status, function, legitimacy: (are) the essentials of the new order."* (emphasis added by Tarrant)

— Peter Drucker in *DRUCKER, The Man Who Invented The Corporate Society* by John J. Tarrant, p. 50, Warner Books, 1976.

Our children long for realistic maps of a future they can be proud of. Where are the cartographers of human purpose?

— Dr. Carl Sagan, prominent astronomer and scientist, "People Digest," *Dayton Daily News* and *Journal Herald,* page 29, November 21, 1987.

Many-to-Many Communication

A Breakthrough in Social Science

Introduction

"WE THE PEOPLE" begins the *preamble* of both the United States Declaration of Independence and the United Nations Charter!

The preamble to these historic documents is history's clue to the ultimate source of power and authority in all organizations and institutions, public and private *everywhere in the world!*

It is our original civic values—the principles of freedom, equality, democracy and justice embodied in the Declaration of Independence, the Constitution and the Bill of Rights that brings us together as a people and enable community enhancement.[4]

What is the responsibility of all citizens in their public churches, neighborhoods, communities, regions, cities, counties, states, and governments and in their private organizations and workplaces today? *It is to discover and communicate their vision of the common good!*[5A] When people can communicate their vision coherently and with growing consensus, then the vision itself begins to steer society toward that objective *naturally.*[5B]

But the question leaders and constituents all face together today is: *how* can that be done? How can citizens and constituents be enabled to communicate with each other and with their leaders constructively? Our historical and cultural reliance on big meetings, which are often at remote distances for people, precludes such communication. Big meetings hold the seeds of their own destruction. Just about the time a leader thinks one has a good program growing, the program usually runs out of space, facilities, parking, staff support,

---

[4] *Dr. Ed Schwartz, "Rediscovering Our Civic Values," an address given at the Good City Luncheon by the Center for Ethical Leadership, Seattle University, Seattle, Washington, March 24, 1998. Dr. Schwartz is the founder and director of the Institute for the Study of Civic Values in Philadelphia. He is a former City Councilman there and was director of the city's Office of Housing and Community Development in which he oversaw the rehabilitation of 4,000 homes for...residents.*

[5A] *Benjamin B. Ferencz, Planethood, 1988, Coos Bay, Oregon: Vision Books, Page 23, PASSIM.*

[5B] *See The Search For ENLIGHTENED LEADERSHIP, Volume 1: Applying New Administrative Theory (1996) Spady and Bell, Theory 10: The Natural Factors of Governance, Administration and Communication (A New Paradigm Toward Civilization Building) Page 91.*

leadership support, or money. But understanding the problem is the first step toward solving it and can lead us to the solution.

Today we have "One-to-One Communication" in both theory and practice. One person writes a letter to another and mails it, or one person composes a message and transmits it electronically via e-mail to one or many persons simultaneously. The world is moving, though, toward "Many-To-Many (MTM) Communication" where many people can communicate their ideas to others, respond to the ideas of others, and understand the values of others and their leaders in a process that increases their own self-awareness about the world around them, i.e., the process itself is inherently good for the individual involved.

> What is occurring is a process—a doing, specifically a process interrelating a person and his (or her) world, bringing new meaning into the human situation. [6]

Sara Baase, author, writes "It is by now almost a cliché to say that the Internet lets us all be publishers. We do not need expensive printing presses. We need only a computer and a modem. Any business, organization, or individual can send comments to news groups and bulletin boards or set up a home page on the World Wide Web. We can "publish" whatever we wish; it is available to be read by anyone who chooses. The dramatic change brought about by computer communications is described by Mike Godwin, an attorney with the Electronic Frontier Foundation."

> It (computer communications) is a medium far different from the telephone, which is only one-to-one medium, ill-suited for reaching large numbers of people. It is a medium far different from the newspaper or TV station, which are one-to-many medium, ill-suited for feedback from the audience. For the first time in history, we have a many-to-many medium, in which you don't have to be rich to have access, and in which you don't have to win the approval of an editor or publisher to speak your mind. Usenet and the Internet, as part of this new medium, hold the promise of guaranteeing, for the first time in history, that the First Amendment's protection of freedom of

[6] *Howard Ellis and Ted McEachern, Reflections on Youth Evangelism, General Boards of Evangelism and Education, The Methodist Church, (1959).*

the press means as much to each individual as it does to Time Warner, or to Gannett, or to the New York Times. [7]

Probably the most sophisticated examples of MTM communication is the Delphi technique which was invented at the Rand Corporation following World War II. The problem was how to make economic administrative decisions on the development of nuclear energy without disrupting the work of the physicists to require their attendance at big meetings at remote distances. There were lots of conflicting opinions among all the expert scientists, and it was very confusing for the government administrators, who had to make the final administrative and technical decisions, to allocate substantial funds. The process was burdensome and expensive. The Rand Corporation hit on the idea to prepare a series of surveys sent to each scientist for a response after a suitable window period. Travel would be avoided and, the process would not interfere with the scientists' regular duties, and overall the process would be significantly lower in costs. The government would evaluate the results statistically, determine the central tendencies, and based on this information, prepare a second iteration of questions—and a third. Then on the basis of this final information, administrative decisions would be made, funds would be provided, and the project of nuclear energy advanced.

The next most sophisticated example of MTM communication is the use of random-sample questionnaires to conduct surveys among people using statistical theory which is based on mathematical theory. This is in common use everywhere today.

The Fast Forum® technique, however, which is being explained in this book, is new and is a part of Many-To-Many communication. It exists at a degree of complexity below the Delphi technique and below typical random-sample polling, but above the use of letter-writing, telephoning, and big meetings. It makes the same contribution, however, to solving system-wide problems as do letter writing, telephoning, and big meetings, but it does it more efficiently, economically, and with greater sensitivity to the human

[7] A Gift of Fire—Social, Legal, and Ethical Issues in Computing *(1997), Sara Baase, Page 200, Prentice Hall publisher. The original footnote given for this quote is: "From a speech by Mike Godwin at Carnegie Mellon University, November 1994, quoted with permission. (The speech is excerpted, including part of the quotation used here in Mike Godwin, "alt.sex.academic.freedom," Wired, February 1995, Page 72.)*

nuances of participants as they paint their tapestry of human values in the visioning process entailed in "civilization building."

Furthermore, the Fast Forum® technique deals only with "statistical universes," not with random samples, e.g., it deals with the whole classroom, the whole school, the whole school district; a whole neighborhood, a region, a city, a county, a state, or a nation; or a section, a department, or an organization as a whole; an association of organizations and the like. It does not deal with random samples. Different rules apply.

People, today, are inundated with information that comes down to them from newspapers, television, radio, magazines, reports, lectures, speeches, sermons etc. These methods of communication are all very important in their own right, but they are all primarily one-way, *downward*, communication systems. Today, with our far larger, diverse and mobile population than was present at the start of our nation, it is all people can do in their organizations and institutions, public and private, to get one simple idea across and upward. *This "social logjam" is devitalizing our society and others in the world at enormous social and economic costs for all organizations and institutions functioning within them.*

> *We are facing an institutional dysfunctioning of the highest order.*
> —Professor David Webb, C-Span

An inability of people to communicate ideas and opinions across and upward lies at the heart of the problem. Freedom of speech, freedom of the press, freedom to peaceably assemble *are hollow rights* if, as a practical matter, people feel unable to be *heard* in their organizations and institutions. There is evidence of this inability to communicate when people plan demonstrations for public media purposes rather than try to communicate their interests and concerns with their political, community, school, and other leader/representatives through meetings, letters, public hearings and other more traditional ways of expressing themselves as citizens.

People reach society through their organizations and institutions, i.e., through governments, politics, economics, education, the church—*and vice versa.* Therefore, the relationships of people in these organizations and institutions with each other and with their leaders and representatives are of vital importance in the administration of a world of increasing instability and tension. This is the domain of administrative theory and new MTM communication theories and technologies.

Most communication is in the subjective, text format. MTM communication theory and computer technology permit many people in an organization or institution to communicate their own values and opinions to themselves as well as to parent, teacher, school, church, business, community, and government establishments of the values and opinions in which they believe.

When many people try to communicate with each other and their leaders primarily in the traditional modes of letter-writing, telephoning, and big meetings, i.e., the *subjective* mode, there is usually "information overload." Leaders with large constituencies can seldom even read their voluminous correspondence let alone synthesize and measure adequately its meaning. Many-To-Many communication, on the other hand uses the *objective* mode. It does not break down simply because large numbers of people participate since it uses mass means of communication, e.g., surveys, small groups, computers and optical scanners to tabulate data. In fact with people responding *objectively* (i.e., yes/no/abstain, multiple-choice, and value-scale questions), as more people participate, the data generated never gets bigger—*it just gets better.* MTM communication allows all members who are interested to participate within their time and energy levels. Furthermore, people can participate in small groups, e.g., four to twelve persons, at convenient times and places, e.g., their homes or businesses. *These are places where people already are*—they don't have to go someplace to attend a big meeting at often remote distances.

While the data generated does not tell anyone what is "right" or "wrong," it does tell what the people who are participating *perceive* is right or wrong. *Natural* organizational dynamics then occur between leaders and constituents which tend to move the organization toward solving its problems and anticipating or adapting to changes in its internal or external environments as effected by administrative theory.[8]

---

[8] See The Search for ENLIGHTENED LEADERSHIP, Volume 1: Applying New Administrative Theory (1996, 160 pages in full detail). A condensation of that book is printed in the front of the Appendix of this book. The condensation was published in MAGISTER No. 1, 1998, pages 80-89, a bi-monthly International Psychological-Education Journal published in Moscow, Russia.

Since 1976 the Forum Foundation has been engaged in the development of research models to fine-tune and test our administrative theories and the Many-To-Many computer communication technology that has derived from our research. The application models are presented in their general concepts next in this book with specific models and examples listed or in the appendix. These are models and examples of the kind of feedback communication that we consider essential in organizations and institutions in the future.

MANY-TO-MANY COMMUNICATION

THE FAST FORUM® TECHNIQUE

"Too many of our scholars have...pointed to the ills and then left us without prescriptions," writes author Irving J. Lee. "In short, we have needs of methods—simple, teachable, and usable—by which to break through the conventionalized, stiffly resistant, and confusing habits of evaluation."

The Fast Forum® is a new groupware technique and methodology that in our organizations, institutions, and societies in the world can:

- restore meaningful and constructive dialogue in organizations and society
- enable people to learn and grow in their abilities through the use of the Socratic Method
- allow all individuals who are interested to participate in the administrative process functions of Diagnose, Theorize, and Review
- project the ideas and opinions of individuals participating through feed-back communications to their leaders through management forums and to themselves and their leaders in leadership forums and
- produce a printed, attitudinal profile report(s) and Viewspaper® of participant opinions and attitudes for

use in the public and private planning processes of governance

- reduce polarization and destructive conflict among people by substituting human responsibility for futile strife and hatreds and thus moving toward peace through improved communications among people as organizational members, constituents, and citizens.[9]

The general characteristics of the Fast Forum® technique which is used in many different models we are proposing next in this book are:

There are no Robert's Rules of Order, no motions, no amendments, no win-lose situations, no controversy, no arguments, no talking at the point of decision-making, thus there is no heat. Instead, there is just light, that is: swift, silent, rational, synaptic, mind-to-mind response to objective *questions posed in writing—hence the name "Fast Forum."*

THEORETICAL FOUNDATIONS

Experiments have been conducted in the Seattle area since 1965 in churches and community organizations with an informal, organizational, and objective feedback communication system. It all began with research by the Seattle District Board of Laity of The Methodist Church. They were trying to find out how to have better meetings other than using Robert's Rules of Order to pass resolutions at big meetings with two or three hundred concerned people who were trying to get their minds around some issue, in or out of the church, controversial or not. Sometimes they would invite a panel of experts to their forum, sometimes they would not. Sometimes they would do this, sometimes they would do that. They were less interested in the issues being discussed than they were in the process itself, and they kept changing the rules about how to conduct the forum. But from that research from 1965 through 1968 emerged the prototype of the "Fast Forum" technique and the new technology of "Many-To-Many" communication detailed here. In 1970 the Forum Foundation was organized to continue the project as a non-profit educational research corporation of Washington state by two

[9] *Frontispiece: The Christian Forum or (Fast Forum) Why and What It Is! (1969) by Richard J. Spady, Lay Speaker, The United Methodist Church.*

ministers and the rest were church laymen. This expanded to a full time "futures research" program in 1971 with the cooperation of the Forum Foundation and the Church Council of Greater Seattle, today a consortium of over 300 local churches within 18 regional denominational judicatories including Catholic and Protestant churches with Jewish observers.[10] The religious community of Seattle thus provided the *arena* of people and organizations in which to conduct the research. Within the Church Council, the Episcopal Church, Roman Catholics, United Church of Christ, and American Baptist Churches/USA participated in active research projects. Futures research was defined, not as forecasting, but rather as the search for ways to improve the sociological and technological future. This futures research in pure and applied social science has included (1) development of programs to strengthen the democratic processes in society, and (2) research in the field of administrative theory.

HOW IT WORKS

The Fast Forum® technique functions similarly to, but at a degree of complexity below, statistical random-sampling but above letter writing, telephoning, and interpersonal dialogue. This system makes the same contribution to solving organizational and societal problems as does letter writing, the telephone, group dialogue, and big meetings, but it does so in a more systematic and economical fashion. This approach uses mass means of communication (printing press, U.S. mail, small groups, cassette tapes, optical scanners, and computers or variations dependent upon the organizational setting) and can involve large numbers of people meeting over great distances in small groups of 4 to 12 persons at convenient times and places. People can meet symbolically rather than being forced to physically attend big meetings at often remote distances with all

---

[10] *Dick Spady, co-author and a self-employed businessman since 1954 (Dick's Drive-In Restaurants in Seattle) served as Seattle District Lay Leader of The Methodist Church from 1965-68 and began the original research there. He became a silent partner of his business in 1968 to enroll in the Graduate School of Business Administration at the University of Washington continuing the research there into 1970 at which time he organized the Forum Foundation. From 1971-1990 he served on the volunteer staff of the Church Council of Greater Seattle essentially full time in coordination with the Forum Foundation. On January 1, 1989 he became the active partner again in his business until August 1, 1991 at which time he bought out his partners when they retired.*

the logistics and expense such meetings involve. Instead of using an objective questionnaire based on statistical and mathematical theory, it uses an objective Opinionnaire® based on participation and administrative theory. Different rules apply.

Using the Fast Forum technique, an administrator or organizational leader can establish a routine, interactive, feedback system for regular use on short notice. This allows administrators and leaders to get feedback from their colleagues or constituents easily, accurately, in a timely fashion, and with relatively little expense. Administrators or regular staff can prepare the questions themselves; the process tends to be self-correcting. The process does not require an inside or outside expert versed in random-sample statistical polling which takes time (to explain the problems requiring the questions) and adds expense. The process is more akin to the leader and staff conducting a meeting than it is to their conducting a survey. Leaders and staff probably have better resources and are better prepared than others to pose questions at meetings. It is just that the meeting is not physical, i.e., in real time and space, rather it is symbolic, i.e., in symbolic time and space. The process can be self-funded in the public or private sector if desired—it need not require taxes or budgets to accomplish.

People participating can be provided printed materials and/or audio or video cassettes through the mail or otherwise through internal distribution facilities. An objective Opinionnaire® is composed of statements or questions posed by the administrator, leader, or staff. Responses can include yes, no, abstain, multiple-choice, or value-scale questions ranging up to five choices, e.g., Strongly Agree, Agree, Neutral, Disagree, Strongly Disagree. Participants can always choose to abstain or object to any of the questions or statements if they are not ready to answer, are undecided, feel they need more information, or object to the wording. Participants can either record their answers directly on their Opinionnaire® for subsequent keying into a computer for processing, or they can record their answers onto a response sheet which can be scanned optically onto a diskette for subsequent computer processing. Either method is timely, accurate, and economical.

The system is designed to accommodate administrators, leaders, and planners of organizations and institutions who must make decisions and who recognize the desirability of allowing participation in their organizational context by colleagues or constituents. The process can be done with a minimum effort of time and expense considering the large numbers of people who can participate in the process.

It is practical to key data up to 1,000 participants. The rate of keying costs is constant and depends upon the number of strokes required to record the data. The strokes required are determined by the number of demographics, questions, and the number of people participating. Beyond 1,000 participants, optical response sheets are usually more practical unless one is dealing with an open system. For example, twenty thousand or more people might receive a typical survey sent to constituents by legislators. In this case, most people (often 90%) would ignore the surveys and would dispose of the specially printed optical scanning sheets if used. The expense would be prohibitive.

If one is dealing with a closed system, however, in which participants have agreed in advance to participate in an ongoing program (such as in schools, churches, cities and other organizations), the optically-scanned, machine-readable forms should be used. They are the most practical, accurate, and least expensive to use and produce more timely reports than when keying of the data is done. Reports can be expected to be 100% accurate in scanning. That is not possible by keying without verification techniques which are cost and time prohibitive. When the numbers of questions and people participating increase, total costs tend to be lower by scanning than by keying. People in closed systems quickly learn the use of optically-scanned sheets.

Generally setup of questions, tabulation of data, and printout of profile reports is accomplished in one of the following ways.

First, users can purchase an instruction packet at nominal cost from the Forum Foundation through the Stuart C. Dodd Institute for Social Innovation (SCDI/SI), tax exempt).[11] From the instructions

---

[11] *E-mail: DrRSKirby@aol.com. Write to: Dr. Richard S. Kirby, Stuart C. Dodd Institute for Social Innovation, 4427 Thackeray Place N.E., Seattle, WA 98105-6124 U.S.A. The phone is (206) 545-0547; the fax is (206) 633-3561. If you need more information about the theoretical and design requirements, contact the Forum Foundation via E-mail: fastforum@aol.com or see World Wide Page at: http://weber.u.washington.edu~forum. You may also write to: Forum Foundation, 4426 Second Ave. N.E., Seattle WA 98105-6191 U.S.A. Their phone is: (206) 634-0420 and fax is: (206) 633-3561.*

given in this book they can then prepare their own Opinionnaire® with demographics, prepare their own computer set-up file for those demographics, prepare their own data file, tabulate their own data by keying (or use their own local scanning facility if available, e.g., in schools), and transmit the Opinionnaire®, setup, and data files via e-mail on Internet or diskette to Seattle via U.S. Mail for processing of desired profile reports. Costs are nominal.

Second, users can negotiate with the Stuart C. Dodd Institute for Social Innovation to do it. While the Forum Foundation is primarily in a research mode and not a service delivery mode, we are attempting with the help of SCDI/SI to provide organizations, governments, church networks, and others with the technology to help them get started during this continuing initial research period. Within its capability, the Forum Foundation will assist SCDI/SI to key and/or scan data when properly prepared and shipped by express, prepare the setup and data files, and tabulate the results on its SCDI/SI computer with profile reports returned by U.S. Mail. This process takes more turnaround time and is more expensive to a user, but it is the most trouble-free and allows an organization to get profile reports without having scanning facilities. It is a good way to start and familiarize oneself with the communication process.[12]

The Fast Forum® program can also generate compound searches and print out very specific profile reports easily. There are 15 demographics in the forum program, most with ten fields. This means that the data is arranged so as to be able to produce whatever unique profile reports are required. Normally only a few direct profile reports are required and printed, e.g., gender, age, cities, counties, states, departments, districts, conferences, counties, role, ethnic family, employment, time zone etc. However, com-

---

[12] *It has been Forum Foundation policy, upon request and within its capability and interest, to assist an organization with its needs to establish a feedback communication system using the Fast Forum® technique. If the application has never been done by the foundation, i.e., the application is "at the frontier of knowledge," and the foundation schedule is such that they can do it, the foundation waives consulting fees but requires all direct costs such as machine-scannable response sheets and travel to be covered. Also, Dick Spady, co-author, as an active United Methodist churchman and within his time and energy levels (he is 74 years old), is willing to meet with United Methodists and with other religious denominations with only direct costs and an honorarium to the Forum Foundation, as they might feel appropriate, to help fund its research. Dick Spady receives no salary for his services, and he donated his royalty interest in the book The Search for ENLIGHTENED LEADERSHIP, Volume 1: Applying New Administrative Theory to the Forum Foundation to help fund its futures research programs.*

pound searches can also be made, e.g., (1) citizens by neighborhoods who live in a specific city compared with other citizens in the same county, (2) youth in churches by gender in a district compared with youth in all other districts. Thus, specific sub-profile reports that are of interest to leaders, teachers, and students can be studied or printed as desired. Detailed applications for further analysis, therefore, are numerous and flexible.

These policies will permit the foundation to continue primarily as a research organization in social science applications, i.e., in the field of administrative theory, which it is best suited to do. The Stuart C. Dodd Institute for Social Innovation, in turn, will be able to support, monitor, and assist in use of the Fast Forum® program to establish and maintain a feedback system through Internet which is available to governmental units, church, and other organizations at local, regional, state, or national levels as well as to business organizations.[13]

We first contracted to develop the Fast Forum® computer program in 1970 with the University of Washington Academic Computing Center to meet the needs of our research.[14] The program has been updated periodically as our research matured. In 1978 the fourth generation change was made to the computer program, FORUM D; some very simple changes technologically were made to the computer program at that time, but they were very advanced in administrative theory (the "objection" feature was added to the Opinionnaire®.) The fifth generation change, FORUM E was completed in 1989. It was upgraded from an exclusively research model to a model which permitted access by Uof W students and faculty electronically without cost for scholarly purposes.

[The first Fast Forum Computer Program was copyrighted in 1971. FORUM E computer program was copyrighted U.C.C. 1989 by the Forum Foundation under Universal Copyright Code. All rights

---

[13] *In May, 1997 the Stuart C. Dodd Institute for Social Innovation was organized as a non-profit, 501(c)(3) tax-exempt organization and is preparing to provide specific services for organizations, schools, and governments which wish to use the Fast Forum® technique. Its address is: 4427 Thackeray Place N.E., Seattle, Washington 98105-6124 U.S.A. Their phone is (206) 545-0547. Richard S. Kirby, Ph.D., is Executive Director.*

[14] *At the time I was a graduate student with few computer skills. As a theoretician, I knew where to go but didn't know how to get there. The computer programmer assigned by the University of Washington Academic Computer Center was John Jacobsen, Ph.D. As a computer programmer, he knew how to get there, but didn't know where to go. Between the two of us we designed and crafted the first Fast Forum® computer program. (RJS)*

were reserved. The program is currently on the Macintosh computer and being updated to run on the PC. Fast Forum®, Opinionnaire®, Viewspaper®, PLAN Forum®, and "A City in Pursuit of Happiness!®" are all registered trademarks of the Forum Foundation, United States Patent Office. Their uses (except when done in the normal processing of data with the Forum Foundation FORUM program), without written permission, are prohibited.]

MANAGEMENT VERSUS LEADERSHIP FORUMS

Basically there are two general kinds of forums. First, are Management Forums which are like regular surveys in that the data generated is to be basically one-way feedback to the manager or initiator for confidential use. Management Forums are used if results should be confidential as in annual performance evaluations by managers or leaders of their organization's performance. Here managers or leaders are trying to improve the organization and themselves and they need anonymous, confidential, and non-threatening feedback as to how they and their organization are doing. An awareness and diagnosis of such problems is the first step in the administrative process of doing something about it. The goal is to offer the opportunity to all members of the organization who are interested to assist in the evaluation. It is not just a random sample of those concerned. Of course how that would be done in any one organization is a function of its size, but different strategies using the basic principles presented earlier can be utilized.

Second, are Leadership Forums which basically are provided for two-way interaction within an organization among leaders and colleagues or constituents. From the start the data generated is meant to be available to all, e.g., in a local or national church or educational setting.

PART ONE

Proposed Groupware/Socialware Application Models

There are a variety of groupware application models, most of which have only been proposed at this time. Nevertheless, each is based on a solid, theoretical foundation. In the years ahead as their strengths and weaknesses are learned, some models will surge forward and others will decline Some models were developed in a research mode in which fundamentals and techniques were explored with little or no money available for promotion. The numbers of people participating in a model and whether it has grown should not be the only criteria to judge its success or possible future application. Each model has its own history and each has made its contribution to understanding. Trying to create a new social context in which people can be responsible is a difficult task.

Sometimes it seems as if one learns more in research from failures than from successes because when one is successful, one stops looking; when one fails, one often keeps trying and keeps learning. Those who are interested in trying any of these new models may have similar experiences. In fact, this is such a prevalent dynamic that, for our theoretical purposes, we have given it a name, the *frustration phenomenon.* The first time one does anything new, whether it be learning to ride a bike, type, dance, study, ski, skate, or a new job and the like, one should expect to be clumsy and inefficient and to expend two or three times as much energy in accomplishing the task at hand as one will do once experience is gained. While we have completed our basic task of research in theory and presented it in volume one of this trilogy and new communication technology in this book, we have no illusions that what we have created, at this point of the application models, is a finished product without problems. That is just not the way with social science. It seems as if there are a million ways to fail, some are just better than others. Nevertheless, we are learning, and if you are a venturesome soul, we welcome you as colleagues in the larger task of civilization building.

The Community Forum

CITIZEN COUNCILOR NETWORK FOR MUNICIPAL, COUNTY, AND STATE GOVERNMENTS

Key Points of Model

• Program is open to any citizen who volunteers to meet on call in small groups of 4–12 persons approximately quarterly but not more than monthly during a 30–45 day window period. People meet usually in their own homes or workplaces; these are places where people already are. They do not have to go to a big meeting at an often remote distance to participate. Their role is as a *councilor—"one appointed or elected to advise a sovereign or chief magistrate"*[15] An ordinance should be passed establishing the program and appointment of any citizen who volunteers to become a *"Citizen Councilor."* With one simple stroke of the pen, this law will create the 3 essential conditions for the successful functioning of the future of society postulated by Peter Drucker.

> No society can function as a society unless it gives the individual member *social status* and *function*, and unless the decisive social power is *legitimate power.* "Status, function, legitimacy: (are) the essentials of the new order." [16]

It will also meet the essential condition postulated by Alvin Toffler.

> I would urge all of us as futurists...to devote some of our energies to finding new ways to destandardize, deconcentrate, descale, delimit, and *democratize* planning (emphasis added).[17]

It also meets the criteria of John Gardner:

> If we are to solve the problems of the cities we must greatly strengthen local government. And given our tradition of private-sector independence, we must invent ways in which local leaders in and out of government can work together to formulate community policies and purposes. [18]

---

[15] *Webster's New International Dictionary, Second Edition, Unabridged.*

[16] *(emphasis added by Tarrant)—Peter Drucker in DRUCKER, The Man Who Invented The Corporate Society by John J. Tarrant, p. 50, Warner Books, 1976.*

[17] *Alvin Toffler; Closing address, 2nd General Assembly, World Future Society, Washington, DC, June, 1975.*

[18] *John W. Gardner, Godkin Lectures, Harvard University, reported in Christian Science Monitor, April 16, 1969.*

• Program is usually funded by the government entity organizing the network. Grants can be limited to the first one, five, or ten thousand citizens who apply to enroll in the network. Above that initial number set, any citizen can participate who contributes to cover the variable direct costs of the program estimated between $10–$15/year. Alternatively, the entire program can probably be self-funded by nominal annual fees of $20–25/year if desired; it need not require tax funds to implement. In effect, a communication network could be established owned by the people but available for use by government officials and planners when citizen participation is desired or required. Provisions can be made for scholarships to assist citizens who are unemployed or handicapped.

• Citizens (and school youth too when desired) can interact symbolically with the Mayor, County Executive, or Governor (i.e., the "chiefs of state") planners, or other officials. A network established and maintained by a municipality can be utilized on occasion by the county, region, or state with approval by the municipality. Citizens will then learn of a variety of topics at all governmental levels and will become increasingly better informed and able, over time, to contribute positively as a citizen to the public planning processes "in pursuit of happiness."

The Citizen Councilor concept is being utilized at this writing at the municipal level by the city of Redmond, Washington which lies within the Seattle metropolitan area. They completed their first application of the PLAN Forum® model in a municipal setting on November 1, 1990. In their first application they produced a video cassette with assistance from their local television cable operator, VIACOM. The video started with a short welcome from the mayor followed by a guided tour of the city by a narrator concerning the topic of "Growth Management." The program was successful. In the first responses received, thirty written comments favored the new process while only four criticized it. Some typical comments:

> The process worked.
>
> The forum was an outstanding idea and ours was very useful as an opportunity to discuss widely divergent views peacefully, respectfully, and insightfully.

> This is a worthwhile process and if sustained, holds promise of revitalizing the political process.
>
> The idea of small group meetings is much more appealing than a larger, and often intimidating community meeting.
>
> I think this is a fantastic idea, and getting the citizens involved is the perfect thing to cure voter indifference.
>
> Excellent way to communicate with others. Should be held every 3-5 months.
>
> I think this is the best thing to happen to Redmond since the stop light at NE 85th and 161st Ave.

The City of Redmond at this writing has completed eleven community forums from December 1990 through October 1997 covering the topics of Growth Management, Downtown Redmond, Transportation, Youth Issues, The Future of Redmond, Regional Transit, Redmond's Economic Strategy, What About Water, Rethinking Rubbish, Dealing with Disaster, and Neighborhoods. Participation ranged from 227 persons at the start to 1,201. The experience in Redmond illustrates that the Fast Forum® technique, which utilizes small discussion groups, does not break down even though large numbers of people participate.[19] See excerpts from "An Analysis of the City of Redmond's Community Forum Program" by Ms. Virginia Balsley following this section. Ms. Balsley, a citizen of Redmond, was also a student in Organization and Environment 302 at the University of Washington School of Business Administration in the Fall of 1997 studying *The Search for ENLIGHTENED LEADERSHIP, Volume 1: Applying New Administrative Theory* as a textbook and chose this research for a term paper.

Washington state was identified as one of five precursor states in social innovation by author John Naisbitt in the best seller

---

[19] *This has been a good start on a workable municipal model, but it hasn't fully matured yet. Now that the initial process is familiar and workable, there is a need to take a next step to more institutionalize the process. Because of the importance of the concept of "mainstreaming" explained later, Redmond should pass an ordinance for the reasons noted above. There might also be provided in the ordinance a Citizen Councilor Commission to work with the elected officials and planners of the city on the process and to encourage citizens to participate. The effort should be to move beyond "citizenship education," "citizen participation," or "public relations" and move resolutely to "democratize planning" in a process of "civilization building." There should be a "symbolic dialogue" between the Mayor (augmented by city council and staff) and citizens.*

MEGATRENDS.[20] It is true. For example, Washington was the only state that emerged from the bicentennial celebration in 1976 with a recommendation and funding by its commission for ongoing programming to try to enable its citizens to participate better in the public planning processes of government. Several states established ongoing programs in volunteerism, while most just turned the key, locked the door, and walked away from their celebration of two hundred years of democracy. Washington, however, was the only state able to discern that where citizenship was concerned, it was not quite volunteerism they were after, i.e., the idea of "give me your time, give me your body, give me your hands." Washington was more interested in "give me your mind!" That is significantly different!

The Citizen Councilor concept is *symbolically* interactive. People meet on call through mailed notices to their group conveners who each arrange for their own small group to meet at times and places convenient to themselves, usually in homes or the workplace where they already are. Citizens then listen to an audio tape (or watch a video) and study printed materials prepared by government planners concerning the issue being discussed. After discussion, each participant responds individually to an enclosed Opinionnaire®. These contain demographics of sex, age, county, city, neighborhood, legislative district, census tract etc. They also contain up to 50 objective questions (yes/no/abstain, multiple-choice questions with up to 5 choices, or value scale questions, e.g., strongly agree, agree, neutral, disagree, strongly disagree, or abstain) or those using "end anchors", e.g., *Not Appropriate 1 2 3 4 5 Highly Appropriate* and the like. The Citizen Councilor bill is an adaptation of the PLAN Forum® model; both use the "Day-in-the-Sun" group process.

The Citizen Councilor model was designed originally to operate at the level of the state with provisions for utilization at the county and municipal levels. That is still the ideal public arena. It is being adapted here, however, to begin at the municipal level with provisions for later compatibility with systems initiated at the higher county and state levels. The reason is that there are more opportunities to start at the municipal level and gain experience rather than start at the state level. The model provides an informal public information system to citizens to allow them to learn about

[20] *John Naisbitt, MEGATRENDS, 1982, Warner Books, NY, NY.*

a public issue and respond with their opinions about it before laws are passed. This is in contradistinction to a formal public information system as is the case with the Washington Voter's Pamphlet which is typical in many states. In the voter's pamphlet all citizens face a choice—vote for the law proposed as it is with all of its complexities or vote against it. There is no middle ground.

Value Reporter

In the process proposed in this model value reporters are assigned by public officials or a steering committee to prepare the cassette or video tapes and develop materials for the citizen councilors network to assist in their discussions. This is a person trained in searching out the facts of an issue much like a reporter, an attorney, or one trained in high school or college debate. A value reporter differs in two significant ways from an investigative reporter. First, a value reporter tries to present all sides of a controversial issue fairly and in an unbiased manner to help groups focus their discussion. The Value Reporter represents the citizens "right to know." The research is not meant to be nor could it ever be exhaustive. It is meant to help stimulate people in their discussion process. The value reporter always returns to the experts and officials interviewed and has them inspect prepared tapes and materials meant for distribution to small groups participating. If a person interviewed is not satisfied with his or her previously recorded statement, the interview is simply done again until the person literally signs off that the statement given fairly represents his or her views. If one mispeaks during an interview, the danger of improper utilization and embarrassment is avoided which might be the case with investigative reporters who often have different agendas. The second difference, as mentioned, is that a value reporter researches only those issues assigned by the government official or steering committee and is representing the people's right to know. An investigative reporter, on the other hand, is usually not so circumscribed and often reports on the sensational. While the role of the value reporter, as we see it, is more deliberate and circumscribed than that of an investigative reporter, both are important.

Convener

Each group has a convener. Usually this is someone who agrees beforehand to act as host or hostess and to convene the group, which is organized earlier, usually to meet within a 30–45 day window period. This allows each small discussion group to arrange their own meeting at a time and place convenient for themselves rather than be asked to attend a big meeting at a remote distance which is the cultural norm. Since there are only about two to five couples in the group, it is not a big task for a convener to get the group together. At their meeting, the person designated as convener helps lead the group through its discussion first by playing a cassette tape. This is usually a 20 to 30 minute audio tape prepared earlier by the organization leader or by his or her staff or "value reporter" with an introduction by the leader followed by a presentation of the issues by others. After listening or viewing the audio or video tape, the convener invites each person in turn to have his or her two-minute "Day in the Sun," if the person wishes to do so.

At least ten minutes before the group is scheduled to leave, each person is given a copy of an objective Opinionnaire® covering the issues under discussion. Each person then individually completes the demographics and answers the questions posed on the optical scanning response sheet provided (or the reproducible Response Sheet if used instead). *The machine-scannable Response Sheet does the same thing as a computer terminal. It allows a human being to interface directly with a machine accurately, swiftly and economically. This application of The Fast Forum® Technique is a breakthrough in social science!*

Response sheets (and tapes for reuse) are returned by mail for optical scanning of responses. A Viewspaper® with highlights of results is returned to each participant by mail and one or more detailed computer profile reports are also returned to each convener for study by participant groups if desired. Results are distributed to public officials and planners as advisory data only. Thus, people act as a sounding board to assist in the public planning process. All reports are properly disclaimed as described later under "Other Fundamentals of the Fast Forum® Technique" and "The Formal Clauses."

If organizational and political leaders want organizational and political stability, they should not be up in the crow's nest just giving orders (authoritarianism) and swaying to each pitch and yaw of the organizational ship of state. Instead, they should be as close as possible to the center of organizational stability, near the keel, where the people are. The closer a leader stays in touch with his or her colleagues and constituents, the more stable the organizational and political relationship is between and among them all. This is why authoritarianism, centralism, and dictatorships are all doomed ultimately to fail; they simply cannot compete with the openness and dynamics of a fully functioning democracy. The Community Forum model has great potential. We commend it to organizational and political leaders everywhere.

We commend this model as revised to Mayor Rosemarie Ives of Redmond together with the analysis given by Ms. Virginia Balsey of the Redmond, Washington Community Forum which follows. [Redmond is a city within the greater Seattle area and is the home office of Microsoft.]

We commended the process to the newly elected Mayor of Seattle, Paul Schell on December 24, 1997 followed by letters of March 21, 1998 and March 23, 1998. They are all printed in Appendix F.

Hopefully, the political and civic leaders of Seattle and Redmond (and Microsoft) will respond. History waits.

THE COMMUNITY FORUM

An Analysis of the City of Redmond's Community Forum Program *[Excerpts used by permission. RJS]*

VIRGINIA BALSLEY
Organization and Environment 302 F
School of Business Administration
University of Washington

DR. RICHARD KIRBY
Fall Quarter 1997

Introduction

This study analyzes the City of Redmond's Community Forum program. This program uses the Fast Forum® technique developed by the Forum Foundation. The City of Redmond uses the Community

Forums to gather citizen input on issues important to the city. There have been eleven Community Forums since they began in 1990, each one addressing a topic important to the City of Redmond. The focus of this study is on the Redmond citizen participants' view of the Community Forum process. As a citizen of the City of Redmond, I want to know if my fellow Redmond citizens feel this process succeeds in allowing them to have their views heard by City officials.

From this research I find that many benefits are gained from this process. Even though I was not able to evaluate how much influence the Forum results have on city decision-making, the benefits gained by both the Redmond citizens and the City are of significant importance.

Research Methods

Documentation on each forum is available at the Redmond City Library and City Hall. For this study, documentation from the first ten forums was analyzed. Research was also accomplished by being a participant in the eleventh Redmond Community Forum in October 1997. During the research, particular attention was paid to the citizen participation, participant comments, and the forum statistical results from participants responses to questions about the forum process....

The proposed forum is announced and advertised in the media, city newsletter, etc. Citizens and businesses are solicited for volunteers to organize a group meeting.

The group meeting volunteer organizers, called "conveners," round-up participants for their meeting (calling, sending invitations, contacting neighbors or fellow employees). The conveners also attend a training session (at) City Hall to pick up the materials for the meeting and share information on how to conduct a meeting. In addition to volunteer citizen conveners, instructors at the local high schools also participate as conveners for their high school classes where students participate in the process.

Participants in the Redmond Community Forum meet for about 2 hours in small groups of 8 to 12 persons. Each group meets at a time and place convenient to that group's participants, usually in the home of the convener, a school, or a place of business. The group meetings are held over a two to three week period.

During each group meeting, the participants watch the video prepared by the City for the forum. In most group meetings the video is followed by group discussion. Each participant is allowed 2 minutes of non-interrupted time to express their views. After the discussion session, each participant fills out the prepared questionnaire.

The results are summarized and included in a newsletter called the Viewspaper®. This newsletter is sent to all past and current participants and provided to all city employees.

Sometimes a follow-up workshop is held to review the results. The workshop is open to everyone and is attended by the Mayor and other City officials....

The cost of each Community Forum is about $13,000.

In 1991, the Association of Washington Cities recognized the Redmond Community Forum with an Honorable Mention in their Municipal Achievement Competition. This award is designed to recognize innovative programs that benefit communities....

FORUM	DATE	TOPIC	TOTAL
1	1990-December	Growth Management	227
2	1991 - April	Downtown Redmond	313
3	1991 - April	Transportation	284
4	1992 -May	Youth Issues	467
5	1992 - October	The Future of Redmond	447
6	1993 - October	Regional Transit	641
7	1994 - July	Redmond's Economic Strategy	611
8	1995 - January	What About Water?	541
9	1995 - July	Rethinking Rubbish	425
10	1996 - February	Dealing with Disaster	1201
11	1997 - October	Neighborhoods	*

** data is not yet available*

Initially the City of Redmond stated their goals for the Community Forum process to be:

- "to make participation in Redmond government easier for citizens by allowing people to meet in small groups at times and places convenient to themselves"

- "to give citizens a chance to meet, discuss and learn more about issues that are important to the City"
- "to go beyond open discussion and gather specific and objective opinions about the topic from every participant"
- "to develop a process that is easily repeated at regular intervals throughout the year....

From reviewing all the comments I have come away with a sense that the majority of the participants think the Forums are a success and they are glad the opportunity is open to them. There are a great number of comments saying simply "thank-you for this process."

"People are interested in government, but have no format other than elections to feel as though they are part of it. The Community Forum helps to provide this."

"This is a great idea to facilitate an involved and collaborative process versus an uninvolved and what usually feels like an antagonistic process when citizens sit back and expect others (government) to solve problems on their behalf."

"The Forum was an outstanding idea and ours was very useful as an opportunity to discuss wide/divergent views peacefully, respectfully, and insightfully. The Forums offer a way to help bond some of our wonderfully divergent citizens."

"Forums are great—input is extremely important—empowerment."

Some people (at least one in most Forums) questioned whether the cost of the Forums were worth the benefit (each Forum costs about $13,000). I don't know if a cost/benefit analysis has been done, but what I have learned from this research convinces me that the benefits gained from this program greatly out-weigh the $13,000 per Forum cost.

Conclusion

As a citizen, I expect to be allowed to participate in city government by offering my opinions and comments to the City officials representing me. In addition, I hope that the City officials listen to me and all my fellow citizens' opinions and comment, taking them into consideration to make wise and prudent decisions on our behalf.

From this research I have come to believe that the Community Forums are very beneficial to the citizens and City officials, but not just because they allow citizens to participate in the government. Nor are they beneficial just because they allow the City officials to collect input to their decision-making processes. The Redmond Community Forums are providing a valuable service to its citizens and city government.

The process is educating students in how to participate constructively in the governing process. It allows them an opportunity to discuss real-life, close-at-hand issues that effect their families' lives.

It educates citizens on issues they need to know about. Disaster preparedness, recycling, and water quality are issues for which all citizens need to be educated.

It builds a sense of community. It gives people the sense they belong to a group of people who are working together for the better of the whole. It gives people an excuse to get to know their neighbors. In our fast-paced mobile society, getting to know the people next door isn't something that is necessarily likely to happen.

The Community Forums allow people to hear other people's opinions and comments on issues. Just as it is important for people to ponder issues and come to opinions for themselves, it is important for people to know what everyone else is thinking and feeling.

Sharing views, ideas, and opinions with others assures that the best ideas will promoted.

The process is invaluable to the Redmond City officials and its residents. This Redmond citizen plans to continue to be involved.

Letter from The Mayor

Together We Create a Community of Good Neighbors *- I hope you have been hearing that statement more and more since the Community Forum in October. During that Forum, we asked you if this statement was a fitting vision for Redmond, if you agreed with our interpretation of it, and how this vision should be implemented to build a greater sense of community in our neighborhoods.*

As with past Forums, I am excited and challenged by what you told us. Two-thirds of you liked the vision statement with few or no changes, and almost three-quarters agreed that our interpretation of this simple statement coincides with your own. So, we feel confident we are moving in the right direction.

As for implementation - building a greater sense of community - you have given us a wealth of ideas from enhancing existing programs like Block Watch and emergency preparedness, to looking at new ideas such as neighborhood liaisons and localized community events. You have told us there are many ways to create a community of good neighbors and our role in city government cannot be to create these elements of "good neighborliness" alone. Rather, our role is to put the vision forward while we demonstrate, through partnerships and programming, ways all segments of the community can create and maintain it together.

Thank you to everyone who participated in this Forum. I invite you to continue staying involved in your neighborhood, through formal or informal means, and also to watch for your ideas to yeild results (with some help from the city and our partners in the community).

!YOUR VIEW COUNTS!

Rosemarie Ives

Rosemarie Ives, Mayor
City of Redmond

Forum Highlights

The 12th Redmond Community Forum, Neighborhoods, was held during the month of October 1997. A total of 383 people participated (222 adults, 161 youths) being surveyed at 23 community-based groups and 8 high school classes. The following were among the survey results.

Feeling the Connection:

Overall, two-thirds of the respondents seemed to know their immediate neighbors (at least by sight), but half wished to be <u>more</u> connected.

Getting Together:

Most respondents either have attended or would attend a neighborhood social gathering or clean-up party.

But Who Has the Time?

Most respondents indicated that the sense of community within our neighborhoods is a casualty of the fast-pace lifestyles of many people.

And What About That Traffic?

Adult respondents overwhelmingly stated traffic speed or noise was the top "de-valuer" of their neighborhoods.

On the Other Hand...

Almost one-third of the respondents had no complaints with their present neighborhood.

A complete written analysis, a sample of the comments received, and a summary of all the Opinionnaire® survey responses are included in this Viewspaper®. For more detailed information including cross-tabulation tables of key questions and copies of all written comments, please see the Community Forum Data Binder. This binder has been presented to the Mayor and City Council members, and is available for public inspection and copying at the Planning Department on the third floor of City Hall and at the Redmond Public Library.

What's Inside...

Analysis .... **page 2**
Comments .... **page 4**
Letter to Participants .... **page 5**
Who's Participating .... **page 6**
Summary Report .... **page 8**

Psycho-Social Education

DEMONSTRATING DEMOCRACY AND CITIZENSHIP IN SCHOOLS

by Richard J. Spady
President, Forum Foundation

Presentations Made To:

WORLD NETWORK OF RELIGIOUS FUTURISTS CONFERENCE
May 23-25, 1997 London, England

RUSSIAN ACADEMY OF EDUCATION
Russia's Open University, May 30, 1997
Moscow, Russia

"CONNECTIONS '97, EDUCATION FOR RESPONSIBLE CITIZENSHIP"
University of Sydney, Australia, July 6-9, 1997

INTERNATIONAL CONGRESS OF UNITED METHODIST MEN
Purdue University, West Lafayette, IN, USA, July 11-13, 1997

"TRENDWATCH, TECHNOLOGY, SOCIETY, AND VALUES"
WORLD FUTURE SOCIETY CONFERENCE
San Francisco, CA, USA, July 17-19, 1997

"THE SOCIAL/MORAL FABRIC OF SCHOOL LIFE"
(INSTITUTIONAL PROCESSES OF SOCIALIZATION)
INTERNATIONAL CENTER FOR CURRICULUM STUDIES
Seattle Pacific University, Seattle, WA, USA, October 2-4, 1997

The Problem: Governance!

> As human systems and organizations grow ever larger, more complex, and more impersonal—in our schools, in our communities, in our churches, in our governments, and in our industries and commerce—the individual shrinks toward facelessness, hopelessness, powerlessness, and frustration.

—DR. STUART C. DODD, Professor-Emeritus of Sociology, University of Washington, and RICHARD J. SPADY, "Citizen Counselor Proposal," *The Seattle Times,* November 10, 1974.

Harvard Professor Elton Mayo, sometimes called the "father of the human relations movement," wrote in the preface of the classic *Management and the Worker* by Roethlisberger and Dixon published in 1943:

> The art of human collaboration seems to have disappeared during two centuries of quite remarkable material progress. The various nations seem to have lost all capacity for international cooperation in the necessary tasks of civilization. The internal condition of the nation is not greatly better; it seems that only a threat from without, an unmistakable emergency, can momentarily quiet the struggle of rival groups....How can humanity's capacity of spontaneous cooperation be restored? It is in this area that leadership is most required, a leadership that has nothing to do with political 'isms' or eloquent speeches. What is wanted is knowledge, a *type of knowledge* that has escaped us in two hundred years of prosperous development. *How* to substitute human responsibility for futile strife and hatreds...(emphasis added).

Notice that it wasn't just more "knowledge" per se for which Mayo was searching, but rather a "type" of knowledge that somehow we have missed. It is my thesis that the new type of knowledge and leadership, for which Mayo was searching, has been found!

The Solution: A>B>C>A (Democracy!)

It's as simple and profound as ABC—**A**dministrators over **B**ureaucrats over **C**itizens over **A**dministrators—Democracy! Our national and global institutions of state, economic, religious, and social enterprises require organization, direction, and administration. *But how and where do these democratic solutions all start?*

The Schools: Psycho-Social Education!

This paper deals with the theory of Erik H. Erikson, a pre-eminent national and international school psychologist, advocating a "Psycho-Social Moratoria" for children. Robert Pranger, a political scientist at the University of Washington in Seattle, wrote a book in 1968 titled *The Eclipse of Citizenship.* In it he stated, "This need of the adolescent for a Psycho-Social Moratoria, as defined by Erikson, is so important, it is of equal importance to the need of a small child for maternal care." This paper will explain how to conduct such a program in schools using new "socialware" communication technology.

The Curriculum: Intellectual Gaming!

A child is told by his or her parents, teacher, and culture, "this is a fact." But when the child reaches adolescence, however, the youth begins to realize there is ambiguity and differences of opinion—everything is not clear cut. We all must realize that teenage youth exist at a *crucible-forming time* in the development of the human personality between childhood and adulthood. And if parents and society "don't get it right then"—they may never get it right. During this special formative time and place, this period and place of *psycho-social moratoria,* there is no "right" or "wrong" answer by young people as they reflect on the "facts" they have learned in a search together for "meaning." What they need is an *educational arena* in which to do it. *It is the responsibility of adults organizationally, locally, regionally, nationally, and internationally to provide this neutral, mentoring, supportive, loving, and caring community.* Moreover, these basic processes of democratization are therapeutic, they reduce organizational and societal tensions among people, that is, they lead to peace!

The process proposed here is a kind of *intellectual gaming* in schools and for exactly the same reason that we have physical gaming. As the children exercise their bodies, they get stronger physically. Similarly, as youth exercise their reasoning abilities with ideas posed about real problems in life and their future, and they share their opinions with each other, their parents and others—they grow stronger intellectually, i.e., *they learn* through the dynamics of the Socratic Method! Socrates didn't "tell" his students as much as he "asked them questions." In the process they achieved their own "insight" that upwelled from within themselves. "Ah-ha, that's the answer to my problem," or "Ah-ha, that's the answer to the question—it's "yes" or it's "no!" *And it makes no difference which is chosen at that time; it has nothing to do with what is "right" or "wrong."* What does occur, however, is that the child's mind becomes "psychologically benchmarked" with the problem or the question and his or her own creative response to it, and *learns!* And when an individual learns "X" amount, the organization and the society of which he or she is a part learns exactly the same amount and all move toward being able to solve problems better in the future.

The moral to the story is that if leaders and educators in society are really interested in improving the abilities and capacities of their citizens and of their children and youth, then *they* must enable *them* to make lots of decisions about lots of real problems in life! Through the dynamics of the Socratic Method—they will learn! The first three steps in the Socratic Method (awareness, frustration, and insight) are personal—just the individual and his or her world; no one else is involved. But there is a fourth step, and it is a group effort. It is called "verification." The individual needs to know, "Are my ideas practical? Will they work? How do they stack up against the thinking of other people? Thus, intellectual gaming requires a systematic feedback component.

Printed or computer reports generated in the process are all disclaimed and do not purport to represent the views of the parent or sponsoring organizations or others not participating. Thus, this allows people to speak; they speak only for themselves which is every person's right. The results are, however, 100% valid for the students, parents and citizens participating. In the final analysis, it allows the parents to say, "Look son or daughter, even though all other students say this or all other parents say that, I want to call your attention to this "additional fact." They then can lay their own value judgment on their own child which is the parental prerogative, and the process ends right there with remaining questions still unanswered, just as in the story of "The Lady and the Tiger." While the adults participating as mentors search for their own "right" answers to the questions posed, *the children participating are not told* by anyone ahead of time which is the "right" answer to the ideas and questions posed. They need to seek their own solutions. Educational leaders will ask. "But how can you assure the children will have the "knowledge" and "right" information to make such choices?"

The Moral Stance: No Right—No Wrong!

There are no "right or wrong" answers for children and youth in their *search for meaning* as they grow to maturity at this point in their lives between childhood and adulthood. They will begin to discern the morality, the diversity, and the insights of their peers, parents, and other citizens as they learn from the process itself using the dynamics of the Socratic Method to gain insights and mature their critical thinking and civil discourse skills.

The process will build in students the essential citizenship and democratic skills of listening, respectfully stating one's own opinion, and interacting respectfully in civil discourse with public officials, planners, and other citizens in their own "pursuit of happiness" with others for a better future. *Governments are not charged with providing their citizens with all the amenities of life they feel they need to make them happy, but all governments are charged with enabling their citizens to pursue their own happiness!*

The Methodology: How It Would Work Using The QUEST Forum™ (Quick Environmental Scanning Test).

Traditionally, in schools, democratic institutions are mimicked by students electing their own officers and representatives. The expectation then is that the officers and representatives will determine school policy and administer projects and that thus this process "teaches the principles of democracy." That is wrong. While this is a valuable and positive learning experience for those few students elected, it is a negative democratic learning experience for those defeated or not even running for office. The democratic and educational philosophy which is really being communicated to our children and youth by this methodology is, "If you are not elected or duly appointed in organizations or society, you don't count." That philosophy is anti-democratic—it strikes at the very foundations of a democratic society. Further, that flawed administrative process produces apathetic citizens instead of interested and informed citizens actively striving to improve the quality of life for themselves, their community, and the society of which they are a part.

(A) What should be done differently in the initial step? (1) After the officers and representatives are elected, they should determine the subject for class or school discussion. Usually at the start of the school year the subject is "What should our class or school do this year?" (2) All students should be invited to print, legibly, on one side of a 3 X 5 inch card an idea or proposal concerning the subject under discussion. *[Note: Do not give students a larger card or paper; they will tend to ramble and fill it up. Instead, by using the smaller 3 X 5 card, students are forced to think— to condense, craft, and refine their thought.]* (3) The officers and representatives should read all cards and select, edit, and rephrase, if required, up to 50 key, representative, "value statements." *[Note: It is all right if statements are similar—even differing by just one word. The important thing is that the statements are typical, from the students, and help illustrate different choices.]* (4) The officers and representatives should prepare and administer an "Opinionnaire®" listing the selected ideas and providing demographics of gender and class such as freshman, sophomore, junior, or senior. In this case participants will respond *Agree, Disagree, Abstain,* or *Object.* To most people, this will look like a typical "Questionnaire" random-sample "survey" using objective yes/no, multiple-choice, and value-scale questions. But a Questionnaire is based on statistical theory which, in turn, is based on mathematical theory. An Opinionnaire®, however, is based on participation theory which, in turn, is based on administrative theory. There are essential differences in some small but critical, theoretical, and practical ways, e.g., an Opinionnaire® *always* allows students to *abstain* or *object* to any question. Different rules apply! (5) Let all students respond to the Opinionnaire® by circling their responses on the Opinionnaire® for keying into the computer or marking their response sheet. Response sheets are either machine-scannable or reproducible in which case the data is keyed also into the computer. When appropriate, ask parents to respond too. (6) The officers and representatives should organize and oversee the hand or computer tabulation of the data and the preparation of printed profile reports using the Fast Forum® technique showing responses to each question or statement by gender and again by grades. It is essential that each report show the Disclaimer Clause which follows.

DISCLAIMER CLAUSE

> The purpose of this informal report is to communicate ideas, issues, and problems among people as a platform for future, meaningful discussions of concerns. Participants are assisted in becoming aware of their own beliefs as well as of those intellectual and moral beliefs of others at a point in time—"the spirit of the time." The views and opinions expressed herein are those of the individuals who participated and do not necessarily represent the official views of the parent group or sponsoring organization. Nor will the views expressed necessarily represent those of the same participants at a later period of time; as humans we each have the ability to receive new information, consider it, and change.

The Disclaimer Clause actually frees all participants to contribute their opinions because everyone knows the societal context in which it is being done; they speak only for themselves which is every person's right. It allows each individual to contribute his or her greatest gift—human thought. Furthermore and statistically, the model deals with the "universe" and not just a sample. (7) A "Viewspaper®" should be prepared, posted, and distributed which is a short summary report of response highlights which also must contain the Disclaimer Clause.

(B) What is the second step? (1) The officers and representatives should study the detailed reports and prepare a second Opinionnaire® iteration listing the representative's opinions of the prevailing consensus of the students. For example, "The elected representatives of (school) have studied the reports generated and discussed the results and the following value statements appear to be the prevailing consensus among the student body. Do you agree?" The Opinionnaire® should list up to 50 statements with the demographics of gender, class, ethnic family, role (e.g., student, parent) and/or other demographics felt appropriate. (2) The officers should then administer and tabulate the second Opinionnaire®.

(C) What is the third and final step? (1) The officers and representatives should organize and oversee the hand or computer tabulation of the data and the preparation of the printed profile reports and the Viewspaper® using the Fast Forum® technique.

Tabulated results are shown for each statement or question posted as a "Polarization-Consensus Rating" (PC Rating) which is shown below in a Viewspaper® from an actual question submitted to a group.

> The Polarization Rating is the % of the participants answering *only* yes or no. The Consensus Rating is the % *positive of those polarized.* For example:
>
> • Some have stated, "Innovation can only take place in the physical sciences, not in the social sciences." Do you agree?
>
> Agree Disagree Abstain Object PC Rating (95%—0)

This is read as "95% had zero consensus." It means, "95% of those participating were polarized (thus 5% abstained or objected). Of those who were polarized, no one answered yes (thus everyone answered no)." The reports generated will not be one line bigger regardless of the size of the group participating, thus students, their officers and representatives, and their parents will not get "information overload." [See "The Four Foundations of the Fast Forum® Technique" later in this book for more information about the "Polarization Consensus Rating".]

At this point, after this third step, the QUEST Forum™ [21] would normally end. However if the elected officers and representatives feel there is still no general consensus or if there are other specific areas that need to be explored, they could continue the iterations. Otherwise it is at this point that the officers and representatives would begin their in depth discussion of the information, make policy decisions, and administer the programs desired.

Notice that in this process, the elected officers and representatives still retain all their prerogatives to make the final decisions, but they just go through the preliminary democratic process first *in order to enable their constituents to participate.* What is the main thing

---

[21] *While Fast Forum, Opinionnaire, and Viewspaper are registered trademarks of the Forum Foundation and the QUEST Forum trademark is pending, they can be used by others as long as they use them properly (i.e., they don't label a random-sample Questionnaire an "Opinionnaire" or vice versa and don't provide questions or statements for response without allowing participants to abstain and object.) Just acknowledge: "Fast Forum, Opinionnaire, Viewspaper, and PLAN Forum are registered trademarks, U.S. Patent Office, and QUEST Forum trademark is pending, of the Forum Foundation, 4426 Second Ave. N.E., Seattle, WA 98105-6191, USA [206-633-3561 Fax; 206-634-0420 phone] and that they are used by permission." Other uses are not authorized unless written permission is obtained.*

to be gained by this approach? "Authority" will begin to flow from the students to their elected officers and representatives making ultimate decisions by the representatives easier and more acceptable to the student body as they "pursue their own happiness."[22]

This model using Psycho-Social Education and Intellectual Gaming in schools holds great promise. It is a model that can be tabulated by hand using arithmetic if a computer is not available in a classroom or school. This itself is an exercise for students that can build skills and learning (and reduce expenses). If paper is scarce, Opinionnaires® can be administered verbally at least to the students with their responses made to reproducible sheets (see example in Appendix D). Finally, as more resources are available, responses can be made onto machine-scannable "Forum Foundation Councilor™ Response Sheet." (Councilor: "One appointed or elected to advise a sovereign or chief magistrate.")[23] The machine-scannable response sheet does the same thing that a computer does but at a fraction of the cost—it allows a human being to interface directly with a machine, accurately, swiftly, and economically.

Further QUEST Forums™ should be held approximately quarterly to expand the psycho-social education curriculum as determined and administered by the officers with topics selected by the representatives. Typical questions which might be considered are:

- How can we tell when a person is "grown up?"
- What makes "growing up" most difficult?
- What "concerns" you about growing up?
- What do you believe is the most difficult part of being a parent?
- How might one become a "successful parent?"
- How might we change the "family" to make it a better place to grow up?[24]

---

[22] *See "The Theory of Authority" in Volume 1: Applying New Administrative Theory, Spady and Bell (1996), page 49.*
[23] *Webster's New International Dictionary, Second Edition, Unabridged.*
[24] *These questions were provided by Mr. Bill Wortman, retired social studies teacher from Interlake High School, Bellevue, Washington in a series of classes conducted at St. Peter's United Methodist Church, Bellevue, Washington USA in March, 1997.*

The Summary: Psycho-Social Education!

> "What is occurring is a process–a doing, specifically a process of interrelating the person and his or her world, bringing new meaning into the human situation."
>
> —HOWARD ELLIS and TED MCEACHERN,
> *The United Methodist Church,* authors

The discussion of ideas *within a constructive, open, democratic context is the mortar which binds* a creative organization or society, i.e., an organization or society which is actively searching for solutions to its problems. Any group, organization, institution, community, society, or world ideology which inhibits (innocently or not) the free flow of ideas among its constituents—up, down, and across its organizational and societal structures, is depriving itself of its greatest asset—human thought—and is in grave danger of being buried in history by the avalanche of the creativity of others!

 The Spiritual Forum Network

UNITED METHODIST COUNCILOR NETWORK PROPOSAL

A Proposed Futures Research Model for United Methodist Men presented at Congress '97, July 12, 1997, Purdue University, West Lafayette, Indiana

—Richard J. Spady
President, Forum Foundation;
Lay Speaker, St. Peter's UMC, Seattle District, Pacific Northwest Annual Conference, The United Methodist Church

The Connection–Futures Research

Wesleyan Transformations: A Study in World Methodism and World Issues by the late Rev. Dr. Earl D. C. Brewer, Candler School of Theology, Emory University in Atlanta, was co-authored with Rev. Dr. Mance J. Jackson in 1988. It was a significant book completed just a few short years before Rev. Brewer's death. It is a small gem of a book that lifts up the history and ministry of The United Methodist Church to the world as a civilizing influence for the future. Rev. Brewer was the first president of the World Network of Religious Futurists, itself a spin-off from the World Future Society, a non-profit, educational-scientific organization, dedicated to the study of the future. I have been a member of the World Future Society since the early 1970's and a member of the Religious Futurists Network beginning at its start in 1980, following the *World Future Society's* "First Global Conference on the Future" held in Toronto. I also served on the volunteer staff of the Church Council of Greater Seattle from 1971-1990 with the portfolio "Futures Research" (which was defined, not as forecasting, but as the search for ways to influence the sociological and technological future), and I have been a Rotarian since 1980 with the active classification of "Futures Research."

The Start of the Church

The Methodist Church started with Rev. John Wesley who lived from 1703-1791 in England. Rev. Wesley succeeded in leading a lively renewal movement in the Church of England. The movement expanded to America where organized Methodism began as a lay movement. Following the famous Christmas Conference in Baltimore in December, 1784, its ministers rode on horseback to meet the religious needs of the many small communities on the frontier. They were called "circuit riders." From the beginning The Methodist Church was interested in the spiritual needs of people but also social issues which affected society. There was great emphasis on education. The church established a significant number of today's colleges and universities throughout the nation. This includes the University of Washington which today is a world class university in Seattle in which I have studied and researched in the field of administrative theory.[25]

Today, The United Methodist Church is one of the largest of the "main line" denominations with nearly nine million members in over 36,000 local churches in the United States. An additional 23 million members in 72 denominations in 108 countries consider themselves autonomously a part of the Methodist family and are related through the World Methodist Council with headquarters in Lake Junaluska, North Carolina.

The Social Principles and The Book of Resolutions

United Methodists are unique among religious organizations in that they systematically take positions on public policy issues through their *Social Principles* and a remarkable religious document called *The Book of Resolutions.* Currently the 1996 book contains 294 resolutions of policy recommendations concerning The Natural World, The Nurturing Community, The Social Community, The Economic Community, The Political Community, The World Community, and Other Resolutions. One Hundred Twenty-Five (43%) of the resolutions were adopted in 1996. Resolutions are usually prepared by the General Board of Church and Society, the General Board of Global Ministries, or others and require approval by the General Conference, the highest governing body of the church, when it meets every four years. Such resolutions are considered as official expressions of the church for twelve years when adopted after which time they are deemed to have expired unless re-adopted. Thus, *the document is visionary and dynamic.*

---

[25] *The Rev. Daniel Bagley was an early driving force to bring the University of Washington to Seattle (Ref: Roots and Branches, David Buerge and Junius Rochester, 1988, page 105).*

Theology is the application of one's religious beliefs in the world. The "Wesleyan Quadrilateral" teaches that theology is derived from scripture, tradition, experience, and reason. Methodist tradition is Protestant—as such they do not believe in the infallibility of the church. Methodists are taught that they are directly responsible to God, through Christ, and there is no other person or institution between them and God—including the church.

This is very powerful theology because it means that every Methodist is free to disagree with any part of The Book of Resolutions *and not be ostracized from the church* for it is the individual parishioner, and not the corporate church, who has the primary responsibility to affect the world in the direction that Christ has taught.

As a member of the church since 1954, Seattle District Lay Leader from 1965–68, and a certified or local church lay speaker each year since 1967, I became very familiar with the Book of Resolutions. But there is a problem. Presently the church treats The Book of Resolutions as a finished document primarily to be used for reference purposes. It isn't a finished document, *but it is truly a great beginning document.*

Next to the Bible, I believe the Book of Resolutions is the greatest written treasure of the church; unfortunately, it may also be the greatest secret because the majority of United Methodists do not seem to know about it. It seems each quadriennium to be placed on the deepest shelf in the church. Bishops don't talk about it, District Superintendents don't talk about it, most ministers don't talk about it—is it any wonder that most United Methodists don't know much about it?

My impression is that the ministerial and lay leaders of the church are fearful that if their parishioners talk about real problems in life, it will be "political and divisive." That is a legitimate concern—however, it need not be divisive if care is taken in establishing a process that is constructive, democratic, and open to all. In fact, the reverse should be true; there should be a release of social and organizational tensions as is similar after most elections. A social, organizational, and institutional bonding should occur. More than any other philosophy of governance, democratic processes are therapeutic and lead to peace.

Parishioners, as well as citizens in society, are hungering for theological and spiritual insight. Who am I? What is my role in life? Where do I fit in? These "identity questions" may be the religious questions of the millennium. Can these questions be answered? I believe they can, but only if we create new social contexts. "But we are all babies at creating context—and babies don't always get it right. But it is only in getting it wrong that we can ever hope to get it right" (Eldon Byrd, scientist, in an address titled "The Transformation of Societal Institutions" given at a session of the "First Global Conference on the Future" and General Assembly of the World Future Society, Toronto, Canada, July, 1980).

The Purpose

The purpose of this research proposal is to help bring theological and spiritual insights to the level of the pew by acknowledging the meaning of our Protestant tradition. As the corporate church and individual laity participate cooperatively in a process of civilization building, any individual member should be able to disagree, in good conscience, with The Book of Resolutions or other proclamations and not be ostracized from the church. Parishioners study the Bible, listen to preachers each Sunday, and pray together. In this process they learn of God's will. People also need, however, to be able to talk together at a level above politics, above economics, and at the spiritual level of civilization building. And what is the contribution of such people to the solution of problems faced by the human race? It is wisdom!

Leadership, like the ability to learn, is a universal human attribute; leadership is not a quality reserved for the titled head of an organization. What does every human being in the world do from the time they get up in the morning until the time they go to bed at night? They try to bring some kind of order out of the chaos that is usually going on around them in their world. This is leadership—it is a positive force, not negative. Most of the knowledge of the world is in books and computer databases, but most of the wisdom of the world is in the minds of people walking the earth, and we have to learn how to reach it. "What is real wisdom? It comes from life experience, well digested" (Erik H. Erikson, New York Times, June 14, 1988, page 13).

United Methodist Councilor Network Proposal[26]

(Councilor: An official advisor to a sovereign or chief magistrate.—Webster)

The General Commission of United Methodist Men should use its good offices to take the lead to organize a grassroots discussion of The 1996 Book of Resolutions, not as a reference document, but as a dynamic document which clarifies the overall theology of The United Methodist Church in its ministry to the world. All meetings would be held in small groups in local churches or in homes weekly, bi-monthly, or monthly and be open to all members who are interested in participating.

Starting as soon as possible, in 1998 hopefully, small packets can be sent by the General Commission of United Methodist Men to local churches participating containing:

(1) An instruction and assignment sheet showing about five resolutions to be studied each month for the next quarter, e.g., January, February, and March;

(2) An Opinionnaire® listing two questions for each resolution studied using "end anchors," e.g., (a) *How appropriate is this resolution?* Participants can respond: *Not Appropriate 1 2 3 4 5 Highly Appropriate;* (b) *All things considered and as now written, can you ratify this resolution?* Participants can respond *Yes, No, or Abstain* (similar to the options provided citizens when they vote in elections);

(3) A Fast Forum® Reproducible Response Sheet on which an individual can record answers (see Appendix D).

Completed response sheets will be returned by the deadline date at the end of each month and tabulated by: (a) a local church "communicator" who keys participant responses into a computer for transmission to the Forum Foundation by e-mail or mailed diskette for tabulation without cost, (b) by mailing the completed response sheets with identifying church letterhead together with a check for 50 cents for each sheet to be keyed by the Forum Foundation, or (c) by replacing reproducible response sheets in advance with machine-scannable response sheets from the Forum Founda-

---

[26] *From the 1996 Book of Discipline, we recommend this research project to the General Commission on United Methodist Men in accordance with ¶ 2302.2 a), c), and f); to the General Board of Discipleship in accordance with ¶ 1102.10; to the General Board of Church and Society in accordance with ¶ 1004; to the General Board of Global Ministries in accordance with ¶ 1302.12; to United Methodist Communications (UMCom) in accordance with ¶ 1806.16, and to the General Council on Ministries in accordance with ¶ 906.17.*

tion @ 25 cents per sheet in packets of 100 sheets.

Results will be tabulated by the Forum Foundation using the Fast Forum® computer "socialware" program that it first designed and created at the University of Washington Academic Computer Center in 1970. Profile reports showing responses by Gender, Age, Ethnic Family, and Jurisdiction will be provided to GCUMM for return to participating churches. A simple, folded Viewspaper® of summary highlights will be prepared for return to local churches for insert in their Sunday Bulletins as ongoing information for all members of the congregation if they desire. Finally, since the response sheet will use only about 10 questions and has room for 50, a local church in any month can append additional survey-type questions concerning its own programming or needs on short notice. The Forum Foundation can then tabulate this data for an additional nominal cost and return it to the local church for its reference.

Costs

Costs of this research proposal should be nominal. If the General Commission on United Methodist Men does not have the budget at this time, the program can be implemented initially by establishing a fee for local churches which want to participate—possibly $75 over a nine month period September through May. Another source would be grants from supportive foundations. While the Forum Foundation was organized in 1970 to do educational research and is non-profit, it does not in itself have the resources to cover all costs of such a large project, but it can help by contributing leadership and technical support.

Other favorable factors

• Inasmuch as The 1996 Book of Resolution adopted a new resolution titled "Realizing Unity Between Lutherans and United Methodist," (page 713) the Evangelical Lutheran Church in America could easily be included in the project if desired.

• Inasmuch as the 1996 Book of Resolution adopted a new resolution titled "Make Evangelism the Number One Priority for the Next Quadriennium," (page 695) the project could be easily expanded to invite citizens from local church communities as "Citizen

Councilors." Anytime, anyone from outside the church comes to a local church for any activity—that is evangelism. The problems and issues under discussion are not just "church" issues, they are national and international issues in which all citizens are interested. The computer can easily keep track of the different responses.

• Inasmuch as the 1996 Book of Resolution readopted a resolution titled "Enlist and Involve Youth in the Life of the Church," (page 735) as a program emphasis for the 1997-2000 quadriennium, this project could easily be expanded to fulfill that objective with important overtones for the youth and citizens of the society at large. [See "Psycho-Social Education, The Future Molding Game, and the Youth Futures Forum™" article on page 149 in the book *The Search for Enlightened Leadership, Volume 1: Applying New Administrative Theory* (1996). See World Wide Web <http://weber.u.washington.edu~/forum> for more information or to order the book.

• This project is also compatible with the Vision 2000 program which the General Board of Discipleship has been developing over the last few years under the leadership of the Rev. Dr. Joe A. Harding who has endorsed this proposal.

Conclusion

As reports are generated over the months ahead, responses will be returned routinely to the General Boards of Church and Society, Global Ministries, and Council on Ministries for their reflection. The responses should help them in their continual task of perfecting the statements and resolutions in the new Book of Resolutions being prepared. Presently, each resolution listed in The Book of Resolutions ends with the word "Adopted" on a line showing the year of adoption or readoption noted. The overall responses of United Methodist Councilors to their study and discussion of each resolution considered could be reported on this same line in the next publication of the book. This would complete the feedback loop for everyone's information and benefit and without adding one line more to the book. In this manner The United Methodist Church will have created a national feedback system in which religious leaders of the church and the laity of the church at large can "talk" symbolically to each other.

This will meet the criteria of administrative theory number nine, "The Zeitgeist Principle," stated in the book *The Search for Enlightened Leadership* on page 79:

> To work most effectively, human organizations and institutions (from the smallest–a husband and wife, up to civilization itself–the largest) require a functional feedback communication capability. This is best accomplished in most organizations by a democratic, open, participative, reliable, viable, anonymous, routine, and objective feedback communication system. *Most organizations, institutions, and governments in the world today have no such system.*

If this research project is successful, the model will be a contribution of The United Methodist Church to the successful functioning of society at large and a significant contribution to the noblest experiment in governance in the history of humanity—democracy!

Summary

"What is occurring is a process–a doing, specifically a process of interrelating the person and his or her world, bringing new meaning into the human situation," [Reflections on *Youth Evangelism*, (1958) Howard Ellis and Ted McEachern, The Methodist Church, authors].

The discussion of ideas *within a constructive, open, democratic context* is the mortar which binds a creative organization or society, i.e., an organization or society which is actively searching for solutions to its problems. Any group, organization, institution, community, society, or world ideology which inhibits (innocently or not) the free flow of ideas among its constituents—up, down, and across its organizational and societal structures, is depriving itself of its greatest asset—human thought—and is in grave danger of being buried in history by the avalanche of the creativity of others!

How To Make Ideas Count

THE "STATE OF THE UNION" ADDRESS AND THE YOUTH OF AMERICA

A Part of the "Millennium Community Project" The White House[27]

ABSTRACT: Using new Many-To-Many and Fast Forum® communication technology, this paper proposes a symbolic national dialogue between the President of the United States and the youth of America in an educational process of "Civilization Building."

A Spiritual Hungering

The citizens and youth of America are hungering today for spiritual insight.[28] Who am I? What is my role in life? Where do I fit in? These "identity questions" may be the spiritual questions of the millennium. Can these questions be answered? We believe they can through new Many-To-Many communication technology as proposed in this book but only if we create new social contexts. "But we are all babies at creating context—and babies don't always get it right. But it is only in getting it wrong that we can ever hope to get it right."[29]

The Future Molding Game[30]*, and the Youth Futures Forum*[31]

Beginning in 1970, the Forum Foundation has conducted research and has identified ten organizational and societal dynamics (administrative theories) which tend to move all organizations and societies, universally, toward solving their problems and anticipating or adapting to changes in their internal or external environments. They are: The Basic Attitude in Civilization Building, The Theory of Learning, The Theory of Leadership, The Theory of Authority, The Theory of Politics, The Self-Fulfilling Prophecy, The Administrative Process Defined, The Helping Professions Defined,

[27] *The Millennium Community Project was announced by White House press release on August 15, 1997. See www.whitehouse.gov/Initiatives/Millennium; E-mail: Millennium@whitehouse.gov.*

[28] *"Promise Keepers" is a current example of this religious surge in men.*

[29] *Eldon Byrd, op. cit.*

[30] *This process was invented by our colleague Dr. Stuart C. Dodd, Professor-Emeritus of Sociology, University of Washington. It was demonstrated to the Evergreen Chapter of the World Future Society in Seattle in the early 1970's.*

[31] *The original paper was presented at the November 18, 1994 conference of The College and University Faculty Assembly, National Council for the Social Studies, Phoenix, Arizona, by Richard J. Spady. These paragraphs were extracted from the article.*

The Zeitgeist Principle; and The Natural Factors. My co-founder and colleague has been Dr. Cecil H. Bell, Jr., Associate Professor, Department of Management and Organization, School of Business Administration, University of Washington.[32] In July, 1996 we published our findings in *The Search for ENLIGHTENED LEADERSHIP, Volume 1: Applying New Administrative Theory*. This book, Volume 2: Many-To-Many Communication, is being published in the spring of 1998. Volume 3: The Civilization of Tomorrow will be published in the year 2000.[33]

Other than the ten administrative theories published in volume one of our trilogy, the essence of over 25 years research in social science for us is the realization that big meetings at often remote distances are the Achilles' Heel of the democratic process which undergirds our society, public and private. People today do not have the time and energy to go to big meetings, especially at remote distances. They are too busy earning a living. Besides they remember the last time they went; the sheer logistics are such that only a few people can speak, most can only listen.

People today are often accused of being apathetic in their responsibilities as citizens to their communities, their schools, and their churches. Our research indicates that people are not apathetic; it is just that they have concluded that such big meetings at often remote distances are not worth their time and effort, and they drop out. But that is not apathy. If the issues are critical enough, they will be there much to the chagrin of their leaders who may not understand that kind of behavior. The Forum Foundation has concluded that in order to get at the organizational and societal problems in society better, *leaders* must enable their members or constituents to meet in small groups (4 to 12 persons for adults but *foursomes* for youth), at times and places convenient to themselves during a one or two month window period in interaction with their leaders using audio (or under some conditions video) cassettes and "Opinionnaires®." But what is gained through interpersonal communication by being and talking in small groups is simultaneously lost among the participants as to who they are and what they be-

[32] *Dr. Cecil H. Bell, Jr. is co-author of the textbook, Organization Development, currently under revision for its sixth edition, Prentice-Hall, publisher. The book has been published in several languages.*

[33] *See World Wide Web <http://weber.u.washington.edu/~forum> for more information.*

lieve *as a whole.* To restore this "lost sense of touch," we have developed the Fast Forum® technique. It is a part of Many-To-Many communications and exists at a degree of complexity below the Delphi technique and below typical random-sample polling but above letter writing, telephoning, or big meetings. The Fast Forum® technique makes the same contribution to organizational and system solutions as those other, more sophisticated survey techniques do, but does it more effectively, systematically, and economically. Furthermore, since all data generated is objective showing percentages of responses to various survey-type questions by demographics of gender, age, geographic, jurisdiction, ethnic family etc., the reports generated never get bigger, they just get better as more people participate. For example, we can easily compare the opinions of groups of persons of 300 with 3,000 with 30,000—thus there is no information overload for officials, planners, teachers, students, and parents involved. Communication, understanding, and "community" are enhanced. In addition the process is never dependent on in-house or external news media which can be involved as much or as little as it wishes.

Mainstreaming

There is a concept in participation theory called "mainstreaming." Unless people perceive that what they are asked to do is mainstream and a part of the decision-making processes of the organization of which they are a part, they won't get too excited. They have to be convinced that their leaders truly want their participation and that the process is beneficial to them personally, to the church, and to the society of which they are a part. Further, the President of the United States is a "system manager."

> Through public policies, government is involved with every technology in a variety of roles. As a result, the president of the United States becomes the nation's systems manager....Since every technological choice poses ethical questions, outcomes are shaped more by the moral vision of political leaders and the electorate than by the technical content....To achieve the goals of a humane, democratic society, large numbers of people need to make thoughtful, realistic choices....We need to know who we are, where we are, and then decide on where we want to go....

> Finally, we need to admit that facing the future is as much ideological as it is technological. The bedrock values that define the nation's behavior depend on people taking responsibility. We are not just consumers of technology. In a high-tech world, we are producers, managers, investors, and sometimes innocent bystanders and victims. We are voters. Unknowingly perhaps, we are all stewards of our natural inheritance and responsible for what we leave our progeny. We are citizens of the world.
>
> —EDWARD WENK, JR., Professor-Emeritus of Engineering, University of Washington, *Making Waves:* p. 198, 230, 237, 240; University of Illinois Press, Urbana and Chicago; 1995.

Conceptually, the model proposed in this paper of "How to Make Ideas Work" recognizes that heads-of-state, e.g., a city mayor, a county executive, a state governor, and the President of the United States, are the only officials elected by all the people to represent their overall interests and are in the position of being also "master teachers." Together with all such elected public officials, *it is the prerogative and responsibility* of the president, as a head-of-state, to articulate and represent what should be done philosophically or politically to enhance the future of society. This is what is done by the president in the "State of the Union" address.

Conversely, it is the youth of society at all levels who hold the longest stake in that future and, in turn, should be enabled to interact in some appropriate manner educationally with the head-of-state. This is in an overall process of "civilization building" which is at a level above politics and above economics but includes them. The new Fast Forum® technique, which we have developed as a part of Many-To-Many communication "groupware" and "socialware" technology, allows the head-of-state to "talk" symbolically to youth and parents participating through a brief 15 to 20 minute audio tape extract of the president's "State of the Union" address. Participating youth listen to the tape and then they break into foursomes. Each youth is given a two-minute "Day in the Sun" period to state his or her opinion. The role of the other youth in the foursome (or threesome or dyad) is to *listen*—not interrupt, not ask questions, not comment, not do gestures of support or opposition but just listen. In our culture we seldom have or take the time to enable young people *to be heard* concerning substantive issues. This is one of those very precious moments for them. Youth discuss their ideas in small, non-threatening, four person, "Future Molding Game" peer discussion groups keeping in mind the "Basic Attitude."

The Basic Attitude in Civilization Building

(An Implied Administrative Imperative.)

One must always treat all persons with dignity, consideration and respect! We can reject or not agree with anything said, but we must always respect another person's right to say it. The process is LISTEN to the other person, WEIGH what is said, and then do one of three things with the idea or information received: ACCEPT it, REJECT it, or MODIFY it, i.e., accept that which fits, and ignore the rest—*but always with consideration and respect for the other person, and his or her views—in order to protect best one's own freedom to speak.*[34]

The Basic Attitude is the modern day idea of "I'm OK, you're OK; it is the biblical idea, "Love thy neighbor as thyself" which is in both Jewish and Christian scriptures.[35] It is the same idea, just millennia apart.

After each young person has had his or her "Day-In-The-Sun, a brief open discussion then follows in the foursome. When the open discussion period is over, each youth responds to objective questions about the head-of-state's ideas using an objective yes/no/abstain, multiple-choice, or value-scale instrument, e.g., Strongly Agree, Agree, Neutral, Disagree, or Strongly Disagree. While the instrument resembles a typical "questionnaire" and random-sample survey based on statistical and mathematical theory, it is instead based on participation and administrative theory—different rules apply! It is called an "Opinionnaire®." The process uses mass means of communication including audio tapes, printing, U.S. mail, small discussion groups, optical scanning (when possible), and computer tabulation of data. It will not break down simply because large numbers of people participate as is now the case with our cultural reliance on big meetings at often remote distances for people.

Again, this research model meets the criteria of "psycho-social

---

[34] *The Search for Enlightened Leadership, Volume 1: Applying New Administrative Theory, Spady and Bell, 1996, Page 35.*

[35] *(Old Testament) Leviticus 19:18 and (New Testament) Matthew 19:19.*

moratoria" as defined by Erik Erikson. "The purpose of psychosocial education as defined by Erikson is to insure the development of healthy citizens who, when they reach the age of legal maturity, are also capable of political maturity."[36]

We believe this educational model is at the frontier of knowledge. It has great potential for the nation, and its people. A national educational research model should be initiated. But we need a place to research and start to institutionalize the civilization-building process envisioned. The Forum Foundation and the Stuart C. Dodd Institute for Social Innovation are willing to assist in conducting a two-year research program to develop this model toward building "community" into the 21st century. It is a process of civilization building. Direct expenses of audio tapes, printed material, postage, and tabulation to participating teachers for the project will be minimal and can be covered by a nominal fee. We will try to obtain a financial grant from a philanthropic foundation to match the Forum Foundation's in-kind services. Thus the project should be self-funded at a nominal fee by those schools and religious groups participating.

How It Will Work

It is recommended that this research project start fall quarter 1998 and continue in fall, winter, and spring to July, 2000 through the following steps:

(1) A 15-20 minute audio tape will be prepared from speeches of the President of the United States by the Forum Foundation Research Team. The team is composed of:

DICK SPADY, President, Forum Foundation, Chair
REV. WILLIAM B. CATE, Ph.D., Social Ethics, Vice Chair
REV. KENNETH BEDELL, Ph.D., Sociology, President, EPIC, Inc. (Ecumenical Programs in Communication), Vice President (Research), Forum Foundation, Team Administrator
MS. JAN CATE, M.A., Values Education, Forum Foundation Board
REV. WILLIAM D. ELLINGTON, Ph.D., Theology, Forum

[36] *Robert Pranger, The Eclipse of Citizenship, 1968. Dr. Pranger was in the Department of Political Science at the University of Washington at the time.*

Foundation Co-founder and Board Member

REV. RICHARD S. KIRBY, Ph.D., Theology, Executive Director, SCDI/SI (Stuart C. Dodd Institute for Social Innovation) and faculty member of the University of Washington, School of Business Administration)

REV. JOHN C. GINGERICH, Ph.D., Christian Education

BERNARD Z. FRIEDLANDER, Ph.D., Visiting Scholar, Dept. of Psychology, U of W, Seattle; Professor Emeritus, Dept. of Psychology, Univ. of Hartford, West Hartford, CT

MR. LEN SCHREINER, Peace Activist Teacher, Seattle

REV. ROBERT F. CRAMER, RFC Communications

JOHN SPADY, Director of Research, Forum Foundation

RON SCHMEER, Staff, Forum Foundation

(2) An Opinionnaire® will be prepared by the Forum Foundation Research Team with questions based on the issues raised by the President.

(3) The cover letter, instructions, audio tape, and Opinionnaire® for (1) A Millennium Community Project packet, and (2) A current "State of the Union" packet will be replicated and mailed by SCDI/SI to those enrolled in the project. Schools and religious groups that want their youth to participate can enroll in the project anytime during the year.

(4) Youth enrolled listen to the tape, split into foursomes, and participate in the "Future Molding Game."

(5) Each youth and adult participating shows demographics, e.g., gender, age, ethnic family, state etc. and responds to questions posed on the Opinionnaire®. All responses are recorded on a Forum Foundation Reproducible Response Sheet (they can be copied on a regular copy machine).

(6) If possible, a new Opinionnaire® and Response Sheet(s) are taken to the parents of the youth participating who also are encouraged to respond to the Opinionnaire® questions.

(7) Preferably the Forum Foundation Reproducible Response Sheets are tabulated by one or more school volunteer "communicators." The communicator tabulates data responses on a computer using a standard word processor. Instructions are not complicated, e.g., a "yes" is tabulated as "1" and a "no" as "2." A multiple choice

question is tabulated "2" through "5" etc. An abstention to a question is tabulated as a space.

(8) The teacher transmits the data tabulated to SCDI/SI (a) via e-mail on Internet at no additional cost, (b) on a diskette mailed to SCDI/SI with a self-addressed, stamped envelope enclosed for return of the diskette, or (c) mails completed Forum Foundation Reproducible Response Sheets to SCDI/SI for their tabulation of data with a check enclosed @ 50 cents per sheet to help cover direct costs for this service. [Note: If desired, a school or church can also purchase Forum Foundation Machine-Scannable Response Sheets in packets of 100 sheets @ 25 cents per sheet in advance from the Forum Foundation through SCDI/SI. Upon completion, machine-scannable response sheets are mailed to the SCDI/SI for tabulation at no additional cost over school or church letterhead and signature for verification.]

(9) The Forum Foundation prepares the directives file, the data file, and generates the profile reports required. The profile reports which will be provided are gender and class. A summary Viewspaper® of response highlights will be prepared also. This will be an 8½X11 sheet folded once to make four pages (see sample format in Appendix G, H, or I).

(10) Profile reports will be mailed to teachers enrolled in the project for discussion with their students. Parents are encouraged also to discuss the results with their youth and make comments they feel are necessary to clarify understanding of the issues or the data responses. The overall discussion process is one of *civilization building*. The basic discussion, then, is above "politics" and above "economics" but includes both in a process of *psycho-social education*. The overall process is a *symbolic* dialogue (i.e., not physical) among the youth and their parents with the President of the United States in an exploration together of the future. Perhaps other citizens, especially the elderly, will also participate as the program matures. Any news media interested can get the information it wants for further analysis and editorials as it wishes.

(11) Reports will be sent to the President and be posted on a web site established for this project. This will allow all interested governments, organizations, and citizens to access and study all reports. The program is capable of almost numberless "compound

searches" which can be made with specific reports generated as desired. For example: How did male and female youth, fathers, mothers, and others in a time zone or state compare with participants in other time zones or states?

Basic Roles of Participating Organizations

MILLENNIUM COMMUNITY PROJECT, THE WHITE HOUSE: Hopefully, and to help energize this proposal, this research project will be designated as an official millennium project which recognizes outstanding proposals to develop "community."

FORUM FOUNDATION: Conducts the research project and oversees preparation by SCDI/SI of the audio tapes, Opinionnaires®, Viewspapers®, and generates profile reports; establishes the web site for the project and posts reports. These in-kind services, as a contribution of the Forum Foundation, will be provided without cost. The Forum Foundation will have the right to publish the overview of research results and Viewspapers® in its future publications of books and articles. [The Forum Foundation is primarily in a research mode and not a service delivery mode. While the Forum Foundation is a non-profit Washington state corporation organized in 1970, it is not tax exempt; all funds are internally generated from the sale of books and services with no public donations accepted.]

STUART C. DODD INSTITUTE FOR SOCIAL INNOVATION (SCDI/SI): Non-profit, tax-exempt organization which will provide follow-on services, as might be required, for schools and churches participating. [SCDI/SI was approved as a 501(c)(3), tax exempt, organization on May 9, 1997. It is gradually building its infrastructure to perform these services for interested organizations and communities. The Rev. Dr. Richard S. Kirby, Ph.D., Theology, is Executive Director. Their address is: 4427 Thackeray Place N.E., Seattle, WA 98105-6124. [Tel: 206-545-0547; Fax: 206-633-3561; E-mail: DrRSKirby@aol.com.]

Summary

"What is occurring is a process—a doing, specifically a process of interrelating the person and his or her world, bringing new meaning into the human situation"[37]

---

[37] *Howard Ellis and Ted McEachern, The United Methodist Church, authors.*

Conclusion

Confrontation of ideas is the mortar which binds a creative organization or society, i.e., an organization or society which is actively searching for solutions to its problems. Any group, organization, institution, community, society, or world ideology which inhibits (innocently or not) the free flow of ideas among its constituents—up, down, and across its organizational and societal structures, is depriving itself of its greatest asset—*human thought*—and is in grave danger of being buried in history by the avalanche of the creativity of others.

PRESIDENT CLINTON'S INITIATIVE ON RACE

Founded in 1970
Non-Profit

April 18, 1998

Dr. John Hope Franklin, Chair
President Clinton's Initiative on Race

Dear Dr. Franklin:

It was good to hear you speak at the Seattle Chamber of Commerce and City Club luncheon on April 13th and to learn more of the work of President Clinton's Initiative on Race. "The Time to Talk" theme with a series of conversations in private homes and community meetings sponsored by the Urban Enterprise Center of the Greater Seattle Chamber of Commerce holds great promise here. I have a suggestion that will amplify their impact in Seattle and similar programs elsewhere in the nation.

We had a forum program in 1969 conducted by the Eastside Inter-Racial Clearing House of which I was chair. It was composed of the Bellevue Area PTA Council, Bellevue Ministerial Association, Bellevue Chamber of Commerce, Eastside Conference on Race and Religion, Eastside YMCA, and Seattle-King County Economic Opportunity board; the program was co-sponsored by the East Madison YMCA and the Rotary Boy's Club in Seattle.

We had 3 black families and 3 white families meeting two hours over 3 Friday nights running. This research was the prototype development of what today is known as the "Fast Forum®" technique in which we discovered two of its four foundations—(1) Social Resolving Power, and (2) the Polarization-Consensus Rating (P-C Rating). [Please note the cover and frontispiece of *The Christian Forum (or Fast Forum), Why and What It Is!* (1969) which is enclosed. It shows the responses by all participants to some statements generated by the dialogue groups.]

I then attended the University of Washington Graduate School of Business from 1968-1970 concentrating in the field of administrative theory and organizational behavior. In the spring of 1970 I took an advanced class in Management Theory and was assigned a term paper with the words, "Just take anything in management theory and make it sound rational." From that broad brush but fun assignment, I came up with 8 theories at the time. These were the identification of those dynamics which tended to move organizations, universally, toward solving their problems and anticipating or adapting to changes in their internal or external environments. I then contracted with the University of Washington Academic Computer Center to write a new program; as a theoretician I knew where to go, but didn't know how to get there. The computer programmer knew how to get there but didn't know where to go. Together we designed and created the first Fast Forum® computer program which today is known as "groupware" or "socialware" programming. It is now on the Macintosh.

I co-founded the Forum Foundation in 1970 as a non-profit, educational research corporation of Washington state with Dr. Cecil H. Bell, Jr. who was my advisor at the time. Most recently he was chair of the Dept. of Management and Organization of the School of Business Administration at the university. He is just finishing a sabbatical to complete the sixth edition of his book *Organization Development* which he has co-authored (Prentice-Hall Publishers).

Seattle Office
4426 Second Avenue N.E. • Seattle, WA 98105-6191 • Fax (206) 633-3561 • Phone (206) 634-0420
http://weber.u.washington.edu/~forum

Forum Foundation April 18, 1998 Page 2

When one does research in social science, one needs (1) people and (2) organizations. I then served on the volunteer staff of the Church Council of Greater Seattle from 1971-1990 with the portfolio "Futures Research" which we defined not as forecasting but as the search for ways to influence the sociological and technological future. We continued to learn from religious groups and schools participating with us in the research to improve communication and thus help build "community."

In 1996 Cecil Bell and I wrote our findings in the book *The Search for Enlightened Leadership, Volume 1: Applying New Administrative Theory* which is enclosed. [Please see the Forum Foundation Fact Sheet on page 117 for further information.] The book is currently being taught as a textbook to undergraduates in the School of Business Administration by Dr. Richard S. Kirby in the class *Organization and Environment*. So we are making progress. The second volume in the trilogy is *Many-To-Many Communication* which was just given to the printer two days ago. The book will be ready in June and will be introduced in July at the annual conference of the World Future Society in Chicago. [See outline enclosed.]

The Fast Forum® technique can be used by you and your committee to establish a "symbolic" dialogue between yourselves (either representing the President or helping him to conduct the dialogue himself using audio tape) and small groups of 4 to 12 persons who are talking about the problems of race in Seattle and throughout the country. Furthermore, the process can be self-funded as direct costs are nominal. Additional tax funds need not be required. The Forum Foundation is willing to contribute its consulting services and provide computer reports of data as an in-kind service to the Seattle dialogues and elsewhere if a two-year research project is initiated. Variable costs are nominal. I am willing to meet with you and your committee at my expense to talk further of the proposal if you or the Seattle groups are interested. Best wishes for success.

Sincerely,

Dick Spady

Richard J. Spady, President

Enclosures: As shown together with a Forum Foundation *Councilor* Response Sheet

cc: Mr. Robert C. Wallace, Chair, Seattle Chamber of Commerce
City Club

cc w/o encl.: Directors, Forum Foundation
Dr. Richard S. Kirby, Exec. Dir., Stuart C. Dodd Institute for Social Innovation and Chair, World Network of Religious Futurists

Census Forum™ & Time and Talent™ Survey

FOR CHURCHES AND ORGANIZATIONS

The purpose of this annual CENSUS Forum™ model is to prepare a series of *specific* program questions to the congregation to help in planning programs for the coming church year. At the same time every member of the congregation is invited to complete the Time and Talent™ Response Sheet (Form K). This is a machine-scannable response sheet that is marked with a pencil; it can be easily updated each year by erasing changes and adding new information. When a current Time and Talent report is required by the nominating committee or committee chairs, the machine-scannable sheets need only be scanned. The response sheet records each person's gift of service to the church—past, present, and of interest in the future. For example, parishioners mark:

A = Presently Serving or Active

B = Interested (but not experienced)

C = Interested and experienced (but not currently serving);

D = Experienced (but not currently interested)

St. Peter's United Methodist Church
Seattle District, PNW Annual Conference, UMC
May/June 1997

1. *CENSUS FORUM '97*

Help Us Plan for Your Religious Journey in the Coming Year!
(For St. Peter's UMC Youth and Adults)

PLEASE PRINT:

CURRENT DATE: ______________________________

LAST NAME FIRST NAME MIDDLE INITIAL ______________________________

STREET ADDRESS (IF NEEDED) ______________________________

CITY STATE ZIP CODE

RESIDENCE PHONE OTHER PHONE

BIRTHDAY-M/D/Y

Pastor Tom and..., Co-chairs of Adult and Youth Education, want to provide relevant programming for all adults and youth at St. Peter's. Please indicate if you are interested now and will probably want to participate in the following programs if they are introduced: *[Please circle your answer. If you are undecided and cannot give a* clear *yes or no answer, please circle abstain.]*

1. Bible Study. Are you interested in attending a Sunday School Bible Study group? (YES NO ABSTAIN)

2. Lectionary Bible Study. (Wed. at noon, Sept-May) (This class, led by the Pastor, studies the assigned scripture for the upcoming Sunday. These are the same scriptures that the Sunday School classes study and that the sermon is based on.) Are you interested in attending? (YES NO ABSTAIN)

3. Sermon "TalkBack." Are you interested in attending? (Sundays from 11:45 A.M.–12:15 P.M.—gather in the Prayer Room to discuss the Pastor's message. A discussion led by....) (YES NO ABSTAIN)

4. Adult Sunday School using Faithlink. (9:00 A.M., Sundays) (Faithlink is a lesson/discussion sheet featuring a current issue, for example—"Taxes: Bane or Blessing" and "Faith and Civil Religion.") Are you interested? (YES NO ABSTAIN)

5. Book of Resolutions, 1996. Are you interested in studying the UMC Book of Resolutions? (Contains the UMC Social Principles and Resolutions relating to The Natural World, Nurturing Community, Social Community, Economic Community, Political Community, and World Community. This class will be led by Dick Spady,...and meet at Dick's home on a Sunday evening or at another time and place if preferred by the group.) (YES NO ABSTAIN)

6. Greater Seattle Citizen Councilor Network Are you interested in participating? (Once a quarter, during a one-hour "community building" period on a Sunday evening, discuss and record your opinions on a community-wide issue as an "Ecumenical Councilor" of the Church Council of Greater Seattle.) (YES NO ABSTAIN)

Adult Class or Discussion

Family Issues: Please indicate whether you are interested in attending an Adult Class or Discussion Group, perhaps evenings, concerning the following topics:

7. Parenting (preschool through elementary) (YES NO ABSTAIN)

8. Communication Between Parents/Teens (YES NO ABSTAIN)

9. Couple Communication (YES NO ABSTAIN)

10. Caring for Adult Parents (YES NO ABSTAIN)

11. Grief Recovery (YES NO ABSTAIN)

12. Are you interested in teaching or working with preschool or elementary classes at St. Peter's? (YES NO ABSTAIN)

13. Are you interested in teaching or working with Junior High students at St. Peter's? (YES NO ABSTAIN)

14. Are you interested in teaching or working with Senior High students at St. Peter's? (YES NO ABSTAIN)

Methodist Related Topics

(as Sunday or evening discussion topics)

15. The Theology of UM Christians (articles of religion) (YES NO ABSTAIN)

16. Spiritual Formation (YES NO ABSTAIN)

17. Missions (example: Cooperative School of Missions) (YES NO ABSTAIN)

Youth Classes or Activities

Please indicate whether you are interested in participating in a

Youth Activity or Group concerning the following areas:

18. The Nursery Program? (YES NO ABSTAIN)

19. The youth Sunday School program in general? (YES NO ABSTAIN)

20. Junior Church and Children's Fellowship? (YES NO ABSTAIN)

21. The Middler Program? (YES NO ABSTAIN)

22.The SPUMY program for high-school youth? (YES NO ABSTAIN)

23. Children's Music? (YES NO ABSTAIN)

24. The Confirmation Class? (YES NO ABSTAIN)

25. The summer program for youth? (YES NO ABSTAIN)

Other Educational and Social Opportunities

26. Are you interested in participating with a young adult group? (YES NO ABSTAIN)

27. Are you interested in participating in "Dinners for Eight?" (YES NO ABSTAIN)

28. Are you interested in participating in "Diversity Dinners?" (YES NO ABSTAIN)

29. Are you interested in participating in "M & M's (Mature Methodists) activities?" (YES NO ABSTAIN)

30. Are you interested in Day Bus Tours with neighboring churches? (Example: trip to Smithsonian Exhibit in Portland.(YES NO ABSTAIN)

31. Are you interested in attending a two-hour, "Stuart C. Dodd Lecture Series" over three Sunday evening periods next fall by The Rev. Dr. Richard S. Kirby, Theologian and Philosopher, Chair, World Network of Religious Futurists? (The series will include the 21st century's needs including the "Graying of America," "Coming of Age of Generation X," "Financial Crisis in Medicare," "Social Security," and "Race Relations.") (YES NO ABSTAIN)

32. Would you attend "A Mini-Course in Christian Theology" by The Rev. Dr. William D. Ellington, UMC Theologian and Fuller

Theological School faculty member? *(This event had to be cancelled earlier by UMM. Dr. Ellington can reschedule to come in late October on a Sunday evening from 4–7 p.m. Are you interested in attending?)* (YES NO ABSTAIN)

Please print or write legibly your comments and suggestions below as to how St. Peter's can better help you on your religious journey in the coming year. Thank you for participating.

TIME AND TALENT SURVEY
St. Peter's United Methodist Church
Seattle District, PNW Annual Conference, UMC
Sept./Oct. 1998

Your Personal Demographics: *(please circle the letter or number of your choice)*

1. GENDER: M = Male; F = Female

2. AGE:_______please enter your age or age decade, e.g., , teens, 20's, 30's...60's, 70's etc. (otherwise you will be recorded as "not identified" on the Age profile report for the above questions.)

3-4. "CLASS YEAR" (Year of Birth +18): [For children and young adult response. For example, a child born before August 31, 1997 in the Bellevue School District will normally be in the "Class of 2015" when graduating from high school. In this way we can always determine the children in each grade for whom the church has a spiritual responsibility without updating church records each year. We need only correct the entry if a child skips a grade or falls behind.]

5. RESIDENT QUADRANT: With a clock centered over St. Peter's and 12 pointing north (1=northeast quadrant, 2=southeast, 3=southwest, 4=northwest)

6. DISTANCE FROM CHURCH: Using map with concentric circles "as the crow flies." (1=under 1 mile, 2=1-2 miles, 3=2-3 miles, 4=3-4 miles, 5=Over 4 miles)

7. ETHNIC FAMILY: In order to best determine the general charac-

teristics of our congregation for planning "Diversity Dinners" and like events, what is your ethnic family? *(please print)*

8. EMPLOYMENT: (1=Employed in Industry, 2=Employed in Govt., 3=Self-employed, 4=Unemployed and looking for work, 5=Homemaker, 6=Student, 7=Retired)

9. FAMILY STATUS: (1=Married; 2=Married w/children at home; 3=Single, 4=Single Parent, 5=Separated, 6=Divorced, 7=Widowed)

10-11-12. CARE AND NURTURE GROUP ASSIGNMENTS (as might be assigned in the future)

Time and Talent Survey Inventory

"Yes, I am interested in sharing my time and talents in furthering the mission of our church in the following areas." *(Please write "A," "B," "C," or "D" when applicable.)*

A = Presently Serving or Active

B = Interested (but not experienced)

C = Interested and experienced (but not currently serving);

D = Experienced (but not currently interested)

LEADERSHIP/ADMINISTRATION

☐ 1. Administrative Council Member

☐ 2. Lay Leader

☐ 3. Lay Member to Annual Conference

☐ 4. Lay Speaker

☐ 5. Treasurer

☐ 6. Financial Sec.

☐ 7. Church Computer Communicator

☐ 8. Worship Committee

☐ 9. Chancel Choir

☐ 10. Bell Choir

☐ 11. Contemporary Worship

☐ 12. Liturgist

☐ 13. Altar Flowers

☐ 14. Communion Preparation

☐ 15. Usher

☐ 16. Greeter

☐ 17. Trustees (Building & Grounds)

☐ 18. Staff-Parish Committee

☐ 19. Mission/Outreach
☐ 20. Membership & Evangelism Com.
☐ 21. Membership Records
☐ 22. Special Gifts/Memorials
☐ 23. Finance Com.
☐ 24. Stewardship Coordinator

GIVING

☐ 25. Pony Express Trail Boss/Agent

EDUCATION

☐ 26. Committee Member
☐ 27. Coordinator, Sunday School
☐ 28. Coordinator, Adult
☐ 29. Teacher (please circle) 1= Nursery, 2=Preschool, 3=Elementary, 4=Jr. high, 5=Sr. high, adult
☐ 30. Vacation Bible School Helper

ADULT GROUPS

☐ 31. Bible Study Class
☐ 32. United Methodist Men
☐ 33. United Methodist Women
☐ 34. Dinners-For-Eight Coordinator
☐ 35. Adult Nurture/Study Group

OTHER GROUPS

☐ 36. Young Adults
☐ 37. SPUMY (Youth)
☐ 38. Middlers

HOSPITALITY

☐ 39. Coffee/Kitchen

FELLOWSHIP/COORDINATION
Helping Hands:

☐ 40. Shut-ins (1=visit, 2=telephoning)
☐ 41. Meal Providing
☐ 42. Providing Transportation
☐ 43. Office Help (please circle below) 1=typing, 2=Keys, 3=mail, 4=telephoning
☐ 44. Gardening/Landscaping

SEASONAL EVENTS

☐ 45. Camp Retreats

☐ 46. Instrument (List)

____

____

☐ 47. Soloist (List)

____

____

☐ 48. Active Hobbies (List)

____

____

☐ 49. Other skills/activities (List)

____

____

TIME AND TALENT SURVEY
St. Peters United Methodist Church
17222 NE 8th Street
Bellevue, WA 98008
(425) 747-3210

Please mail or return this Census Forum and Time and Talent survey to the church office. Thank you.

St. Peter's Time and Talent

Name	Phone	Sex	Birth Month	Birth Day	Birth Year	Class Year	Demographics Quad	Miles	E.F.	Empl	F.S.	Nurture Groups	Talents 1 through 50 ==> 1	2	3	4	5	6	7	8	9	10	11	12	13	14	15	16	17	18
Alphabetical Report																														
Time and Talent Format **(Machine scannable sheets are filed alphabetically in a "tub file" for easy reference at any time or scanned for current, printed reports.)**																														
Family 1: Father		M					4	1	3	3	1		A														A			A
Family1: Mother		F	1	14	44		4	1	3	1	2				D	D		D	D	D					A				A	
Family1: Son 1		M	3	16	80	1998	4	1	3	5	3					B			A											
Family1: Daughter 1		F	1	10	83	2001	4	1	2	7	3																			
Family1: Daughter 2		F	11	13	86	2005	4	1	3	5	3																			
(additional families - etc)		M							3																					
Member		M							3																					
Member		F	12	12	38		1	1	3	4	9					A														
Member		F	5	8	38		3	5	3	3	6		A	A	C	A	B	C		A		C								
Member		M	4	2	26		4	5	3	6	1																			
Member		F	9	12	25		4	5	3	1	6																			
SPADY, RICHARD J	(206) 634-0420	M	10	15	23		2	1	3	3	1		A	D	D	A			A											
Member		F	8	5	29		1	1	3	3	2					D			B						B	B	C		C	
Member		F	10	20	42		1	2	3	4	1		A	D		C						A			D	A	D	A	D	
Member		M	2	21	34				3		1																			
Member		M					4	1	3	3	1		A					A	A	A	A	A					A			A
Member		F	1	10	83	2001	4	1	2	7	3																			
Member		F	11	13	86	2005	4	1	3	5	3																			
Member		F	1	14	44		4	1	3	1	2				D	D		D	D	D					A				A	
Member		M	3	16	80	1998	4	1	3	5	3					B			A											
Member		F	6	22	84	2002			3																					
Member		M	4	14	36		3	2		3	1		A			A				D		A			D		D	D		C
Member		F	12	28	34		3	3	7	6	1						A													
Member		F	9	14	80	1998			3																					
Member		M					4	5	3	6	1								A											
Member		F					4	5	3	6	1										A									
Member		F	11	10	89				3	7	3																			
Member		F	8	27	46		3	2	3	2	3																D			
Member																														
Member		F	9	27	37		1	1	3	1	5		D			A		B	D	D										
Member		F	10	29	32		4	1	3	6	1																			
Member		F	8	7	16		4	2	3	6	6														D		D	C	D	
Member		F	12	6	27		3	2	3	6	6																			
Member		F	4	19	25		4	5	3	6	1		D			A		D					D						D	
Member		F	7	22	2		1	5	5	6	6																			
Member		M	3	11	26		4	5	3	6	1		D			A		C		D	D				D	D	D	D	D	D
Member		M	3	14	34		3	5	3	6	1		A	A					D			D								
Member		F	6	19	36		3	5	3	6	1		C	D	D	A		A		A	D				D		D			
Member		F	7	31			1	2	7	2	2					A														
Member		M	11	15	85	2004		2	7	5	3																			
Member		M					1	2	7	2	2																			
Member		F					3	2		6	1								A											
Member		F	8	24	22			5	3	6	6											A								

September 22, 1997
St. Peter's United Methodist Church

St. Peter's Time and Talent

Name	19	20	21	22	23	24	25	26	27	28	29	30	31	32	33	34	35	36	37	38	39	40	41	42	43	44	45	46	47	48	49	50
Alphabetical Report																																
Family 1: Father				A			A																									
Family1: Mother	D	D			D	D	D												D	D	D								D			
Family1: Son 1				A					A		A	A													A	A					A	A
Family1: Daughter 1									A			B																				
Family1: Daughter 2																																F
(additional families - etc)																																
Member																																
Member	A			A											A					A												
Member	C		A			C	C					C		A	C				B										C	C	C	C
Member											D	D																				
Member	D										D	D																				
SPADY, RICHARD J	D	D					D				C	D	D	A			C															
Member	A	D			C	C	C		D	D		D		C	C	A		A	C				C	A							A	C
Member													D		D				D										D			
Member																																
Member				A			A											A														
Member									A			B																				
Member																																F
Member	D	D			D	D	D												D	D	D								D			
Member				A					A		A	A													A	A					A	A
Member																																
Member															A														D			
Member															A					A												
Member																																
Member												A																	A			
Member	A											A		A			A															
Member																																
Member	A	A	A		A										B	B							C									
Member																																
Member	D	A																												A		
Member																																
Member						C	C					C		C			C						C				D					
Member	B	A												B	C																	
Member	C	A				D												D			A					A			D	D	A	A
Member																															A	
Member		A				D												C	A							C			D		A	A
Member											C	C				A					C											
Member		A	A			D	D									A			D			D							C	B		
Member	A	A									A												A									A
Member										B																						B
Member																																
Member	A		A									A			A																	
Member												A																				

QUEST Forum™ *(For Organizations)*

(QUICK ENVIRONMENTAL SCANNING TEST)

Key Points of Model

The QUEST Forum™ (**QU**ick **E**nvironmental **S**canning **T**est) model is designed to get quick survey-type information from constituents without their meeting with others.

The idea of the QUEST Forum™ is to send out an Opinionnaire® to a closed, organizational constituency quickly by mail without the need for small discussion groups or any other supporting information. It is a quick, simple, uncomplicated way to scan and test a specific constituency individually about current issues without using discussion groups. It can be either a management forum where the data returned is kept confidential or a leadership forum where the data is open to all.

For example, a QUEST Opinionnaire® sheet could be sent by mail directly to local church pastors nationally, regionally, or in a smaller conference or district who were members of a denomination. They could be asked to make copies of the Opinionnaire® for each ministerial associate and for four key laity in leadership positions. This permits tabulation to compare results of pastors, associates, and key lay persons. The data should be interesting and credible to church leaders. Completed responses using optical scanning sheets could be used and returned in a church envelope with a secretary's signature authenticating the data as long as participants remain anonymous by categories. In this manner, the denomination can best assure the validity of the data returned if required.

Another example is that a network could also be established in an "annual conference" or regional group composed of local church officers and/or specific constituencies, e.g., stewardship, education, youth, or music committees. Conference or group leaders could talk symbolically with key local church constituents.

We would expect that if any group in society would encourage participation of their constituents in a process of questing to improve organization and civilization building, it would be clergy and church members.

This model has never been used as designed to date of this writing, but the format is a viable research proposal. The model has great flexibility in program design and should be of immense use to improve communications in appropriate situations in church and society. A proposed QUEST Forum™ format for churches follows.

ST. PETER'S UNITED METHODIST CHURCH
QUEST FORUM™
[QUick Environmental Scanning Test]
Date:________1st Sunday

On February 1, 1997 the Administrative Council met from 8:00 am to noon in a church planning session with the theme: "FINDING THE WAY FORWARD—St. Peter's A Church of Vision." The following ideas were selected as our primary goals. Please circle as you agree or disagree. *(No circled response = abstain)*

1. Increase visibility of St. Peters to the community.
   STRONGLY DISAGREE DISAGREE NEUTRAL AGREE STRONGLY AGREE

2. Increase St. Peter's awareness of community's needs and how to best service those needs for worship and outreach.
   STRONGLY DISAGREE DISAGREE NEUTRAL AGREE STRONGLY AGREE

3. Focus on children and youth through worship and outreach.
   STRONGLY DISAGREE DISAGREE NEUTRAL AGREE STRONGLY AGREE

4. Expand adult programming.
   STRONGLY DISAGREE DISAGREE NEUTRAL AGREE STRONGLY AGREE

Please print your own best idea for FINDING THE WAY FORWARD—at St. Peters. New ideas surfacing from this request will be provided for your response next week. Please place your response sheet in the collection plate.

Please state anonymously your own best idea for FINDING THE WAY FORWARD—at St. Peters. What are our needs? What are the problems we need to solve? What could we do better? What programs would you like to see at St. Peter's? [Please stick to proposals and observations and avoid any personal references.]

INSTRUCTION: Please think through and carefully craft your statement as clearly as possible since we will not be editing your statement except when absolutely necessary. If you do not carefully craft your statement or have too many different ideas, people responding will either *abstain* or *object* which will defeat your and the congregation's purpose. We can include up to 50 statements on both a "Proposals" Opinionnaire® and an "Ideas" Opinionnaire®. This is a total of 100 possible statements for consideration by the congregation. If the committee receives more than this, the committee will eliminate duplicate or similar statements and then select a representative set of statements from the balance submitted. Thank you.

Please print legibly *and stay within the borders.*(3X5" card equivalent)

Thank you for participating in this QUEST Forum™. If you have any general comments you would like to make about process or St. Peters, please print them below.

ST. PETER'S UNITED METHODIST CHURCH
QUEST FORUM™
[QUick Environmental Scanning Test]
Date:_______2nd Sunday

On February 1, 1997 the Administrative Council met in a church planning session with the theme: "FINDING THE WAY FORWARD—

St. Peter's A Church of Vision." Last week parishioners responded to goals proposed. The results are on the back of this insert.

A representative selection of ideas from parishioners follow. Please circle a number 1–5 indicating the intensity of your disagreement or agreement. (3 = neutral; no circled response = abstain)

1. xxxxxxxxxxxxxxxxxxxxxxxxxxxxxxxxxxxxxxxxxxxxx
xxxxxxxxxxxxxxxxxxxxxxxxxxxxxxxxxxxxxxxxxxxxx.
xxxxxxxxxxxxxxxxxxxxxxxxxxxxxxxxxxxxxxxxxxxxx.

Strongly Disagree 1 2 3 4 5 Strongly Agree

2. xxxxxxxxxxxxxxxxxxxxxxxxxxxxxxxxxxxxxxxxxxxxx
xxxxxxxxxxxxxxxxxxxxxxxxxxxxxxxxxxxxxxxxxxxxx.
xxxxxxxxxxxxxxxxxxxxxxxxxxxxxxxxxxxxxxxxxxxxx.

Strongly Disagree 1 2 3 4 5 Strongly Agree

3. xxxxxxxxxxxxxxxxxxxxxxxxxxxxxxxxxxxxxxxxxxxxx
xxxxxxxxxxxxxxxxxxxxxxxxxxxxxxxxxxxxxxxxxxxxx.
xxxxxxxxxxxxxxxxxxxxxxxxxxxxxxxxxxxxxxxxxxxxx.

Strongly Disagree 1 2 3 4 5 Strongly Agree

4. xxxxxxxxxxxxxxxxxxxxxxxxxxxxxxxxxxxxxxxxxxxxx
xxxxxxxxxxxxxxxxxxxxxxxxxxxxxxxxxxxxxxxxxxxxx.
xxxxxxxxxxxxxxxxxxxxxxxxxxxxxxxxxxxxxxxxxxxxx.

Strongly Disagree 1 2 3 4 5 Strongly Agree

5. xxxxxxxxxxxxxxxxxxxxxxxxxxxxxxxxxxxxxxxxxxxxx
xxxxxxxxxxxxxxxxxxxxxxxxxxxxxxxxxxxxxxxxxxxxx.
xxxxxxxxxxxxxxxxxxxxxxxxxxxxxxxxxxxxxxxxxxxxx.

Strongly Disagree 1 2 3 4 5 Strongly Agree

6. Etc.

Back of Insert:

On February 1, 1997 the Administrative Council met in a church planning session with the theme: "FINDING THE WAY FORWARD—St. Peter's A Church of Vision." They selected the following ideas as primary goals; congregation reaction was:

1. Increase visibility of St. Peters to the community.

STRONGLY	DISAGREE	DISAGREE	NEUTRAL	AGREE	STRONGLY AGREE
xx%	xx%	xx%	xx%	xx%	(xx% Abs/Obj)

2. Increase St. Peter's awareness of community's needs and how

to best service those needs for worship and outreach.

STRONGLY DISAGREE	DISAGREE	NEUTRAL	AGREE	STRONGLY AGREE	
xx%	xx%	xx%	xx%	xx%	(xx% Abs/Obj)

3. Focus on children and youth through worship and outreach.

STRONGLY DISAGREE	DISAGREE	NEUTRAL	AGREE	STRONGLY AGREE	
xx%	xx%	xx%	xx%	xx%	(xx% Abs/Obj)

4. Expand adult programming.

STRONGLY DISAGREE	DISAGREE	NEUTRAL	AGREE	STRONGLY AGREE	
xx%	xx%	xx%	xx%	xx%	(xx% Abs/Obj)

5. Etc.

Thank you for participating in this QUEST Forum™. If you have any further insights or suggestions based on the information above, please print them below for possible consideration next Sunday.

ST. PETER'S UNITED METHODIST CHURCH
QUEST FORUM™
[QUick Environmental Scanning Test]
Date:_______3rd Sunday

On February 1, 1997 the Administrative Council met in a church planning session with the theme: "FINDING THE WAY FORWARD—St. Peter's A Church of Vision." For the past two weeks parishioners responded to goals proposed and ranked ideas. The QUEST Forum committee of the Administrative Council, including church officers and Pastor Tom, have drafted the following statements which, in their view, reflect the consensus and vision to date. Do you agree with the vision, disagree with it, or abstain?

1. xxxxxxxxxxxxxxxxxxxxxxxxxxxxxxxxxxxxxxxxxxxxxxxxxx xxxxxxxxxxxxxxxxxxxxxxxxxxxxxxxxxxxxxxxxxxxxxxxxxx xxxxxxxxxxxxxxxxxxxxxxxxxxxxxxxxxxxxxxxxxxxxxxxxxxx.

AGREE DISAGREE ABSTAIN

2. xxxxxxxxxxxxxxxxxxxxxxxxxxxxxxxxxxxxxxxxxxxxxxxxxx xxxxxxxxxxxxxxxxxxxxxxxxxxxxxxxxxxxxxxxxxxxxxxxxxx xxxxxxxxxxxxxxxxxxxxxxxxxxxxxxxxxxxxxxxxxxxxxxxxxxx.

AGREE DISAGREE ABSTAIN

3. xxxxxxxxxxxxxxxxxxxxxxxxxxxxxxxxxxxxxxxxxxxxxxxxxxxx xxxxxxxxxxxxxxxxxxxxxxxxxxxxxxxxxxxxxxxxxxxxxxxxxxxxx xxxxxxxxxxxxxxxxxxxxxxxxxxxxxxxxxxxxxxxxxxxxxxxxxxxxxxxxx.
AGREE DISAGREE ABSTAIN

4. xxxxxxxxxxxxxxxxxxxxxxxxxxxxxxxxxxxxxxxxxxxxxxxxxxxx xxxxxxxxxxxxxxxxxxxxxxxxxxxxxxxxxxxxxxxxxxxxxxxxxxxxx xxxxxxxxxxxxxxxxxxxxxxxxxxxxxxxxxxxxxxxxxxxxxxxxxxxxxxxxx.
AGREE DISAGREE ABSTAIN

5. xxxxxxxxxxxxxxxxxxxxxxxxxxxxxxxxxxxxxxxxxxxxxxxxxxxx xxxxxxxxxxxxxxxxxxxxxxxxxxxxxxxxxxxxxxxxxxxxxxxxxxxxx xxxxxxxxxxxxxxxxxxxxxxxxxxxxxxxxxxxxxxxxxxxxxxxxxxxxxxxxx.
AGREE DISAGREE ABSTAIN

6. Etc.

Thank you for participating the past 3 weeks in the QUEST Forum™ theme "FINDING THE WAY FORWARD—St. Peter's A Church of Vision." Final results will be reported next week. If there is a lack of overall consensus, further queries may be needed.

ST. PETER'S UNITED METHODIST CHURCH
QUEST FORUM™
*[**QU**ick **E**nvironmental **S**canning **T**est]*
Date:_______4th Sunday

On February 1, 1997 the Administrative Council met in a church planning session with the theme: "FINDING THE WAY FORWARD—St. Peter's A Church of Vision." For the past three weeks parishioners responded to goals proposed and ranked ideas. The final results of last week's queries are listed below. [The Polarization Rating is the percentage of participants responding either agree or disagree (i.e., yes or no) excluding those who abstain; the Consensus Rating is the percentage positive of those who were polarized and agreed or disagreed. Thus a P-C Rating of (85%-66) is read "85% had 66 consensus." It means 85% were polarized and felt able to respond (thus 15% abstained); of those responding, 66% (2 out of 3) were favorable to the idea.] *Thank you for participating!*

1. xxxxxxxxxxxxxxxxxxxxxxxxxxxxxxxxxxxxxxxxxxxxxxxxxxxxxxx
xxxxxxxxxxxxxxxxxxxxxxxxxxxxxxxxxxxxxxxxxxxxxxxxxxxxxx
xxxxxxxxxxxxxxxxxxxxxxxxxxxxxxxxxxxxxxxxxxxxxxxxxxxxxxx.
P-C RATING (xx%-xx)

2. xxxxxxxxxxxxxxxxxxxxxxxxxxxxxxxxxxxxxxxxxxxxxxxxxxxxxxx
xxxxxxxxxxxxxxxxxxxxxxxxxxxxxxxxxxxxxxxxxxxxxxxxxxxxxx
xxxxxxxxxxxxxxxxxxxxxxxxxxxxxxxxxxxxxxxxxxxxxxxxxxxxxxx.
P-C RATING (xx%-xx)

3. xxxxxxxxxxxxxxxxxxxxxxxxxxxxxxxxxxxxxxxxxxxxxxxxxxxxxxx
xxxxxxxxxxxxxxxxxxxxxxxxxxxxxxxxxxxxxxxxxxxxxxxxxxx
xxxxxxxxxxxxxxxxxxxxxxxxxxxxxxxxxxxxxxxxxxxxxxxxxxxxxxxxx.
P-C RATING (xx%-xx)

4. xxxxxxxxxxxxxxxxxxxxxxxxxxxxxxxxxxxxxxxxxxxxxxxxxxxxxxx
xxxxxxxxxxxxxxxxxxxxxxxxxxxxxxxxxxxxxxxxxxxxxxxxxxxxxx
xxxxxxxxxxxxxxxxxxxxxxxxxxxxxxxxxxxxxxxxxxxxxxxxxxxxxxx.
P-C RATING (xx%-xx)

5. xxxxxxxxxxxxxxxxxxxxxxxxxxxxxxxxxxxxxxxxxxxxxxxxxxxxxxx
xxxxxxxxxxxxxxxxxxxxxxxxxxxxxxxxxxxxxxxxxxxxxxxxxxxxxxxxxx
xxxxxxxxxxxxxxxxxxxxxxxxxxxxxxxxxxxxxxxxxxxxxxxxxxx.
P-C RATING (xx%-xx)

6. Etc.

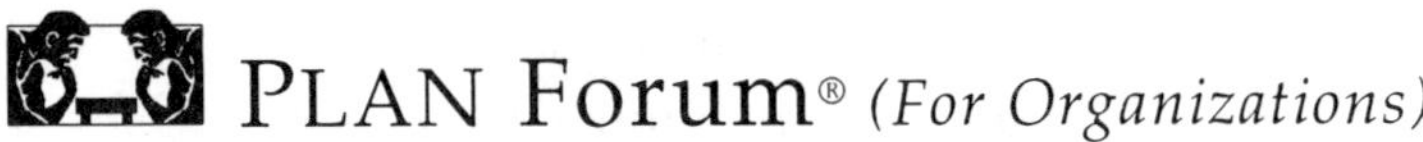

PLAN Forum® *(For Organizations)*

[PLANNING LONG-RANGE ASSESSMENT NETWORK]

Key Points of Model

- Program enables people in organizations, e.g., business, fraternal, church, school, government and the like to meet in small groups of 4 to 12 during a 30 or 45 day window period; they will meet usually in their own homes or workplaces; these are places they already are. People do not have to go to big meetings at often remote distances to participate. Their role is to participate as citizens and constituents in a symbolic dialogue with the organization leaders.
- It is highly adaptable and can be tailored to allow organization leaders to symbolically "talk" informally to constituents and for them to "talk" back.
- The network is maintained by the organization. Members will learn of a variety of topics and will become increasingly better informed and able to contribute as the program continues over time.
- The program uses mass means of communication, i.e., printed materials and Opinionnaires®, audio tapes by a leader or committee, postal service if needed, small discussion groups meeting at various places and times, optical scanning or reproducible response sheets, and computer tabulation. Video, instead of audio tapes, can be used if the dedication, commitment and money are all available. It is important that the frequency be at least quarterly otherwise people will have little sense of a symbolic dialogue. Once a process is established and has proved workable in an organization and they have worked through the initial problems, a lower frequency might be established. That is, the network would function like a fire truck—everyone knows it is there. When it is needed, the leader can just truck it out and use it, and everyone would know what to do.

The PLAN Forum (Planning Long-range Assessment Network) model was proposed originally to the U.S. Air Force in 1976 at USAF Personnel Headquarters, Dept. of Research, Randolph AFB as the PAN Forum (PANoramic Forum)[38]. The purpose was to suggest new ways that the military could utilize the basic principles of the administrative theories that were emerging from our research. The PAN Forum model suggested a cluster of four small discussion groups of senior and junior officers and senior and junior enlisted personnel rotated every six months in a temporary duty assignment. They would meet on call of their base commander when convened by the Office of Primary Responsibility (OPR) of a higher command. The purpose was to design a system that could act as a sounding board to generate feedback information on personnel policies being considered for decision by a commander or after a command decision had been made, to implement it by subordinates through regulations. This model was to supplement the current methodology used by Air Force Human Affairs Laboratories which was primarily dependent upon random-sample polling techniques and tabulation by high-speed optical scanners and computers for the information needed.

While the colonel of the Research Department was impressed with the concept and proposed it to the general in charge for consideration, the general was not impressed. He had had no exposure to administrative theory and could not understand why a new approach was being suggested. He was just exposed to the methodology. His reaction was "Darn if I'm going to have small discussion groups trying to tell my managers what to do." The general missed the whole point. The general and his peers were taught that the "management process" was *plan, organize, motivate, and control.* The military has modified that to: *plan, organize, coordinate, direct, and control.* Both concepts are wrong and do not correctly define the administrative process in which peacetime and wartime commanders are involved. It was because of this failure to elicit the support of the commanding general that we were energized to write the paper, *"A New View of Authority and the Administrative Process"* which was published in 1980.[39] The experience highlights how crucial the

[38] *I was an Air Force reserve officer at the time on a one week training tour to brief the Research Department on administrative theory. I retired the following year with 29 years active and reserve military service and with service in two wars, World War II and Korean. It was in the military that I learned by experience the characteristics of highly authoritarian and bureaucratic organizations. RJS*

[39] *Richard J. Spady, Dr. Cecil H. Bell, Jr., and Dr. Gary A. D'Angelo, "A New View of Authority and the Administrative Process," FUTURICS, Vol 4 No 2 pp 143-157, 1980, Pergamon...*

perceptions, paradigms, and theories held by the top leader of an organization are to its success or failure. It suggests if one is looking for causal responsibility for action or inaction in an organization, look at the attitudes (paradigms and theories) of the administrative leader at the top of the bureaucracy.

However, the Air Force model was subsequently put to very good use. A few months later the Forum Foundation was asked, through the Church Council of Greater Seattle, for assistance in futures research programming for a major denomination in its own long-range planning. The national denomination had just been reorganized within the five states centered in Seattle and was trying to get its long-range planning efforts off the ground.

The Air Force PAN Forum program model was suggested to the denomination as a way to avoid the problem of having big meetings at remote distances. While they adopted the proposal, they changed the name because of the negative connotation ("thumbs down") of the word "pan." They changed the name to PLAN Forum which stood for: Planning Long-range Assessment Network. It was an innovative idea and more descriptive of the model.

The Long Range Planning Committee of the denomination used the model successfully for nearly four years and it involved several hundred people participating in local churches throughout the region. Cassette tapes articulating issues were prepared by the committee and mailed with supporting papers and Opinionnaires® and response sheets to the conveners of small groups in participating local churches. Small groups would listen to the tapes, discuss the issues, respond individually on their own response sheets, and mail responses (and tapes for later reuse) back for tabulation and review by the planning committee. Subsequent reports to the executive committee were an ongoing process.

It was here in the field test research with a religious denomination that it was learned that the small discussion group process worked over large geographic areas, as advocated in the PLAN

---

[39] *Continued...Press Ltd. This article predated and predicted the movement away from authoritarianism and centralism five years before Mikhail Gorbachev even came to power. As such we feel the article has credibility. We updated the article in 1993 to reflect the change in our understanding of administrative theory since 1980. There were relatively few changes. "A New View of Authority and the Administrative Process—Revisited," (1995) is printed in the Appendix of The Search for Enlightened Leadership, Volume 1: Applying New Administrative Theory, page 123, which is our first book in this trilogy.*

forum technique. At the end of the third year the process itself was evaluated by those participating; it had over an 80% positive response and was a further indication that the model was on the right track. When the executive minister of the denomination was interviewed about the process just before his retirement, he reported that the thing he liked most about it was that the process was able to generate data about controversial issues without itself exciting controversy. That was a significant achievement for research in social science at that time.

The National Debate Opinionnaire® Network Forum

(FOR HIGH SCHOOL DEBATERS)

The National Forensic League

The National Forensic League's national high school debate program has been ongoing since 1925. In addition to building a variety of forensic speaking skills such as oratory, extemporaneous speech, dramatic interpretation, Lincoln-Douglas and team debates, it uplifts the importance of the study and discussion of public issues and provides a model for the role of a citizen in a representative democracy.

Nationally high school team debaters take one public issue and study it for an entire academic year. They spend countless hours in the library researching to get expert and official opinions about their topic. Then they debate the issues involved with their peers, pro and con. They are probably the largest, best informed, lay, citizen-group in the nation on the subject of their study.

But when educators fail to ask these bright, dedicated, young citizens for their opinion after all that effort, the educational philosophy that is being communicated in our nation's school systems is:

> *It makes no difference if you have done your homework and are well informed or not. If you are not an expert or public official, nobody wants to know how you feel about an issue.*

If educators do not give high school debaters the recognition they deserve for a good piece of citizenship, i.e., the study and discussion of public issues, then they have just communicated the same philosophy to every student whether they are debaters or not. Other students pick it up through a kind of social osmosis.

Then all students graduate and become citizens. Now our educational system has communicated that same philosophy to every citizen. That philosophy is undemocratic, it strikes at the foundations of our culture, and it produces apathetic citizens instead of interested, informed citizens actively searching for ways to improve the quality of life in their community, in their state, nation, and in the world.

At the National Debate Tournament held each year, debate coaches should prepare an Opinionnaire® asking questions about the current National Forensic League topic and Lincoln-Douglas debate topics. All debaters attending should respond. The demographics can show the students who participated in those events as against those who did not, i.e., they participated in other skill events such as oratory, extemporaneous speech and the like (and more representative of the general high school population). Then the opinions can be tabulated. The profile reports generated will show the differences and similarities of response between debaters, who have studied the topic in depth, and students who have not done so but have opinions based on their own experiences and knowledge to that time. The reports should be very interesting and provide debate, social studies, civic and other teachers and their students and parents much fruitful information for enlightening their later reflections and discussions.

Debate coaches should be encouraged to contact local community service organizations, such as Rotary Clubs [and vice versa as has been done by the Bellevue (Washington) Overlake Rotary Club since 1982]. Debate teams make presentations to their club sometime during May after all competitive debate tournaments have been completed.

The best program format at a community service club seems to be a short introduction of the National Forensic League and its purpose. This is followed by a few examples of high school debate skills, e.g., dramatic interpretation, humorous interpretation, oratory, extemporaneous speech, Lincoln/Douglas debate, or team debate presentation by students. The balance of the program can be devoted simply to the fielding of direct questions from the floor to the debaters who are invited and honored at the program. The Bellevue Overlake Rotary Club typically makes a small contribution to each student who qualifies for nationals to help on their expenses. It is simple, dynamic, and effective and helps to build new bridges between young, articulate, citizens and the community at large. It is citizenship programming at its best.

 The Therapeutic Forum

This research model has not been tried to this date. Methods could be utilized to permit groups of patients (perhaps those trying to cope with alcoholism or drugs), to dialogue their common problems in a group therapy situation, generate their own ideas, respond to ideas of their peers, permit former patients who have been cured to respond through materials received by mail for response, and then compare the results reported by each group to continue the dialogue. People would not have to meet physically (i.e., those successfully rehabilitated) but would meet symbolically with their ideas and insights. As patients achieve their own new insights and understandings, helped by their therapists, their mental and physical health should improve.

It is a model we would very much like to see implemented and be successful.[40]

---

[40] *Contact the Forum Foundation if you think you could help in this research model. See the Forum Foundation Fact Sheet in Appendix J.*

 "Communicate for Peace"

(ROTARY INTERNATIONAL IDEA BANK PROPOSAL)

Key Points of Model

Rotary International is a worldwide community service organization of nearly one million two hundred thousand business and professional men and women in 158 countries in the world plus 35 more geographic areas. Their worldwide scholarship programs in 1996-97 provided 1,277 full university scholarships to study in 60 countries at an estimated cost of $18 million. This included travel, books, tuition, board, and room averaging $22,000 per student. Approximately one half of the scholarships bring foreign students to the United States for study and one half send American students to reciprocating nations. The purpose is to achieve peace through understanding in the world. Their monthly magazine, The Rotarian, goes to every Rotarian in the world and is available in several languages. In the February, 1988 issue of The Rotarian, an article was printed establishing a "Rotary Idea Bank" soliciting individual Rotarians everywhere to submit their ideas, in less than 100 words, for a better program, system, etc.

We think that this peace proposal is a legitimate proposal that is within reach and would be helpful to the process of civilization building and bringing peace to the world. A process of recording worldwide opinion with the participation of citizens is needed in the world. We hope our fellow Rotarians (some day perhaps) will agree. The following was submitted:

TO: ROTARY IDEA BANK: February 11, 1988
From: ROTARIAN RICHARD J. SPADY
(Classification: Futures Research)
Bellevue Overlake Rotary Club
(Bellevue, Washington, USA)
District 5030, Rotary International

Communicate for Peace!

The free enterprise system as we know it exists only within the larger context of a healthy, free, open, democratic society; it does not exist under totalitarianism—fascist or communist.

Rotary Districts and International should enable Rotarians to respond quarterly as a "sounding board" to objective questions about moral/ethical issues facing business, governments, and the world. "Advisory only" results should be published of world opinion in The Rotarian and of district opinion in district newsletters and club announcements. New Forum Foundation "Many-To-Many" communication computer technology and the Fast Forum® technique can effect it.

Viable participation is therapeutic and leads to peace![41]

[41] *Rotary International is an organization of business and professional men and women, dedicated to humanitarian service, ethical standards of business and professions, that works toward promoting community, national, and world understanding and peace. There are nearly 1,200,000 Rotarians in the world represented by 28,531 local Rotary Clubs in 158 nations (The Rotarian April, 1998). Rotarians were solicited to submit ideas to the Rotary Idea Bank in 1988. I submitted this basic idea then. I have been a Rotarian since 1980 and now hold the active classification of Senior Active (Futures Research). I have found Rotary to be a super organization. Perhaps someday they will become aware of this idea and act on it. I'm always hopeful. RJS*

 Moving Toward the Future!

I (RJS) have been a member of the World Future Society since 1974 and a member of their Professional Members Forum as well. In the early 1970's I was an officer and active in the Evergreen Chapter of the World Future Society in Seattle. In 1970 I organized the Forum Foundation as a non-profit Washington state corporation to do educational research, specifically in the field of administrative theory. I consider this work itself to be in the general field of futures research and futures research a part of social science. In 1971 I joined the volunteer staff of the Church Council of Greater Seattle essentially doing full-time research. I had the portfolio of "Future Research" which we defined not as "forecasting" but rather as the search for those dynamics to help organizations and society influence their sociological and technological future. I am a charter member of the Bellevue Overlake Rotary Club (1980) and had the active classification of "Futures Research." I am currently a "Senior Active" in Rotary International with that classification.

My wife and I were at the RI Annual Conference in Glasgow, Scotland in June, 1997, I attended a meeting in which advance planning was being done for ways to honor the founder of Rotary, Paul Harris, at the 50th year anniversary of his death. The talk was to organize Rotary Paul Harris Universities for World Peace and Understanding in six or seven universities in the world. Probably there would be two in the United States. The chair, Cliff Dochterman, Past President of Rotary International and the General Secretary of RI, Mr. S. Aaron Hyatt, ended the meeting with a request for persons to recommend to the committee those universities which might be suitable. I wrote the following letter:

July 30, 1997

Mr. S. Aaron Hyatt, *General Secretary, Rotary International*
One Rotary Center
1560 Sherman Ave.
Evanston, IL 60201

Dear Mr. Hyatt:

I attended the Rotary International Conference in Glasgow last month. On the last afternoon I attended a session considering the Rotary Paul Harris Universities for World Peace and Understanding as a fifty-year commemoration of the death of Rotary's founder. Past RI President Cliff Dochterman was chair. The talk was of six universities with Rotary Scholars at each networked in the world. The panel was stimulating and Rotarians attending were enthusiastic.

You were on the panel and at the end asked those present to recommend to the committee those universities which might be suitable for this designation. You mentioned the university must have the essentials of an international school and extensive computer resources.

I would like to recommend the University of Washington in Seattle for the committee's consideration. The University of Washington is a world class academic institution. It has the Henry M. Jackson School of International Studies (see brochure enclosed). It also has extensive computer resources to support its complete academic program. In addition, Redmond in the Seattle area is the home of Microsoft and Microsoft Foundation recognized as software leaders in the world. Bill Gate's mother served many years as a regent at the university, and he has been very supportive of it. I believe he would be open to collaboration with Rotary in its objectives.

There are two other local resources of which the committee should be aware. One is the *Foundation For the Future* organized in 1996 with headquarters in Bellevue here in the Seattle area. Walter Kistler, a physicist and inventor, is president and benefactor. The goals of the Foundation for the Future and Rotary International are very similar and would be symbiotic (see brochure enclosed).

Finally, another non-profit, 501(c)3 organizations that was just organized in May, 1997 in Seattle is the *Stuart C. Dodd Institute for*

Social Innovation. The institute will encourage interdisciplinary research by scholars in the archives of Stuart C. Dodd (1900-1975) who was Professor-Emeritus of Social Science at the University of Washington. In his career he had over 200 scholarly papers published. Scholars will pursue research in the areas of intellectual, moral and civil legacies of Dr. Dodd in the fields of sociology, business administration, education, urban planning, sustainable communities, statistics and mathematics. The SCDI/SI is affiliated with both the University of Washington and Seattle Pacific University through Richard S. Kirby, Ph.D. Executive Director, who is on the faculty of both. He teaches ethics to undergraduates in the School of Business Administration at the University of Washington in "Organizations and the Environment." He also has taught in the School of Education at Seattle Pacific University.

Thank you for your consideration and best wishes to you, Cliff Dochterman, and the committee for success in your quest.

Sincerely,
Richard J. Spady, President
Senior Active (Futures Research)
Bellevue Overlake Rotary Club

Enclosures: as shown

cc w/o encl:

MR. CLIFFORD L. DOCHTERMAN, Past President RI
MR. WALTER KISTLER, President, Foundation for the Future
DR. RICHARD S. KIRBY, Executive Director, Stuart C. Dodd Institute for Social Innovation
MR. STAN DICKISON, District Governor RI #5030
MR. JIM HATHAWAY, DG-Elect RI #5030
MR. RICHARD F. CLARKE, Past DG RI #5030
MR. DICK GRADDON, President, Bellevue Overlake Rotary Club

Dr. Virginia Nordby, a member of the RI Paul Harris Centers Committee, traveled to Seattle to visit with faculty at the Henry M. Jackson School of International Studies to assure that they would meet the criteria set by Rotary International for students on scholarship there. Dr. Richard Kirby, Executive Director, Stuart C. Dodd Institute for Social Innovation and I had breakfast with Dr. Nordby on Monday, March 9, 1998 to offer what assistance we could to her in her quest.

On December 17, 1997 Dr. Richard Kirby and my son, Jim, and I were invited to a morning meeting with Dr. Walter Kistler, president, Foundation for the Future and his staff. It was a fruitful meeting. They asked Dr. Kirby to draft a scenario for a meeting of key futurists of the World Future Society to attend a meeting in Bellevue on February 4–6, 1998. He did so, and was invited to participate in that conference to begin planning for the "First Humanity 3000 Planning Meeting" to meet in the year 2000 in Seattle. [Dr. Kirby has been a long-time member of the World Future Society and is chair of the Professional Member's Forum youth committee. He is also chair of the World Network of Religious Futurists and on the faculty of the School of Business Administration of the University of Washington. He teaches "Organization and Environment" in the Dept. of Management and Organization.]

That too proved fruitful for Dr. Kirby has been retained by the Foundation for the Future to help them interface their programs with the University of Washington. I just heard today, April 10, 1998, that the contract was approved.

As a part of the continuing saga, I wish to acknowledge and cite the work of Peter and Trudy Johnson-Lenz of Portland, Oregon who attended the February 4–6, 1998 meeting. They also have been retained by the Foundation for the Future as a spin-off of that meeting.

Peter and Trudy Johnson-Lenz have been long involved in computer programming and tabulating the opinions of people. They are concerned with "How can we use cyberspace to increase and disseminate futures knowledge." They have worked on a way for people to think together in large groups (and remote) same-time facilitated electronic meetings (brainstorming and rating). They are CEOs of *"Awakening Technology"* and their address is 695 Fifth Street, Lake Oswego, Oregon 97034. Tel. (503) 635-2615; fax: 503-636-0106. *e-mail:* p+t@awaken.com; www.awaken.com.

Another key reference is the work of Dr. Ed Schwartz, Director, Institute for the Study of Civic Values, 1218 Chestnut St. Suite 702, Philadelphia, PA 19107; and 215-238-1434; and fax: 215-238-0530; edcivic@libertynet.org; http://libertynet.org/community/phila/natl.html. He spoke recently in Seattle at the Good City luncheon sponsored by the Center for Leadership and Transformation of which Dr. William Grace is the Director and founder.

Some other noteworthy connections of which we were made aware by Peter and Trudy Johnson-Lenz are:

Vision 2010: Universities in the 21st Century (web based discussion of scenarios); http://www.si/umich.edu/V2010/.

MIT Initiative on Inventing the Organizations of the 21st Century (2+ year scenario planning process—drafting and review); http://ccs.mitedu/21C21CWP001.html.

Foresight Exchange (FX) (collaborative valuation by betting on how others will value future ideas, predictions—like commodities market); http://www.ideosphere.com/summary.html.

PART TWO

The Four Foundations of the Fast Forum® Technique

Social Resolving Power

One is struck in studying most responses, especially those with two or three profile reports, with a strong overall feeling of confidence in analyzing the way people are thinking about the issues. We call this phenomenon "social resolving power" because it seems as if one is able to peer into the group's thinking and more clearly perceive or resolve the attitudes that are really there. The reason this phenomenon occurs is for the same scientific principle that an electron microscope can resolve or see more than an optical microscope looking at exactly the same field. The unit of measure is shorter.

An optical microscope cannot see anything shorter than the wavelength of visible light, which is its unit of measurement. The electron scope's unit of measurement is the electron, which is much shorter than the wavelength of visible light. When a large group of people meet to convey their opinions, they will usually use Robert's Rules of Order to pass resolutions because that is probably the only democratic process they know. If there is already a substantial consensus there will be no problem. If the problem considered is somewhat controversial, however, it might be very difficult to convey their overall thinking objectively.

If a resolution just barely passes by 51% of the people, it means that while they won, 49% lost and yet the resolution might well give the impression, to others not present, that everybody feels the same way that the resolution was worded. The degree of consensus is seldom conveyed in Robert's Rules of Order and minority reports are usually not done. The resolution in such cases, i.e., a single unit of measurement, is often clumsy and awkward and often downright misleading.

In early applications of the Fast Forum® technique, statements or questions were solicited from persons for response by others in the group. There would be several similar statements or questions. However, each was a little different. There was an emphasis or shade of meaning here that was missing there etc. There was ambiguity; one word made a difference.

While individuals struggle and experience frustration with such ambiguity in making their decisions, the group is better able to discern the overall meanings inherent in the situation in projecting its views. This is done through the polarization-consensus rating that we have developed and is explained next in this book. This is because the group as a whole has much more experience than any of the individuals who comprise it. Thus, the administrators and leaders analyzing the data often have a strong feeling of objectivity and confidence in their diagnosis of the group's thinking. This is exactly what the people in the group wanted to convey in the first place—their thinking.

Since responses are always anonymous and done individually, no one is ever put into a win-lose situation. This keeps tensions at a minimum while communication and understanding are high. Again, the data doesn't tell anybody what is right or wrong at this point. However, it does tell what the participants *perceive* is right or wrong at that point in time, i.e., the Zeitgeist, and sets into motion the natural dynamics of governance of diagnosis, learning, and peace that eventually work themselves through to solutions in the organization.

The Theory of Learning

We consider the Socratic Method, i.e., the Theory of Learning, to be one of the foundations of the Fast Forum® technique. All the theories are important; furthermore, they constitute a coherent set. Nevertheless, we consider the Theory of Learning "first among equals." Therefore, we return to it here, for it offers some additional insights. Its goal is the enlightenment of the mind. The Socratic Method can be regarded as a creative thinking process. It has four steps: awareness, frustration, insight, and verification. Individuals who are searching for solutions to problems and have agreed to respond to objective questions posed in a forum are thus thrust into the dynamics of the Socratic Method. They cannot avoid it. It is one of history's proven learning techniques. In the process individuals participating learn as do their organizations and society itself.

For example, in responding to a question an individual becomes *aware* of the problem (in this case a statement or a question).

The individual then experiences *frustration*, the second step in the process, because one must think of what is the correct answer, and thinking is hard, not easy. This all sets the stage for the third, and most important step, *insight*. The individual says, "Aha! That's the answer to the question. It is yes (or no)!" At that point in time it has little to do with what is "right" or "wrong." At that very moment the person's mind becomes "psychologically benchmarked" in the same manner that one would blaze a trail through a forest with an ax as one would progress through it. The individual becomes a brand new person, psychologically speaking—*the person is what he or she was* plus *the new insight*. The individual has just graduated from the "first grade" into the "second grade" *and learned.*

Then when a new problem comes along which is related, the individual does not just use the information possessed in the first grade, but uses that new bit of information gleaned in going to the second grade. If the new problem is beyond the individual, again the dynamics of the Socratic Method come into play. When the individual achieves insight into the new problem, again there is a graduation but now into the "third grade" and so it continues. The individual grows through new insights; that is, *the individual learns.*

So as a person continues the process of answering questions and being frustrated and gaining insight to each question posed, the individual resolutely moves along with the overall problems posed in the area of discussion and decision and learns. The individual gains more insights, gets stronger psychologically, and decisions begin to come easier as personal understanding matures. *Thus in the Socratic Method an individual not only learns something new, but the individual* becomes someone new—*a brand new person, psychologically speaking, and spiritually renewed.*

The most dynamic questions and most beneficial for the individual participating are those determining right from wrong, i.e., yes or no questions. These can be used to respond to complex issues as we do now in voting for or against laws at election time. Less dynamic for the individual, but still very important to the process, are those involving a value scale such as strongly agree, agree, neutral, disagree, or strongly disagree. It is the decision through insight that is most important in the Socratic Method. The Fast Forum® setting just allows all of it to happen for the individual and organization.

The first three steps in the Socratic Method involve only an individual and his or her problem or question, no one else in the world is involved! But there is a fourth step involving other people. The fourth step in the creative thinking process is verification. The insights of the individual need to be tested against those of other people. The learning process continues as these secondary insights occur within an individual and group. In the Fast Forum® technique, all models provide finished profile reports for managers (leaders) in management forums and for both leaders and participants in leadership forums where such verification can take place.

Considering these dynamics which involve the Socratic Method, it is very important that young people, as well as adults, have opportunities to answer questions and make decisions about real problems in their organizational and institutional lives. They learn and grow psychologically while permitting the organization and institution of which they are part to learn and grow psychologically too. When citizens do not have a meaningful organizational experience, they often leave. In the case of their employment, if they don't leave, they drag their feet. The social and economic costs can be enormous.

Mainstreaming

Today, most citizens inhabit a busy and complex world. Their capacity to participate in civic and organizational affairs is limited by time and opportunity. In fact, they will not participate unless they believe their leader(s) truly want their involvement. If people are asked their opinions, however easy and objective the questions are phrased, few will take part if the poll appears to be part of a general study or academic survey and somewhat unrelated to where they are. *Leaders at the top must be involved and show their interest, otherwise constituents will not participate.* If people believe that a telephone they have is not working properly—and that no one could hear at the other end—no one will take the time and energy to talk into it. The same is true if people believe that their leaders (church, school, political, community) do not want to hear and listen—in fact, are not even interested—people will not take their time and energy to participate. Could this be the reason that most people today do not vote in elections? Perhaps so.

The need today is for a continuing and close interaction between leaders/planners/bureaucrats and their colleagues and constituents. It is not enough for people to participate simply by voting for a public official every two, four, or six years. The cultural dependence on big meetings at remote distances makes it physically impossible for leaders representing large constituencies to get closer to people using conventional thinking and processes. Nor is it much help for leaders to be willing to go into a local neighborhood and hold a "town meeting" in an effort to be more representative. These are helpful, but not adequate. The logistics are still the same—only a few people can talk (usually the leader) and all most people can do is just listen. But leaders and people can get closer together, not physically, but symbolically using the small-group techniques and new concepts of participation theory suggested here. Indeed, the leader must be involved in the program; if not, the people will not usually participate.

Because of this, apathy among people may be less a function of people's attitudes and more a function of leadership style. At this stage, mainstreaming is essential. *Leaders must show their support and be involved in the process with their colleagues or constituents.* The wonderful thing about the emerging concepts of participation and administrative theory, is that the physical demands on the leaders, as well as on the people, are much less. There are *fewer* big meetings and *more* small-group discussions as leaders are met symbolically. It is much more pleasant for all concerned. Indeed, it is very important to the process to help leaders and people have more fun, interesting, and worthwhile meetings. At the same time that meetings are substantive, communication and understanding as a whole and all the dynamics of the natural factors of governance will be effected.

The Polarization-Consensus Rating

One special feature of the computer program includes the use of a new statistical symbol that we invented in 1969 called the polarization-consensus rating (PC rating). A problem arose because our first use of the technique in a community setting in 1969 involved only responses to yes/no questions.[42] With several hundred people participating what does it really mean if large numbers of people respond yes or no or abstain? The numbers were so vast one's mind could not easily comprehend them. We didn't want to use conventional statistical symbols such as standard deviation or variance because whenever that was done, the public would turn itself off. The whole purpose of participation theory was to be able to communicate data back and forth between and among leaders and people. Everyone had to be able to understand it easily.

We reasoned that the most widely understood statistical symbol among non-technical people was the percentage and second to that was the arithmetic mean, the average. After about a month of trial, the Polarization-Consensus Rating was created which consists simply of two percentages in juxtaposition to each other.[43]

The first figure, the *polarization rating,* is a measure of the *weight* given a question by those participating in order to get a sense of the importance of the overall response to the question. It is the number of people who were "polarized" and answered either yes or no (excluding those who abstained or objected), divided by the total number of participants being tabulated, multiplied by 100.

The second number, the *consensus rating,* is a measure of the *opinion* for a given question by those participating in order to get a sense of the overall consensus and response of those who were polarized and answered. It is the number of people who answered yes, divided by the total number of participants being tabulated who were polarized and answered yes or no (excluding those who abstained or objected), multiplied by 100. Thus, the consensus rating is the percentage of the positive response of those who were polarized and answered.

---

[42] *The Eastside Inter-Racial Clearing House program called the "Family Inter-Racial Dialogues" was conducted in the fall of 1968 and through spring 1969 in Bellevue, Washington. It was co-sponsored by the Seattle East Madison YMCA, Seattle Rotary Boy's Club, Eastside Conference on Race and Religion, Bellevue Ministerial Association, Bellevue Public Schools, Bellevue Area PTSA Council, Eastside YMCA, and Bellevue Chamber of Commerce. I was Chair (RJS).*

[43] *Everything is "simple" after one learns how to do it. It is true that while the PC rating is "simple" in mathematical technique, it is "profound" in theory because it turns out to be a highly efficient way to communicate complex data and opinions about and among people from various categories, i.e., by sex, age, residence, organization, legislative district, etc. regardless of the number of people participating in the various groups. The more people who participate in the Fast Forum only makes the reports better—never bigger—so that leaders and constituents are not overwhelmed by "information overload." There is a theory in Gestalt Psychology called the Theory of the Obvious which says, in effect, "the obvious isn't always so obvious." When we were struggling with the problem in 1969, the solution was anything but obvious.*

For example, assume 1000 participants were tabulated:

YES	NO	ABSTAIN	OBJECT	PC RATING	READ AS
1000	0	0	0	(100%-100)	"100% had 100 consensus."
750	250	0	0	(100%- 75)	"100% had 75 consensus."
500	500	0	0	(100%- 50)	"100% had 50 consensus."
250	750	0	0	(100%- 25)	"100% had 25 consensus."
0	1000	0	0	(100% 0)	"100% had zero consensus."
0	0	1000	0	(0%- 0)	"Zero% had zero consensus."
600	200	100	100	(80%- 75)	"80% had 75 consensus."
600	200	200	0	(80%- 75)	"80% had 75 consensus."
600	200	0	200	(80%- 75)	"80% had 75 consensus."
250	250	400	100	(50%- 50)	"50% had 50 consensus."

similarly if 781 persons participated:

YES	NO	ABSTAIN	OBJECT	PC RATING	READ AS
652	84	35	10	(94%- 89)	"94% had 89 consensus."

Since 94% were polarized and answered yes or no, it simultaneously conveys that 6% abstained or objected to the question. Since the consensus rating of 89 shown above is the percent positive response of those polarized in answering yes or no, it simultaneously conveys that 11% of those polarized answered no. Therefore, any consensus rating above 50 means the people answering were favorable to the idea up to 100 which means unanimously favorable. Any consensus rating below 50 means they were unfavorable to the idea down to zero which means unanimously unfavorable. A consensus rating of 50, means those polarized and answering yes or no were split "fifty-fifty;" half said yes and half said no. Since the Forum computer program can rerank the questions by polarization rating, if desired from their original order, additional insights are gained in analysis. One then learns also the kinds of questions people feel able to answer (which rise toward the top of the list) as against those questions where people abstain or object (they may need more information or the wording is not clear which then drops the questions toward the bottom of the list). If a polarization rating falls below 70%, from our experience, we take the consensus rating measuring the opinion with a grain of salt because significant numbers of people feel unable to answer yes or no, but the consensus rating can still provide much insight. Experience shows that the polarization rating of most responsible questions is generally over 70.

The above table demonstrates the principle behind the calculation of the polarization-consensus rating. The actual data shown on a computer profile report shows the percentage of yes and no responses—not the actual raw numbers. For example instead of:

YES	NO	ABSTAIN	OBJECT	PC RATING	MEANING
600	200	100	100	(80%- 75)	"80% had 75 consensus."

it would show:

TOTAL	YES	NO	ABSTAIN	+OBJECTION	PC RATING	CATEGORY
1000	60%	20%	10%	10%	(80%— 75)	Youth

Another example, in an actual profile report from middle school students, with results by classes showed the following:

01-01 (ORIGINAL QUESTION NO. 6)

Have you ever been pressured into taking drugs?

TOTAL	YES	NO	ABSTAIN	+OBJECTION	PC RATING *	CATEGORY
65	6%	91%	3%	0%	(97%—6)	6TH GRADE
98	10%	85%	5%	0%	(95%—11)	7TH GRADE
84	18%	81%	1%	0%	(99%—18)	8TH GRADE
71	18%	79%	3%	0%	(97%—19)	NOT IDENT.
318	13%	84%	3%	0%	(97%—14)	Total

02-01 (ORIGINAL QUESTION NO. 9)

Have you ever experimented with drugs?

TOTAL	YES	NO	ABSTAIN	+OBJECTION	PC RATING *	CATEGORY
65	8%	89%	3%	0%	(97%—8)	6TH GRADE
98	7%	90%	3%	0%	(97%—7)	7TH GRADE
84	21%	75%	4%	0%	(96%—22)	8TH GRADE
71	21%	72%	7%	0%	(93%—23)	NOT IDENT.
318	14%	82%	4%	0%	(96%—15)	Total

Results by sex showed the following:

01-01 (ORIGINAL QUESTION NO. 6)

Have you ever been pressured into taking drugs?

TOTAL	YES	NO	ABSTAIN	+OBJECTION	PC RATING *	CATEGORY
110	14%	81%	5%	0%	(95%— 14)	MALE
135	10%	89%	1%	0%	(99%— 10)	FEMALE
73	19%	78%	3%	0%	(97%— 20)	NOT IDENT.
318	13%	84%	3%	0%	(97%— 14)	Total

02-01 (Original Question No. 9)

Have you ever experimented with drugs?

TOTAL	YES	NO	ABSTAIN	+OBJECTION	PC RATING *	CATEGORY
110	16%	81%	3%	0%	(97%— 17)	MALE
135	9%	87%	4%	0%	(96%— 9)	FEMALE
73	21%	73%	7%	0%	(93%— 22)	NOT IDENT.
318	14%	82%	4%	0%	(96%— 15)	Total

From the above data, one can quickly see that students are pressured to take drugs as they move from 6th grade at 6 consensus to 7th grade at 11 consensus to 8th grade at 18 consensus and that boys at 14 consensus are more highly pressured than girls at 10 consensus. Similar trends can be seen as to experimentation with drugs by class and sex in the second question.

When the computer reranks all questions by polarization rating, one can quickly find whether most questions fall within the range desired, i.e., above 70%. Thereafter, one can pay less attention to the polarization rating as the questions above a certain level are all considered "good data" although they are all relative. Then one need only compare the single consensus rating with other ratings above and below it. It is much easier to compare single consensus ratings with each other than to have to study the same data in four columns of percentages of Yes, No, Abstain, and Objection which would normally be the case without the PC rating format. The percentages of yes, no, abstain, and objection become merely a reference base if needed. As a practical matter, they need seldom to be used except to zero in on abstentions or objections when required. Analyzing data in this manner to tap the minds of people to reveal their thinking and their wisdom is highly efficient after one gets used to it. Most people master it in a short time.

The program can record up to 15 demographic or psychographic categories such as those participants who might identify themselves as expert, above average, average, or below average on the issue under discussion etc. Participants usually mark their personal categories of sex and age and in addition demographic and geographic information such as their organizational department, neighborhood, legislative or congressional district, city, county, state, and other psychographic information if appropriate. Organizations can be listed by number or divisions or other breakdown. The limit that can be recorded in any one field is 10. Choices in any one field are mutually exclusive, i.e., one cannot make two or more choices in any one field. One field can record up to 10 organizations, two fields up to 99 organizations, three fields up to 999 organizations. Fields can be compounded and searched simultaneously if further insights are needed. For example, a profile report showing how people in their 20s and 30s, living within a specific geographic area who are members of a specific organization answered as compared to others who participated and are not in the group selected. While it is possible literally to generate millions of different profile reports from any one iteration with the computer, as a practical matter usually only two or three profile reports are generated for any one iteration. That seems to do the job most of the time. The Fast Forum® program deals only with a "universe" of an organization, a school or school district, a local or national church, a government entity and the like; it does not deal with "random samples."

Throughout use of the various profiles, the polarization-consensus rating is calculated for all yes or no answers. The polarization rating is set most of the time to re-rank all yes/no questions, but it can be set to print the questions in the order they were originally posed to participants and not be reranked. Even multiple-choice questions give additional insights when ranked by the polarization rating. It ranks the questions with the fewest abstentions plus objections at the top and the most at the bottom. It gives leaders and people studying the responses additional insights by showing the kinds of questions in which participants felt able to respond as against those in which they felt more unable by abstaining or objecting. These additional insights sometimes suggest that people feel they need more information before answering, i.e., high abstentions, or are not satisfied with the construction of the questions, i.e., high objections.

An individual marks his or her personal and organizational categories requested on the Opinionnaire® and then can respond to up to 50 objective questions. Since the computer can track all the variables, the individual on one response sheet can simultaneously "participate" with his or her opinions in up to 15 "networks" (i.e., different profile reports showing how similar groups of sex, age, department, role, residence, legislative district etc. responded).

We conducted a nine-week research program from January 16 to March 13, 1994. About 400 parishioners in The United Methodist Church throughout the country participated in a study of issues considered by The Book of Resolutions. The Book of Resolutions is approved by the General Conference (the highest governing body) every four years. The current 1996 edition has 294 resolutions of policy statements concerning moral issues faced by an individual, the church, and the society itself within which the church functions. The nine weeks included Program Orientation, Authority in the Church, The Family, Children, Aging, Health Care, Racism, Economic Justice, and Program Evaluation. An example of various profile reports from that research follows. Notice how the totals for the 380 people participating do not change from question to question and profile to profile. But note the additional insights that are gained from being able to compare the polarization-consensus ratings by gender, age, ethnic family, role, geographic and the like. This additional insight, projected by the Fast Forum technique, enables groups to "talk symbolically" to each other, i.e., by gender, age group, ethnic family, role or geographic (jurisdictional) *all at the same time!* The process, in which people meet in small groups, enhances communication of ideas among all participants in a routine manner that otherwise could not be done over such vast distances. Please study the following examples.

MANY-TO-MANY COMMUNICATIONS
—— Fast Forum (R) Technique ——
Attitudinal Profile Report March 13, 1994

What United Methodists Believe #9

FINAL REPORT ON EVALUATION *EXAMPLE* PROFILE REPORTS

DISCLAIMER CLAUSE: The purpose of these informal reports is to communicate ideas, issues, and problems among people as a platform for future, meaningful discussions of concerns. Participants are assisted in becoming aware of their own beliefs as well as of those intellectual and moral beliefs of others at a point in time—the Zeitgeist. The views and opinions expressed herein are those of the individuals who participated and do not necessarily represent the official views of the parent group or sponsoring organization. Nor will the views expressed necessarily represent those of the same participants at a later period of time; as humans we each have the ability to receive new information, consider it, and change.—*The Forum Foundation*

**Legend: Example-Polarization-Consensus Rating for yes/no questions*

PC RATING

"POLARIZATION RATING" (75% — 80) "CONSENSUS RATING"

A measure of the weight given an idea or question by the people participating. The polarization rating is the percentage of people participating who answered yes or no (excluding those who abstained or objected) *Thus:* A polarization rating of 100% means everyone participating answered yes or no. A rating of 50% means half answered yes or no. A rating of 0% means no one answered yes or no (thus, everyone abstained or objected)

A measure of the opinion given by those people answering yes or no. The consensus rating is the percentage of people answering yes of those who answered yes or no, i.e., the % positive response (excluding those who abstained or objected) *Thus:* A consensus rating above 50 means the people answering favored the idea—up to 100 which means unanimously favorable. A rating below 50 means they were against the idea, down to zero which means they were unanimously against it.

Read the PC rating cited above as "75% had 80 consensus" meaning: 75% of those persons participating were polarized and answered either yes or no. Therefore, of those persons who answered yes or no, 80 out of 100 answered yes (thus 20 out of 100 answered no). The P/C Rating, therefore, allows accurate and easy comparison of responses between different-sized groups and also total responses.

For further insights on the kinds of questions people feel able to answer within a grouping of related questions, questions can be ranked and reordered by the P/C rating showing the weight. That is, both yes/no and multiple-choice questions can be ranked and reordered by the percentage of people who answered the question with clear yes/no or multiple-choice responses—excluding those who abstained or objected. This magnifies the analysis of the data to better resolve the social attitudes of those who participated, i.e., "Social Resolving Power."

---

1 Evaluation Questions
GENDER PROFILE REPORT EXAMPLE:

1-1 (ORIGINAL QUESTION NO. 1)

At the start of this series were you familiar with the UMC Social Principles?

TOTAL	YES	NO	ABSTAIN	OBJECT	PC RATING *	CATEGORY
168	41%	52%	4%	3%	(93%— 44)	Male
198	40%	58%	2%	1%	(98%— 41)	Female
14	14%	71%	14%	0%	(86%— 17)	Not Identified
380	**40%**	**56%**	**3%**	**2%**	**(96%— 42)**	**Total**

2-1 (ORIGINAL QUESTION NO. 2)

Do you feel that you are familiar with the UMC Social Principles now?

TOTAL	YES	NO	ABSTAIN	OBJECT	PC RATING *	CATEGORY
168	77%	15%	6%	2%	(92%— 84)	Male
198	82%	12%	5%	1%	(94%— 87)	Female
14	43%	36%	14%	7%	(79%— 55)	Not Identified
380	**78%**	**14%**	**6%**	**2%**	**(92%— 85)**	**TOTAL**

3-1 (ORIGINAL QUESTION NO. 3)

At the start of this series were you familiar with the UMC Book of Resolutions?

TOTAL	YES	NO	ABSTAIN	OBJECT	PC RATING *	CATEGORY
168	29%	67%	2%	2%	(96%— 30)	Male
198	27%	71%	3%	0%	(97%— 27)	Female
14	14%	64%	21%	0%	(79%— 18)	Not Identified
380	**27%**	**69%**	**3%**	**1%**	**(96%— 28)**	**TOTAL**

4-1 (ORIGINAL QUESTION NO. 4)

Do you feel that you are familiar with the UMC Book of Resolutions now?

TOTAL	YES	NO	ABSTAIN	OBJECT	PC RATING *	CATEGORY
168	68%	23%	5%	4%	(91%— 75)	Male
198	74%	15%	9%	3%	(88%— 83)	Female
14	64%	14%	21%	0%	(79%— 82)	Not Identified
380	**71%**	**18%**	**8%**	**3%**	**(89%— 80)**	**TOTAL**

AGE PROFILE REPORT EXAMPLE:

1-1 (ORIGINAL QUESTION NO. 1)

At the start of this series were you familiar with the UMC Social Principles?

TOTAL	YES	NO	ABSTAIN	OBJECT	PC RATING *	CATEGORY
1	100%	0%	0%	0%	(100%—100)	19 years and under
10	70%	20%	0%	10%	(90%— 78)	20 - 29 years
49	27%	73%	0%	0%	(100%— 27)	30 - 39 years
107	41%	54%	3%	2%	(95%— 43)	40 - 49 years
71	44%	54%	1%	1%	(97%— 45)	50 - 59 years
78	47%	49%	3%	1%	(96%— 49)	60 - 69 years
45	29%	64%	4%	2%	(93%— 31)	70 - 79 years
7	43%	43%	14%	0%	(86%— 50)	80 years and over
9	22%	78%	0%	0%	(100%— 22)	
3	0%	33%	67%	0%	(33%— 0)	Not Identified
380	**40%**	**56%**	**3%**	**2%**	**(96%— 42)**	**TOTAL**

2-1 (ORIGINAL QUESTION NO. 2)

Do you feel that you are familiar with the UMC Social Principles now?

TOTAL	YES	NO	ABSTAIN	OBJECT	PC RATING *	CATEGORY
1	100%	0%	0%	0%	(100%—100)	19 years and under
10	70%	20%	10%	0%	(90%— 78)	20 - 29 years
49	92%	8%	0%	0%	(100%— 92)	30 - 39 years
107	86%	8%	4%	2%	(94%— 91)	40 - 49 years
71	77%	15%	4%	3%	(93%— 83)	50 - 59 years
78	73%	19%	6%	1%	(92%— 79)	60 - 69 years
45	64%	22%	11%	2%	(87%— 74)	70 - 79 years
7	71%	0%	29%	0%	(71%—100)	80 years and over
9	67%	22%	11%	0%	(89%— 75)	
3	0%	33%	33%	33%	(33%— 0)	Not Identified
380	**78%**	**14%**	**6%**	**2%**	**(92%— 85)**	**TOTAL**

3-1 (ORIGINAL QUESTION NO. 3)

At the start of this series were you familiar with the UMC Book of Resolutions?

TOTAL	YES	NO	ABSTAIN	OBJECT	PC RATING *	CATEGORY
1	100%	0%	0%	0%	(100%—100)	19 years and under
10	40%	60%	0%	0%	(100%— 40)	20 - 29 years
49	27%	73%	0%	0%	(100%— 27)	30 - 39 years
107	26%	70%	3%	1%	(96%— 27)	40 - 49 years
71	32%	66%	0%	1%	(99%— 33)	50 - 59 years
78	31%	63%	5%	1%	(94%— 33)	60 - 69 years
45	13%	84%	2%	0%	(98%— 14)	70 - 79 years
7	43%	43%	14%	0%	(86%— 50)	80 years and over
9	22%	67%	11%	0%	(89%— 25)	
3	0%	33%	67%	0%	(33%— 0)	Not Identified
380	**27%**	**69%**	**3%**	**1%**	**(96%— 28)**	**TOTAL**

4-1 (ORIGINAL QUESTION NO. 4)

Do you feel that you are familiar with the UMC Book of Resolutions now?

TOTAL	YES	NO	ABSTAIN	OBJECT	PC RATING *	CATEGORY
1	100%	0%	0%	0%	(100%—100)	19 years and under
10	70%	20%	10%	0%	(90%— 78)	20 - 29 years
49	86%	14%	0%	0%	(100%— 86)	30 - 39 years
107	75%	15%	7%	4%	(90%— 83)	40 - 49 years
71	73%	20%	3%	4%	(93%— 79)	50 - 59 years
78	69%	15%	12%	4%	(85%— 82)	60 - 69 years
45	49%	36%	11%	4%	(84%— 58)	70 - 79 years
7	71%	0%	29%	0%	(71%—100)	80 years and over
9	67%	22%	11%	0%	(89%— 75)	
3	33%	0%	67%	0%	(33%—100)	Not Identified
380	**71%**	**18%**	**8%**	**3%**	**(89%— 80)**	**TOTAL**

ETHNIC FAMILY PROFILE REPORT EXAMPLE:

1-1 (ORIGINAL QUESTION NO. 1)

At the start of this series were you familiar with the UMC Social Principles?

TOTAL	YES	NO	ABSTAIN	OBJECT	PC RATING *	CATEGORY
2	0%	50%	50%	0%	(50%— 0)	African-American
6	17%	83%	0%	0%	(100%— 17)	Asian/Pacific Island
348	41%	56%	1%	1%	(97%— 43)	Caucasian
0	0%	0%	0%	0%	(0%— 0)	Chicano/Latino
6	33%	50%	17%	0%	(83%— 40)	Native American
4	50%	25%	0%	25%	(75%— 67)	Other Ethnic Family
14	14%	57%	29%	0%	(71%— 20)	Not Identified
380	**40%**	**56%**	**3%**	**2%**	**(96%— 42)**	**TOTAL**

2-1 (ORIGINAL QUESTION NO. 2)

Do you feel that you are familiar with the UMC Social Principles now?

TOTAL	YES	NO	ABSTAIN	OBJECT	PC RATING *	CATEGORY
2	100%	0%	0%	0%	(100%—100)	African-American
6	83%	17%	0%	0%	(100%— 83)	Asian/Pacific Island
348	80%	14%	5%	1%	(94%— 86)	Caucasian
0	0%	0%	0%	0%	(0%— 0)	Chicano/Latino
6	33%	50%	17%	0%	(83%— 40)	Native American
4	50%	0%	25%	25%	(50%—100)	Other Ethnic Family
14	43%	21%	29%	7%	(64%— 67)	Not Identified
380	**78%**	**14%**	**6%**	**2%**	**(92%— 85)**	**TOTAL**

3-1 (ORIGINAL QUESTION NO. 3)

At the start of this series were you familiar with the UMC Book of Resolutions?

TOTAL	YES	NO	ABSTAIN	OBJECT	PC RATING *	CATEGORY
2	50%	50%	0%	0%	(100%— 50)	African-American
6	33%	67%	0%	0%	(100%— 33)	Asian/Pacific Island
348	27%	70%	2%	1%	(97%— 28)	Caucasian
0	0%	0%	0%	0%	(0%— 0)	Chicano/Latino
6	33%	67%	0%	0%	(100%— 33)	Native American
4	50%	25%	0%	25%	(75%— 67)	Other Ethnic Family
14	14%	50%	36%	0%	(64%— 22)	Not Identified
380	**27%**	**69%**	**3%**	**1%**	**(96%— 28)**	**TOTAL**

4-1 (ORIGINAL QUESTION NO. 4)

Do you feel that you are familiar with the UMC Book of Resolutions now?

TOTAL	YES	NO	ABSTAIN	OBJECT	PC RATING *	CATEGORY
2	100%	0%	0%	0%	(100%—100)	African-American
6	67%	33%	0%	0%	(100%— 67)	Asian/Pacific Island
348	72%	18%	7%	3%	(91%— 80)	Caucasian
0	0%	0%	0%	0%	(0%— 0)	Chicano/Latino
6	67%	17%	17%	0%	(83%— 80)	Native American
4	50%	0%	25%	25%	(50%—100)	Other Ethnic Family
14	50%	14%	29%	7%	(64%— 78)	Not Identified
380	**71%**	**18%**	**8%**	**3%**	**(89%— 80)**	**TOTAL**

ROLE PROFILE REPORT EXAMPLE:

9-1 (ORIGINAL QUESTION NO. 9)

Each week in the Viewspaper the editor wrote, "However, we treat The Book of Resolutions as a "finished document." It is not. But it is a "great beginning document if we can learn to use it." Do you share this belief?

TOTAL	YES	NO	ABSTAIN	OBJECT	PC RATING *	CATEGORY
12	92%	0%	8%	0%	(92%—100)	Ordained Ministry
7	86%	0%	14%	0%	(86%—100)	Gen Bd of C & S
4	100%	0%	0%	0%	(100%—100)	Conf. Bd Chrch & Soc
11	82%	0%	9%	9%	(82%—100)	District Bd Chch & S
51	75%	8%	10%	8%	(82%— 90)	Local Church Bd C&S
58	88%	10%	2%	0%	(98%— 89)	Local Officer/Chair
207	76%	10%	10%	4%	(86%— 89)	Local Church Laity
30	57%	13%	30%	0%	(70%— 81)	Not Identified
380	**77%**	**9%**	**10%**	**3%**	**(86%— 90)**	**TOTAL**

JURISDICTIONAL PROFILE REPORT EXAMPLE:

6-1 (ORIGINAL QUESTION NO. 6)

Each week in the Viewspaper the editor wrote, "We are taught that our responsibility is directly to God through Christ and there is no institution or person between us." Do you believe this theology is true?

TOTAL	YES	NO	ABSTAIN	OBJECT	PC RATING *	CATEGORY
59	93%	3%	2%	2%	(97%— 96)	NE Jurisdiction
39	92%	0%	5%	3%	(92%—100)	SE Jurisdiction
102	89%	9%	2%	0%	(98%— 91)	North-Central Juris.
94	94%	4%	2%	0%	(98%— 96)	South-Central Juris.
66	77%	11%	8%	5%	(88%— 88)	Western Jurisdiction
20	70%	0%	30%	0%	(70%—100)	Not Identified
380	**88%**	**6%**	**5%**	**1%**	**(94%— 94)**	**TOTAL**

23-3 (ORIGINAL QUESTION NO. 23)

Paragraph 610. The 1992 Book of Discipline reads "Speaking for the church.

1. No person, no paper, no organization, has the authority to speak officially for the General Conference under the Constitution. Any written public policy statement issued by a general church agency shall clearly identify either at the beginning or at the end that the statement represents the position of that general agency and not necessarily the position of the United Methodist Church (Paragraph 817). [See Judicial Council Decision 458.]

2. Any individual member called to testify before a legislative body to represent The United Methodist Church shall be allowed to do so only by reading, without elaboration, the resolutions and positions adopted by the General Conference of The United Methodist Church."

Would you be supportive of an additional paragraph similar to the following in italics and underlined to further clarify authority in our church?

3. We acknowledge from our Protestant tradition that we do not believe in the infallibility of the church. Accordingly, the General Conference, in its turn, does not have the authority to speak for any individual United Methodist. We believe that our individual responsibility is directly to God through Christ and there is no other institution or person between us. Thus, any individual United Methodist is free to dissent in accordance with the Holy Spirit within himself or herself from passages in the Social Principles and The Book of Resolutions without being ostracized from the church.

TOTAL	YES	NO	ABSTAIN	OBJECT	PC RATING *	CATEGORY
59	75%	10%	14%	2%	(85%— 88)	NE Jurisdiction
39	74%	10%	10%	5%	(85%— 88)	SE Jurisdiction
102	74%	5%	16%	6%	(78%— 94)	North-Central Juris.
94	73%	3%	21%	2%	(77%— 96)	South-Central Juris.
66	71%	6%	20%	3%	(77%— 92)	Western Jurisdiction
20	50%	0%	35%	15%	(50%—100)	Not Identified
380	**72%**	**6%**	**18%**	**4%**	**(78%— 93)**	**TOTAL**

THE FORUM FOUNDATION AND THE FAST FORUM® TECHNIQUE

The Forum Foundation is a non-profit, educational/research corporation dedicated to strengthening democratic processes through improved feedback communication. The Fast Forum® technique enables interested persons to more effectively and meaningfully communicate their individual opinions. By summarizing these opinions in written reports, the Fast Forum® technique communicates to participants the values in which they believe. This important information can then be communicated simultaneously to parent, teacher, school, church, business, community, and government organizations, i.e., "the establishment." *The Forum Foundation firmly believes that by improving feedback communication in this manner, society can reduce apathy, improve community well-being, and address better the problems and opportunities we all face together.*

Forum Foundation Philosophy:

A creative society (or organization) actively searches for solutions to its problems. *The open exchange and discussion of ideas is the mortar that binds society together during this creative process.* This exchange, in turn, leads naturally toward improved decision making, consensus, and spontaneous collaboration. *Any organization or society which inhibits the free movement of ideas among its members (whether innocently or not) deprives itself of its greatest resource: human thought. Such a society is in grave danger of being buried in history by an avalanche of the creativity of others.*

The data utilized in this report was submitted on individual Forum Foundation or other response sheets by the user organization and recorded by optical scanning or was keypunched from Opinionnaires® provided. The information contained herein is certified correct barring unintentional errors.

Inquiries are invited from interested organizations and persons who may wish to establish, experiment, or participate in this Many-To-Many Communication process and Fast Forum® technique. "Zeitgeist" and "PC Rating" are registered trademarks. "Fast Forum", "Opinionnaire", and "Viewspaper" are registered trademarks of the Forum Foundation, United States Patent Office.

RICHARD J. SPADY, President
JAMES R. SPADY, Executive Vice President
Forum Foundation (Seattle Office)
4426 Second Avenue N.E.
Seattle, Washington 98105-6191
PHONE: (206) 634-0420; FAX: (206) 633-3561

[END OF REPORT]

The polarization-consensus rating is a very efficient statistical symbol. Data can be calculated by hand easily in small groups by arithmetic or by calculator and in any sized group by computer. We commend its use to you in summarizing the opinions of people.

Someone has said, "If we can measure it, we can improve it!" It is true.

OTHER FUNDAMENTALS OF THE FAST FORUM® TECHNIQUE

An Opinionnaire®

Today most people who look at a valid "Opinionnaire®" say, "Oh, that's a survey." Most people already think they know everything about surveys so they often drop the idea from their mind. But there are some significant differences in a "Questionnaire" which seldom allows abstentions to questions and an Opinionnaire® which always allows abstentions and objections. Also, Fast Forum® reports always provide disclaimer, philosophy, and trailer clauses and the polarization-consensus rating underlying the processes being utilized. These all are based on participation and administrative theory instead of statistical and mathematical theory which underlie objective, random-sample, questionnaire, survey instruments. There is a need to break through the stiffly resistant, stereotyped thinking of leaders and people to open up all to the new possibilities inherent in the new communication technology of Many-To-Many communication which is emerging. One way to do this is to differentiate the processes, techniques, and theories through their names.

The basic thrust of questions from a pollster using statistical theory is to question others about their opinions for his own or others' purposes. The basic thrust of questions from a leader using participation theory is to gain the opinions of constituents for better organizational or institutional decision-making while also building community and cooperation within the constituency. Both approaches are valid and have their place.[44]

Instead of using random-sample objective questionnaires based on statistical and mathematical theory, The Fast Forum® groupware technique uses objective Opinionnaires® based on participation and administrative theory. Different rules apply as the

[44] *See also Forum Foundation website <http://weber.u.washington.edu/~forum>. It contains an example of an Opinionnaire administered to women attending the United Nations Fourth World Women's Conference held in Beijing, China September 4-15, 1995. The Opinionnaire was administered in English, Chinese, French, and Spanish but was tabulated in a single "Language of Opinionnaire" Profile Report. This was a first for the Forum Foundation and a major breakthrough in communication and social science. It was administered in China by "Everywoman's Delegation of Seattle, Washington, USA; Ms. Jan Cate, coordinator. (Jan Cate is also a research team and board member of the Forum Foundation).*

Fast Forum® technique deals with the "statistical universe" and not a random sample. It is for this reason that the Forum Foundation has taken extra pains to differentiate between these methods which equally provide valid social indicators. The term, "Opinionnaire" is a copyrighted registered trademark of the Forum Foundation, United States Patent Office. It is a very simple and effective method to let others know that these concepts are new, important, and different. It can be used by others within the proper context of participation theory (but not statistical theory) with credit given to the Forum Foundation, 4426 Second Ave. N.E., Seattle WA. 98105-6191.[45]

Abstention and Objection to the Question

It is important that every objective instrument provide an opportunity for the individual responding to abstain if the person feels unable to respond because he or she is undecided, feels the need at that time for more information before deciding, or has another reason. An abstention is an equally valid response if it accurately records where that person is with that idea at that point in time. It is also a way for people to communicate to a leader posing the question, that there might be a need for more information before making a decision, especially if the abstention rate is high. The effort is always to get as high a polarization rating as possible with the highest consensus rating before making decisions. The leader who makes decisions where colleagues or constituents agree with a high consensus is on firm ground. The leader who makes decisions contrary to colleagues or constituent consensus is not on firm ground and is instead involved in acts of statesmanship. This may or may not be appropriate in the long run; only time will tell.

In 1978 after eight years of research, a very slight technical change was made to the earlier Fast Forum® computer program and format of the profile reports. Again, while it was a very slight change to the computer program, it was a very great advancement in theory. The format of both the Opinionnaire® and the profile reports was changed to allow individuals participating to object to the wording of a question or statement if they felt that the word-

---

[45] *If not sure that a use of "Opinionnaire" is sanctioned as explained here, write to Forum Foundation, 4426 Second Ave. N.E., Seattle, WA 98105-6191 explaining your situation and ask for permission.*

ing was not clear or that a question or statement was misleading or inappropriately worded.

The problem stemmed from complaints by some persons who felt the questions were biased. They would say, "You can't use the data generated from that survey. The questions are loaded. They just beg the question. They are terrible," and the like. Who was right? No one knew because it was a value judgment. The leader who prepares the questions and statements or collects them from others and places them before the total participants may think the questions or statements are highly appropriate. But if someone disagrees, who is right? It is a standoff, because it is a value judgment for both. It makes little difference if one has the expertise of a George Gallup and Louis Harris all rolled into one. The design of an objective instrument seldom evades some criticism like this; often, there is someone who complains.

Administrators and leaders are seldom trained in the preparation of objective surveys, they usually need help from an outside expert. The essential thing is that the leader (or staff in name of the leader), interact with his or her own constituents and not be reluctant to do so because he or she lacks the expertise to pose questions. The leader probably knows his or her own organizational problems and issues better than any outside expert would. To get around this problem, participants are permitted to object to any Opinionnaire® question posed to them. Now there is a difference.

If someone objects to the wording of a question, one can reply, "Well, let's see how the people who participated felt about that." If only 4 or 5 percent objected to the question or questions challenged, one can place the criticism in its proper perspective, i.e., simply ignore it. But if one sees that a question has 20 or 25 percent of the participants objecting to it, one knows there is a problem. It is not necessary to be told. The response is not a random-sample based on statistical theory like a relationship between a pollster and people that is one time and gone forever. Instead, usually the response is participatory and an ongoing feedback communication system. In the next iteration the defective questions can be rephrased or additional questions submitted for further clarification. This can be continued until the administrator or leader reaches a point in his or her thinking and says, "There is no point in asking these people any more questions about this topic. We already know how they feel."

When that judgment is reached, then the objective of the program has been achieved because the Zeitgeist, the "Spirit of the Time," has just been identified. It will not necessarily tell what is "right" or "wrong," but it will tell what those people participating perceive *is right or wrong at that point in time. And the leader and group move forward to new areas of consideration.*

"Day-in-the-Sun"

The Fast Forum® groupware technique, in most applications, uses small discussion groups that use "Day-in-the-Sun" to get the discussion started in the small group.[46] Each person is invited to speak for up to two minutes as to his or her reaction to what has been presented in the tape—and the role of others in the group is to LISTEN—not find fault, not to criticize, not to comment, not to use body English, e.g., thumbs up or down showing approval or disapproval—but just to listen. After a person has spoken one minute, the convener places a small stone on the table (or holds up one finger). After another 30 seconds, the convener places a slightly larger stone on the table (or crooks the finger). After the final 30 seconds and signifying the end of the two minute "Day in the Sun" period, the convener places a third and larger stone on the table (or holds up two fingers). Suggest that this third stone is a part of the old Irish "blarney stone" (the convener can even color it green to help the symbolism). In any event it's a reminder to all that up to two minutes, that's one's opinion, and that's good, but after two minutes, it's getting into the "old blarney" and the speaker should wind it up as soon as possible. The purpose is to keep things moving and light. After everyone, including the convener, has had an opportunity to have his or her "Day in the Sun," the open discussion continues informally as the group considers questions about the ideas and reactions raised. The first general theory, *The Basic Attitude,* should always be observed. No one has to agree with anything said, but everyone should always respect other person's right to say it.

---

[46] *This model was first observed in a workshop conducted by Sidney Simon, author of Value Education, at the Bellevue, (Washington) Community College in the early 1970's. RJS*

The Formal Clauses

THE DISCLAIMER CLAUSE

Because we are involved in participation theory based on administrative theory and not in statistical theory based on mathematical theory, every profile report generated on the Fast Forum® computer program contains a disclaimer clause at the start which typically reads as follows:

> The purpose of these informal reports is to communicate ideas, issues, and problems among people as a platform for future, meaningful discussions of concerns. Participants are assisted in becoming aware of their own beliefs as well as of those intellectual and moral beliefs of others—the Zeitgeist—"The Spirit of the Time." The views and opinions expressed herein are those of the individuals who participated and do not necessarily represent the official views of the parent group or sponsoring organization. Nor will the views expressed necessarily represent those of the same participants at a later period of time; as humans we each have the ability to receive new information, consider it, and change. —The Forum Foundation

The Disclaimer Clause in effect frees people participating to speak because they speak only for themselves which is every person's right. Thus, the data generated is 100% valid for those persons participating! The data generated is just as valid as letters sent to legislators and public officials. The data is just as valid as telephone messages, just as valid as personal meetings, and just as valid as information gathered in testimony at a public hearing none of which is necessarily "statistically valid" and indicative of the values held by the public at large. It is also much easier to understand where people stand on issues of concern to them because the data can include demographics such as gender, age, geographic, or organization. As more and more people participate in the process, the data reported just gets better; it never gets bigger. The process also avoids the problem of "information overload" which is especially burdensome to leaders who must deal often with voluminous amounts of correspondence.

A Disclaimer Clause is always printed on every profile report generated by the Forum Foundation and released to users. Similarly, users should be careful, in turn, to disclaim the results to their colleagues or constituents to help avoid criticism by others who might be trying to find reasons to do so. Users should always print a Disclaimer Clause in any Viewspaper® they produce. See Appendix G and H for examples.

The use of the disclaimer clause as a function is the key to being able to send the reports to others within or without the organization. For example, it permits reports from leadership forums to be used without the stilting, and perhaps even dehumanizing experience, of having to have the reports approved first by an administrative board, an executive committee, or anyone else. Such a requirement is an abridgment of the basic human rights of the people participating: freedom to assemble (symbolically), freedom of speech, freedom of the press, freedom to petition, and we believe, *"freedom to be heard." These are constitutional rights of every citizen; they apply in all contexts including government, business and industry, education, church, and community.*

All such communication is advisory only to elected or appointed organizational and societal leaders who have the tactical, legal responsibility, for decisions in our republic—a representative democracy. However, organizational and institutional members and citizens have an equally strategic moral responsibility to help their leaders and planners by participating with their thinking, i.e., opinions.

THE PHILOSOPHY CLAUSE

The Fast Forum® computer program and profile reports always contain a philosophy clause which provides an additional frame of reference for those participating and which typically reads as follows:

> A creative organization or society is one that actively searches for solutions to its problems. The *open exchange and discussion of ideas is the mortar that binds such a society together during this creative process.* This exchange, in turn, leads naturally toward improved consensus, decision-making and spontaneous collaboration. Any group, organization, community, or society which inhibits the free movement of ideas of its members up, down, and across its organizational and societal structures

(whether innocently or not) is depriving itself of its greatest resource—*human thought*—and is in grave danger of being buried in history by an avalanche of the creativity of others. (Emphasis added)

THE TRAILER CLAUSE

The Fast Forum® computer program and profile reports always contain a trailer clause which provides an additional frame of reference for those participating and which typically reads as follows:

> The Forum Foundation is a nonprofit educational-research corporation of Washington state. It conducts research in pure and applied social science—specifically in the field of Administrative Theory, which is a subset of Organization Development. The foundation is dedicated toward strengthening the democratic processes of our society through improved feedback communications from people. This Fast Forum® technique assists interested persons in our society and among its institutions and organizations to participate more meaningfully by expressing their individual opinions. Through written reports, as attached, these opinions assist those persons participating to illustrate to themselves, as well as to parent/ teacher/ school/ church/ business/ community, and government establishments, the values in which they believe. It is hoped that the overall communication process established will reduce apathy among people, improve community mental health, and assist in solving the human problems we face together in our society and world.

THE CERTIFICATION CLAUSE

The Fast Forum® computer program and profile reports always contain a certification clause which provides an additional frame of reference for those participating and which typically reads as follows:

> The data utilized in this report was submitted on individual Forum Foundation machine-scannable or other response sheets by the user organization and recorded by optical scanning or was keyed from Opinionnaires® provided by the Forum Foundation. The information tabulated by the Forum Foundation contained herein is certified correct barring unintentional errors.

The purpose of this clause is to acknowledge that the data is as accurate as possible under the processes being followed. The Forum Foundation tries its best to report accurate data, but can not be responsible for inaccurate data supplied by others in the course of their participation in a project. Of course, keying data in itself, without verification, will have some errors, however, verification (like that required for bank transactions) is prohibitively expensive and, in this case, experience indicates that verification does not provide significant differences. The Fast Forum® computer program will abort if it detects keying errors over one half of one percent. The certification clause alerts all participants to accept the data within this context.

FORUM FOUNDATION *COUNCILOR*™ RESPONSE SHEET*

(A *FAST FORUM*® MACHINE-SCANNABLE SOCIALWARE PRODUCT)

E-Mail: fastforum@aol.com SIDE A WWW: http://weber.u.washington.edu/~forum

Mark Reflex® by NCS MM217043-1 654321 HR04 Printed in U.S.A.

INSTRUCTIONS:
1. Make a dark mark, using only a regular No. 2 pencil.
2. Do not use ink pens.
3. Make a dark mark that fills the bubble completely. (RIGHT ● WRONG ⊘⊗◒⊙)
4. Cleanly erase any mark you wish to change.
5. Do not fold or write comments on this sheet; write all comments on a separate sheet.
6. It's IMPORTANT that you indicate your personal and organizational categories as requested.
7. Please respond to each statement or question, as follows:

FILL IN:
- Y (Yes) if you can identify with the statement or question without reservation – a clear Yes.
- N (No) if you cannot identify with the statement or question, also without reservation – a clear No.
- ● (The One Best Choice) if the statement or question is multiple choice.
- OBJ (Object) if you believe that the statement or question is misleading or inappropriate in some manner.

MAKE NO MARK IF YOU ABSTAIN TO A QUESTION OR STATEMENT, i.e., if you are undecided or feel unable to respond at this time. For example, if you feel you need more information before answering, you should abstain.

YOUR PERSONAL AND ORGANIZATIONAL CATEGORIES:

1 SEX	MALE M FEMALE F	6	0 1 2 3 4 5 6 7 8 9	11	0 1 2 3 4 5 6 7 8 9
2 AGE	10 20 30 40 50 60 70 80+ / 1 2 3 4 5 6 7 8 / 19 29 39 49 59 69 79	7	0 1 2 3 4 5 6 7 8 9	12	0 1 2 3 4 5 6 7 8 9
3	0 1 2 3 4 5 6 7 8 9	8	0 1 2 3 4 5 6 7 8 9	13	0 1 2 3 4 5 6 7 8 9
4	0 1 2 3 4 5 6 7 8 9	9	0 1 2 3 4 5 6 7 8 9	14	0 1 2 3 4 5 6 7 8 9
5	0 1 2 3 4 5 6 7 8 9	10	0 1 2 3 4 5 6 7 8 9	15	0 1 2 3 4 5 6 7 8 9

YOUR OPINION OF EACH QUESTION OR STATEMENT:

1 2 3 4 5 6 / A B C D E	1 2 3 4 5 6 / A B C D E	1 2 3 4 5 6 / A B C D E	1 2 3 4 5 6 / A B C D E	1 2 3 4 5 6 / A B C D E
1 Y N OBJ	11 Y N OBJ	21 Y N OBJ	31 Y N OBJ	41 Y N OBJ
2 Y N OBJ	12 Y N OBJ	22 Y N OBJ	32 Y N OBJ	42 Y N OBJ
3 Y N OBJ	13 Y N OBJ	23 Y N OBJ	33 Y N OBJ	43 Y N OBJ
4 Y N OBJ	14 Y N OBJ	24 Y N OBJ	34 Y N OBJ	44 Y N OBJ
5 Y N OBJ	15 Y N OBJ	25 Y N OBJ	35 Y N OBJ	45 Y N OBJ
6 Y N OBJ	16 Y N OBJ	26 Y N OBJ	36 Y N OBJ	46 Y N OBJ
7 Y N OBJ	17 Y N OBJ	27 Y N OBJ	37 Y N OBJ	47 Y N OBJ
8 Y N OBJ	18 Y N OBJ	28 Y N OBJ	38 Y N OBJ	48 Y N OBJ
9 Y N OBJ	19 Y N OBJ	29 Y N OBJ	39 Y N OBJ	49 Y N OBJ
10 Y N OBJ	20 Y N OBJ	30 Y N OBJ	40 Y N OBJ	50 Y N OBJ

YOUR COMMENTS: If you have any comments or suggestions, please use a separate sheet, or the comments page of the Opinionnaire® and return it to your convener or mail directly to the Forum Foundation. Please print or write clearly. *Thank You!*

***"Councilor" is defined by Webster as "an official advisor to a sovereign or chief magistrate."**

FORUM FOUNDATION *TIME & TALENT*™ RESPONSE SHEET

(A *FAST FORUM*® MACHINE-SCANNABLE SOCIALWARE PRODUCT)

SIDE B

RIGHT ● WRONG ⊘⊗◒⊙

LAST NAME	FIRST NAME	MI
A–Z	A–Z	A–Z

PHONE NUMBER
( ) -
0–9

BIRTH DATE

Month	Day	Year
Jan.	0	0 0
Feb.	1	1 1
Mar.	2	2 2
Apr.	3	3 3
May	4	4 4
June	5	5 5
July	6	6 6
Aug.	7	7 7
Sept.	8	8 8
Oct.	9	9 9
Nov.		
Dec.		

CLASS YEAR

SPECIAL CODES

A	B	C	D	E	F	G	H	I	J

TIME & TALENT RESPONSES:

A B C D E

1–100 ○○○○○

E-Mail: fastforum@aol.com

WWW: http://weber.u.washington.edu/~forum

The Viewspaper®

The Forum Foundation computer profile reports are designed to be complete reports showing titles, dates, organization, questions, data, legend, disclaimer, philosophy, and trailer clauses. Those profile reports selected can merely be reproduced, and distributed as might be appropriate. They are designed to stand alone. They can be summarized also and highlighted in a "Viewspaper®" if appropriate.

A newspaper is a *feedforward* communication instrument designed to report news to people including the views and opinions of leaders, officials etc. A "Viewspaper" is just the reverse. It is a *feedback* communication instrument designed to report the views of people participating! A Viewspaper® is similar to an editorial statement of the people participating. A Viewspaper® can range from a one-sheet summary highlighting results of a forum to an elaborate stand-alone document for wide distribution and used over time as a reference. See example "What United Methodists Believe (1994) Viewspaper®" in Appendix H.

An example of a more elaborate document is any of the Redmond, Washington Community Forum Viewspapers®. See excerpts from "An Analysis of the City of Redmond's Community Forum Program" completed by a Redmond resident and University of Washington student, Ms. Virginia Balsley (in the "Community Forum" model on page 56).

Tabulation of Data (General)

Participants in a Fast Forum® can record their responses in three ways. First, they can mark their Opinionnaire® directly which is then returned for key tabulation to the user or the Forum Foundation. Second, they can mark a Forum Foundation Reproducible Response Sheet which is then returned for tabulation and the participants can retain their Opinionnaire®, if provided, for future reference. This allows the convener of the group to make as many Reproducible Response Sheet copies as are needed for the group on short notice. Third, they can mark a Forum Foundation Machine-Scannable *Councilor*™ Response Sheet which can be returned and scanned optically by machine by the Forum Foundation and the results tabulated by computer accurately, timely, and economically.

Both the second and third ways listed allow the participants to keep a copy of the Opinionnaire for personal reference to compare with overall results when returned or they allow the convener to read a single copy given to the group to reduce expenses if desired. The group's time, interest, and resources will determine the choice. If the group is operating in a closed system where they are organized and funded or self-funded in advance and the size of the group is known, they can use the Fast Forum® groupware response sheets that are machine-scannable by an optical scanner.

These forms are not reproducible on a copy machine, nor are they usually available from printers locally. Their timing marks and registers from the edge of the paper are critical and they require a special non-magnetic ink.[47] If people are in a group that is operating in an open system where they are not organized individually in advance and the size of the group(s) are unknown and they may or may not be funded or self-funded (such as in a church group), the group may use both machine-readable and a Fast Forum® Reproducible Response Sheet that can be reproduced on any copy machine. Data from reproducible response sheets are keyed either by the organization's communicator or by the Forum Foundation for subsequent tabulation. Data from non-reproducible, optically-scanned, response sheets are either scanned by the organization (for example by school districts where most have such a capability) or by the Forum Foundation. [See Appendix D for examples of reproducible and machine scannable Fast Forum® response sheets.]

Tabulation (Keying of Demographics and Data)

Users can tabulate their own response data using a computer word processor. The data file is then transmitted to the Forum Foundation via E-mail on the Internet or by diskette by U.S. mail for tabulation. This process is the least expensive to the user and most practical for normal purposes where under 1,000 people are participating. If optical scanning is required, the Forum Foundation can do this, or it can be done locally by the user if a scanner is available. Many school systems in the United States use the National Computer Services (NCS) optical scanners; the Forum Foundation re-

---

[47] *The National Computer Systems, 1-800-533-0518, prints these forms. They are readable by NCS scanners which are utilized in many of the school districts of the nation.*

sponse sheets were designed by NCS. Service agreements may be able to be worked out with local school districts to allow use at nominal costs. Electronic results of data on computers can then be transmitted by e-mail via Internet or diskettes which can be mailed or expressed to the Forum Foundation for processing and return of profile reports generated. It is hoped that optical scanning by schools would be an option provided for government agencies at least. Schools have a social responsibility to society, as do universities, to assist educational research in the social sciences in their communities.

ENTERING FAST FORUM® DATA RECORDS INTO A FILE: EXAMPLE (A)

(For transmission to Forum Foundation via Internet or Diskette)

Legend: A Field is a collection of Characters.
A Record is a collection of Fields
A File is a collection of Records.

An asterisk in column one indicates a comment paragraph (not line) and can consist of several lines as follows.

*The Fast Forum® computer program will ignore comment paragraphs.

*The Fast Forum® program allows a maximum of 15 columns (1-15) for demographic and alphanumeric character responses plus a maximum of 50 more columns for question numeric character responses. Any characters entered beyond column 65 are considered comments by the program and ignored. [Note: It may be easier to use the numeric keypad to record data.]

*For example a Youth Opinionnaire® might be set up as follows:

*COLUMN ONE will designate Gender, i.e., 1=male, 2=female;
*COLUMN TWO will designate Age, i.e., 1=teenager, 2=20-29, 3=30-39 years etc.
*COLUMN THREE could designate Ethnic Family, i.e., 1=African-American, 2=Asian-American, 3=Caucasian American, 4=Chicano/Latino American, 5=Native American, 6=Other Ethnic Family, 7=Pacific Islander, 8=Multi-Ethnic Family
*COLUMN FOUR could designate Role, i.e., 1=Teenage Student, 2=Parent, 3=Grandparent, 4=Other Citizen

*COLUMN FIVE could designate State Region, i.e., 1=Region One, 2=Region Two, 3=Region Three etc...."0" (Zero)=Region Ten.

*Protocol: Any *demographic* column left unmarked, should be keyed as a blank (not identified). If the tabulator knows the answer, from other information, for example, the State Region number designated because of the return address, it should be keyed. Any *question* column left unmarked, should be keyed as a blank (abstention).

A "." (period) can then be entered in *column 6* denoting the end of the demographic responses and the beginning of the question responses. A "+" is entered after the last character in the record denoting the end of the data string. If a non-proportional font is used (such as Courier), the strings will all align on the right and alert all when keying errors of skipping or duplicating have been made.

Up to 50 numeric character responses to corresponding questions can then be entered beginning in *column 7*, e.g., 1=yes, 2=no; 1, 2, 3, 4, or 5 for multiple-choice or value scale questions, i.e., 1=Strongly Agree, 2=Agree, 3=Neutral, 4=Disagree, 5=Strongly Disagree.

To denote an abstention to a question, key a space stroke; to denote an objection to a question use a "0" (zero) or "6" (six).

Thus, for a participating local church to record a female, teenager, whose ethnic family is Caucasian, a student, who lives in jurisdiction 7 and who answers the first 5 questions Yes, the second five questions No, marks "3" on the next four multiple-choice questions except that she abstains to question number 15, and answers the last five questions "2" (Agree) except that she objects to the next to last question, a typical data setup sheet and keyed character string would be:

DATA SETUP SHEET

*TO: The Forum Foundation Data Center
4427 Thackeray Place
Seattle, WA 98105-6124

*Date:____________ Forum #___________ Subject:

*From Local Church or Organization: #xxx, City, State, Zip.

*Church/Organization Communicator (or Teacher):

*Phone:____________; Fax:_____________e-mail:

*Comment: I would like a copy of each profile report by (date).

*START OF DATA (Use Courier non-proportional font)

21317.1111122222333 22202+
*etc.
*END OF DATA
*Church Secretary:________________________
*Phone:_____________; Fax_____________e-mail:

As another example, the following might be transmitted by a church or organizational communicator once communication has been established through Internet to the Forum Foundation:
For example a Local Church Opinionnaire® might be set up as follows:

COLUMN ONE designates Gender, i.e., 1=Male, 2=Female.
COLUMN TWO designates Age, i.e., 1=Teenager, 2=20-29, 3=30-39 years etc.
COLUMN THREE could designate Ethnic Family, i.e., 1=African-American, 2=Asian-American, 3=Caucasian-American, 4=Chicano/Latino American,*5=Multi-Ethnic Family, 6=Native American, 7=Other Ethnic Family, 8=Pacific-Islander American.
COLUMN FOUR could designate Role, i.e., 1=Laity, 2=Clergy.
COLUMN FIVE could designate Time Zone, i.e., 1= Eastern, 2=Central, 3=Mountain, 4=Pacific/Alaska/Hawaii.
COLUMN SIX could ask: Are you a church member? 1=Yes, 2=No.
COLUMN SEVEN could ask: A member over 5 years? 1=Yes, 2=No.
COLUMN EIGHT asks: Are you a church officer or committee chair? 1=Yes, 2=No.
COLUMN NINE asks: Are you a committee member (but not an officer or chair)? 1=Yes, 2=No.
COLUMNS 10-14 could designate Geographic Areas showing up to 10 "Jurisdictions" in column 10, up to 99 "Annual Conferences" in columns 11-12, and up to 99 "Districts" in Columns 13-14.

Note: Any demographic column left unmarked, should be keyed as a blank (not identified). If the tabulator knows the answer, from other information, for example, Annual Conference or District number because of the return address on the envelope, it should be keyed. Any question column left unmarked, should be keyed as a blank (abstention).

A "." (period) can then be entered in column 15 denoting the end of the demographic *responses and the beginning of the question responses. [Note, column 15 could still be used for one more demographic if required in which case there would be no "." (period) as a separator.] Up to 50 numeric character responses to corresponding questions can then be entered beginning in column 16 e.g., 1=yes, 2=no; 1, 2, 3, 4, or 5 for multiple-choice or value scale questions, i.e., 1=Strongly Agree, 2=Agree, 3=Neutral, 4=Disagree, 5=Strongly Disagree; and a space for all abstentions or a "0" zero or "6" for objections.

A "+" is entered after the last character in the record denoting the end of the record string. If a non-proportional font is used, such as Courier, the strings will all align on the right and alert all when keying errors have been made.

Thus, to key in data recording a female, 48 years old, whose ethnic family is Caucasian, a laywoman who lives in the Pacific Time Zone, who has been a member of the church over 5 years, who is not an officer or chair but is a committee member, who lives in the Western Jurisdiction (designated 5), in the Pacific Northwest Annual Conference (designated 06), in the Seattle District (designated 03) and who answers the first 5 questions of an Opinionnaire® Yes, the second five questions No, answers 3 to the third five questions except she abstains to the next to last, and answers the last five questions "Agree" except that she objects to the next to last question, the character string keyed after identifying the data would be:

DATA SETUP SHEET

*TO: The Forum Foundation Data Center
4427 Thackeray Place
Seattle, WA 98105-6124

*Date:____________ Forum #__________ Subject:

*From Local Church: #xxx, City, State, Zip.

*Church Communicator (or Teacher):________________________

*Phone:______________; Fax:____________e-mail:

*Comment: I would like to receive a copy of each profile report by (date).

*START OF DATA (In Courier non-proportional font)

```
24314112140506.1111122222333 322202+
```

*END OF DATA

*Church/Organization Secretary:________________________

*Phone:__________; Fax:______________e-mail:

[END OF VOLUME TWO]

APPENDICES

A. GENERAL ADMINISTRATIVE THEORIES (WHY)

A Condensation of *The Search For ENLIGHTENED LEADERSHIP Volume 1: Applying New Administrative Theory*

INTRODUCTION

The Ten Dynamics of Governance and Administration

I was invited to make a day-long presentation of our book on May 30, 1997 in Moscow at Russia's Open University by Dr. Boris Bim-Bad, President, and by the Russian Academy of Education. This was attended by a small group of top educational administrators in Moscow including Dr. Alexander Asmolov, Deputy Minister of Education of the Russian Federation. It was a very stimulating experience. This article was published in English in MAGISTER, No. 1, 1998, pp 80-89 by Dr. Nikolai Nikandrov who was Chief Editor; he is now president of the Russian Academy of Education. MAGISTER is a bimonthly International Psychological-Educational Journal published in Moscow. A Russian translation by our translator, Prof. Tatyana V. Tsyrlina, will be published later in 1998 in PEDAGOGICS, Dr. Vladimir Borisenkov, Chief Editor. In this section we present the ten administrative theories from our research findings in condensed form as concisely as possible and with the briefest transition between theories. For a complete explanation of all the theories you are referred to Volume 1 of this trilogy: *Applying New Administrative Theory*, 1996, 160 pages.

These theories also form a paradigm.

> Paradigms are sets of rules and regulations that do two things. First they establish boundaries....Second, these rules and regulations then go on to tell you how to be successful by solving problems within these boundaries....Paradigms filter incoming experience. We are viewing the world through our paradigms all the time. We constantly select from the world that data that best fits our rules and regulations and try to ignore the rest. As a result, what may be perfectly obvious to a person with one paradigm, may be totally imperceptible to someone with a different paradigm. I call this phenomenon, the Paradigm Effect....Sometimes your paradigm can become

> the paradigm—the only way to do something. And when you are confronted by an alternative idea, you reject it out of hand. Now that can lead to a nasty disorder. I call that disorder Paradigm Paralysis. Paradigm paralysis is a disease of certainty.[48]

Hopefully, these theories will provide a better grasp of how to administer "us" and avoid the effects of "Paradigm Paralysis" in the future. We invite you to become "Paradigm Pioneers" with us in a search together for more effective administration in all organizations and in the processes of governance everywhere in the world.

The ten natural dynamics of governance and administration are listed below. These ten dynamics constitute our view of administrative theory.

1. THE BASIC ATTITUDE—An implied administrative imperative.
2. THE THEORY OF LEARNING—The source of individual creativity.
3. THE THEORY OF LEADERSHIP—The source of organizational creativity.
4. THE THEORY OF AUTHORITY—The source of organizational power.
5. THE THEORY OF POLITICS—The source of collaboration and action.
6. THE SELF-FULFILLING PROPHECY—The generator of theories and the determinant of individual and organizational capacities.
7. THE ADMINISTRATIVE PROCESS—A definition.
8. THE HELPING PROFESSIONS—A definition.
9. THE ZEITGEIST PRINCIPLE—The Supreme Governor.
10. THE NATURAL FACTORS—A new paradigm shift toward civilization building.

---

[48] *Joel A. Barker and Ray J. Christensen, "Discovering the Future—The Business of Paradigms," Video, 1989, produced by Infinity Limited and Charthouse Learning Corporation, 1-800-328-3789, based on the book by the same name by Joel A. Barker.*

The Search For ENLIGHTENED LEADERSHIP Volume 1: Applying New Administrative Theory

A CONDENSATION

Abstract—The following administrative theory in Part 1 is a condensation of Volume 1 presented by Richard J. Spady to Russian educational leaders on May 30, 1997 at a conference convened by the Russian Academy of Education at Russia's Open University in Moscow. It was published in the Russian International Psychological-Education Journal MAGISTER in No. 1, 1998. It contains the ten natural dynamics of administrative theory for more effective families, churches, education, business, government, and society. [Note: Ellipses "...." denote portions of the original book of 160 pages that were deleted from this condensation.]

The Ten Dynamics of Governance and Administration—Introduction

In this section we present the ten administrative theories from our research findings as briefly and concisely as possible. Most are followed in this condensation by a brief comment; for a complete explanation, please reference the book itself (160 pages in the English version). The book can be obtained also in a Russian translation from references in Appendix P of this book. Where passages have been deleted in this condensation from the original book, the ellipse "...." at the end of a sentence or "..." within a sentence has been shown....

We have been formulating and measuring these theories since 1970 and first published an article on them in 1980, others in 1984 and 1986, as well as a prepublication manuscript titled Administrative Theory in 1986.[49] The articles and book were written before we had heard of the concept of glasnost (openness) and perestroika (re-

[49] *Richard J. Spady, Cecil H. Bell, Jr., and Gary A. D'Angelo, "A New View of Authority and the Administrative Process," FUTURICS, Vol 4 No 2 pp 143-157, 1980, Pergamon Press Ltd. "The Participative Heterarchy A>B>C>A; The Administration of Church and Society in the Future" by Richard J. Spady, was published by the Forum Foundation, 1984. The prepublication edition of the manuscript of this book titled Administrative Theory was published in January 1986 as part of our research to get initial feedback and reaction of our general theories from scholars and leaders. "A New View of Authority and the Administrative Process—(Revisited 1995) is reprinted in the Appendix of this book. (This article was also presented at session W3-13 on the theme "Reinvigorating Democracy" of the Seventh General Assembly of the World Future Society, June 27-July 1, 1993 in Washington, D.C. The article was titled, "A New View of Authority and the Administrative Process—Revisited.")*

structuring) proposed by Mikhail Gorbachev, General Secretary of the Soviet Union, who came to power in 1985. Our earlier writings all predate and predict the movements in the world toward democracy as exemplified in the former Soviet Union and in Eastern Europe and buttress our arguments. From our experiences and scholarship these new general theories seem true. We hope that you, the reader and final judge, will agree and use these theories of administration and governance that apply in an increasingly complex, dangerous, but hopeful world. In the words of the cartoon character Pogo, "We have met the enemy, and he is us." Hopefully, these theories will provide a better grasp of how to administer "us"...in the future. We invite you...to participate with us in a search together for more effective administration in all organizations and in the processes of governance everywhere in the world...

THE BASIC ATTITUDE

1. The Basic Attitude in Civilization Building
(An Implied Administrative Imperative.)

One must always treat all persons with dignity, consideration and respect! We can reject or not agree with anything said, but we must always respect another person's right to say it. The process is listen to the other person, weigh what is said, and then do one of three things with the idea or information received: accept it, reject it, or modify it, i.e., accept that which fits, and ignore the rest—but always with consideration and respect for the other person, and his or her views—in order to protect best one's own freedom to speak.

We must discern that we can reject the ideas of another person without in any way rejecting or diminishing the person himself or herself. This is the modern-day idea, "I'm OK, you're OK;" it is the biblical idea, "Love thy neighbor as thyself" which are in both Jewish and Christian scriptures.[50] It is the same idea, just millennia apart....

Our culture is rooted in Judeo-Christian religious concepts, and a basic tenet of the Christian religion is, "Everyone is unique and is just as important before God, *but no more* than anyone else." This principle, helped form the basic tenet of "equality of citizen-

[50] *(Old Testament) Leviticus 19:18 and (New Testament) Matthew 19:19*

ship" for this democracy as shown in our Declaration of Independence, "We hold these truths to be self-evident, that all men are created equal." As a nation of people which takes seriously its democratic and religious traditions, it is imperative to adopt this "Basic Attitude" of universal respect based upon equality in all our relationships with each other and others in the world. This helps people search together, as citizens, for ways to implement national and international objectives as well as more limited objectives in organizations and institutions which vitalize our society....

THE THEORY OF LEARNING

2. The Theory of Learning—The Creative Thinking Process

(The Source of Individual Creativity—the process of bringing a new idea into an individual's mind.)

When an individual is exposed to a problem (or is asked a question—which is just a small problem but is still problem oriented), the individual is thrust into the dynamics of The Socratic Method, one of history's proven learning techniques; it has four steps: Awareness, Frustration, Insight, and Verification. In the process an individual not only learns something new, but literally becomes someone new psychologically speaking. This ability to learn through the dynamics of the Socratic Method is a universal human ability.

Creativity is a process that brings a new idea into an individual's mind. It is the ability to learn, and it is a universal human capability. Socrates would not tell his students the answers to problems; he would just ask them questions and send them to ferret out the answers themselves. In the process of doing so, they became aware of the problem (i.e., Socrates' question) and experienced frustration, apparently a necessary prerequisite of success....

It is hard to think. An individual must ponder the problem, must worry about the problem; if one does not worry about a problem, one will not generate enough psychic voltage to give light to it. But this frustration sets the stage for the most important third step—insight, which wells up from within the individual. The individual says, "Ah ha! The answer to my problem is....," or the answer to the question is "Yes" or "No." At that moment it makes no difference which is chosen, yes or no. At that very microsecond, the individual's mind becomes psychologically benchmarked with the problem or the question and his or her own creative response to it and *learns.* And it can be a simple yes or no answer, even to very complex moral and value question oaths, e.g., Let what you say be simply "Yes" or "No;" anything more comes from evil, (Matthew 5:37).

The first three steps (awareness, frustration, and insight) are personal. It's a relationship between the individual and his or her problem in the world. No one else is involved. However, the fourth step, verification, is a group effort. Here morality and values and "right" or "wrong" answers of the individual are best tested anonymously against the responses of others who are participating in solving the problem. Secondary insights are then gained by the individual who continues to learn. All of this is done without putting anyone in a "win-lose" situation which makes it an ideal learning climate. We must enable people (including young people) to make lots of real decisions about lots of real problems in life; in the process of doing that, they will learn! When an individual learns "X" amount, the organization or society of which he or she is a part learns exactly the same amount, and both move toward being better able to solve their problems in the future. The principal authority for the Theory of Learning is Socrates....

If we accept that all original thinking and all new ideas came from the mind of some individual at sometime and someplace, then the importance of a "creative climate" in organizations and institutions everywhere that permits individuals to participate with their thinking is better appreciated. The role of administrators (governors) should be understood, not as directors or authoritarian figures, but as members of the "helping professions" similar to teaching, counseling, and ministry.[51]

3. THE THEORY OF LEADERSHIP

The Source of Organizational Creativity—the process that brings new ideas into an organization's or institution's "mind."

Leadership—like creativity, the ability to learn—is a universal human attribute; leadership is a function and not a quality reserved for the titled head

[51] *This idea will be developed later in the theory and definition of The Helping Professions.*

of an organization. To develop leadership properly, all decisions in an organization or institution should be made at the lowest level possible, consistent with two basic premises. First, adequate information is available with which to make a valid decision. Second, adequate resources are available to implement the decision reached. If either adequate information or resources is not available, the decision should be moved up one level higher in the organization or institution until both valid information and adequate resources to implement the decision are available.

The question arises, "But how can a person at the bottom be a leader? By definition there is no one else to lead." Yes, there is. Even the individual at the bottom level of a bureaucracy or a society has to "lead" himself or herself through the labyrinth of solving organizational and societal problems, as he or she perceives them, by using his or her own time and resources to solve those problems.

Adopting a conscious policy to decentralize decision-making in organizations and institutions in which higher levels assign problems to lower levels produces enormous amounts of leadership. As individuals are assigned problems, they are thrust into the dynamics of the Socratic method and the creative-thinking process; they can not avoid it. They become aware of the problem, experience frustration in solving it, achieve insight, and learn. The organization and society of which the individual is a part then move toward better problem resolution in the future. And all people involved become engaged in an overall process of civilization building. . . .

Because there is so much knowledge in the world today, it is a truism to say that most people, including ourselves, are just plain ignorant about most things and anybody who is considered to be an "expert" in anything is indeed fortunate. So within a culture where "becoming an expert" is a process of knowing more and more about less and less, the implications are that the answers people seek in the increasingly complex future are not likely to be found in any one person or small group of people, but are more likely to be found somewhere among all of us in the totality of our knowledge and experiences. Does that mean "expertise" is not needed? Not at all. There is a need for more, not less, but in addition, there is a need to differentiate between "knowledge" and "wisdom." William Cowper, 18th century English poet, captured one subtlety of this difference in his insightful poetry: *Knowledge is proud that it knows so much. Wisdom is humble that it knows not more.*

Thus, it is necessary to learn how knowledge can be distilled to produce the wisdom needed for making organizational and societal policy decisions. This will become a whole new organizational and cultural skill requiring its own expertise after the administrative theory has been worked through. And who is the main repository of this wisdom? The people are—people in organizations and people in society and people in the world. Most of the knowledge in the world is in books in libraries and in computer data banks, but most of the wisdom in the world is in the minds of people walking the earth. We need to learn how to reach it. What does every human being in the world do from the time they get up in the morning until they go to bed at night? They try to bring some kind of order out of the chaos that is often going on around them in their world. That is leadership, and it is a positive force—not negative.

We like the insights of Erik H. Erikson, pre-eminently recognized national and world psychologist, and his wife Joan.

> What is real wisdom? It comes from life experience, well digested. It's not what comes from reading great books. When it comes to understanding life, experiential learning is the only worthwhile kind; everything else is hearsay[52]...

Along a similar theme which points to the wisdom of people, George Gallup, in an August 1978 article in Reader's Digest, wrote:

> In conducting thousands of surveys on almost every conceivable issue for nearly half a century, I have learned three significant things about our fellow citizens. One is that the judgment of the American people is extraordinarily sound. Another is that the public is nearly always ahead of its leaders. The third is that the electorate has become better educated and more sophisticated politically than ever before.

---

[52] *Erik H. Erikson, "Erikson, In His Own Old Age, Expands His View of Life," New York Times, June 14, 1988, page 13.*

Our more limited research experience verifies Mr. Gallup's conclusions. When people are trusted and enabled to be responsible in their organizations and society by their leaders, they use good judgment, they are rational, they are wise.

However, we have been struck also by a counter-theme among legislators and public officials. Our impression is that most such officials espouse a philosophy of, "Keep your ear close to the ground." They try to keep very close to the moods of their electorate with surveys, phone calls, letters, meetings and the like. And that is good. But if that administrative style is also coupled with an unwillingness to study and use the extra information that is usually theirs as political leaders and to propose new and innovative solutions to problems in acts of statesmanship {to their constituents and colleagues}—simply because the public is not clamoring—then one must wonder: Who is doing the leading, and who is doing the following? People must be brought into planning processes at all levels in organizations, institutions, and governments through new theories and communication techniques that enable them to participate within their time and energy levels. Society needs the knowledge provided by experts {and officials}, but it also needs the wisdom and leadership provided by {the} people within the contexts of their organization, economic, and political arenas in their overall search for meaning and in the ongoing process of civilization building....

Centralization of decision-making (i.e., authoritarianism and totalitarianism) actually suppresses the "leadership" function in an organization or institution. Many believe that authoritarianism provides the strongest "leadership," but that is not the case. That is, centralization strategies to "control" or "take charge" and the like tend to suppress "leadership" in general. This is why decentralization, freedom, and participative democratic processes are the wave of the future for the human race in public and private organizations, institutions, and governments. Such dynamics simply provide at all levels a more effective "leadership" function, which is a universal human capability, and are thus more effective and efficient....

There are extremely important and direct links between administrative theory and economics and politics. Administration cuts across and transcends economics and politics. It is not simply a separate matter of "economics" or "politics" per se. Freedom and a democratic context are required for effective "leadership and administration" of complex organizational, institutional, and societal problems which economics and politics are. The fundamental issue is not "capitalism versus communism in nationalism;" the issue is "freedom versus totalitarianism in civilization building."

What does this all imply for the future of military and other dictatorships in third world countries and other highly centralized and authoritarian nations? It is extremely important for them that they begin to adapt themselves to becoming more free and open societies. Fortunately, this is what all people in all nations in the world will tend to do naturally. Dictators and authoritarian leaders cannot prevail. Time itself will see them fall due to the liberating energies of these natural, worldwide, cultural trends toward freedom. Therefore, it is better for them to embrace the trend and help shape their country constructively using their power transitionally to move to democracy.[53]

4. THE THEORY OF AUTHORITY

(The Source of Power in Organizations)

> *"Those who govern derive their power from the consent of the governed."*[54]

> *"Authority lies always with him to whom it applies.... Authority is another name for the willingness and capacity of individuals to submit to the necessities of cooperative systems."*[55]

> *"...it is the governed who determine the governing of men."*[56]

---

[53] *Unfortunately, the leadership of China took a step backward with its military suppression of students in 1989 in Tiananmen Square. With this episode they stepped away from democracy and back toward dictatorship and centralization of control. Hopefully, the political leadership of China in the future will learn from their mistake and make amends. Theirs has been a great nation in the history of the civilization of mankind and the world has long respected that.*

[54] *Thomas Jefferson, The Declaration of Independence, July 4, 1776.*

[55] *Chester Barnard, The Functions of the Executive, Harvard University Press, 1938 and 1968, Chapter 12, pages 183 and 184.*

[56] *Alexander Leighton, The Governing of Men, Octagon Books Inc., New York, 1964, page 367.*

This theory is probably the most widely misunderstood of all the theories presented in this book. Through the years, most people have believed that "authority lies in the office," i.e., in the president, in the governor, in the public official, in the general or admiral, in the policeman, in the administrator, in the manager, in the supervisor, in the boss and the like. This was the prevailing view for years among scholars. Then, as insights came to those contemplating the problem, this view changed. The nature of authority was realized to be more complex than originally perceived. The view expanded to recognize that the authority of leaders resides in their "task," or again later, in their "knowledge," from their "charisma," i.e., their personal ability to instill confidence in their constituents, or from the "situational ethic" of the leader. While all of the above are not without truth, the evidence of our studies, experiences, and research suggests that a more definitive and accurate description of the seat of "authority" and power in all organizations, public and private, (and applying to all persons from parents to heads of state), is: "those who govern derive their power and authority from the consent of the governed."

> We hold these truths to be self-evident, that all men are created equal; that they are endowed by their Creator with certain unalienable rights; that among these are life, liberty, and the pursuit of happiness. That, to secure these rights, governments are instituted among men, deriving their just powers from the consent of the governed...[57]

Chester Barnard, a transitional writer in the field, has best analyzed "authority". . . .

> Authority lies always with him to whom it applies....Authority is just another way of talking about the willingness of people to submit to collaborative systems.

Barnard's propositions were verified by the research of Alexander Leighton, psychologist, anthropologist, and naval reservist who studied Japanese-American citizens interned during World War II from the West Coast. The significance of Leighton's work seems to have been missed by most scholars. Leighton con-

---

[57] *Thomas Jefferson, The Declaration of Independence, July 4, 1776.*

cluded in his book, The Governing of Men:

> It is the governed who determine the governing of men....

(These views) have important meaning to all "governors."

It means if children are not willing to be "parented," then parents cannot "parent" them; if students are not willing to be taught by a teacher, then the teacher cannot teach; if students (or teachers) are not willing to be "principaled" by a principal, then the principal cannot "principal" them; if employees are not willing to be managed by an employer, then the employer cannot manage them; if bureaucrats are not willing to be administered by an administrator, then the administrator cannot administer them; if soldiers and sailors are not willing to be commanded, then a commander cannot command; and if citizens of a nation are not willing to be led by a government, then a government cannot lead them (be they kings, tyrants, or dictators and the like). If the people of the United States were not willing to be governed by the President and the Congress, then the President and the Congress could not govern them, Constitution or no Constitution, army or no army! All of the power of the President and the Congress is derived, like that of all leaders, merely by the willingness of the people in their constituency to be governed by them. This principle applies equally from parents of children to the heads of state everywhere. . . .

It is not just rhetoric that the Constitution of the United States and the preamble to the United Nations' Charter both begin, "We the People...." It is history's clue to the ultimate source of power and authority in all organizations everywhere in the world. This has been a long, hard, lesson to learn and one which petty organizational and institutional tyrants as well as military dictators of developing nations had better heed in the future.

5. THE THEORY OF POLITICS

(The Source of Collaboration and Action in Organizations)

A political relationship is defined as one between or among equals, and progress in a political relationship comes only from agreement, or failing that, from compromise through collaboration; otherwise there is stalemate.

Progress in a political relationship is best reached by increasing interaction and improving communication, and thus understanding, between or among the participants. It is a misnomer to consider any human organization as "non-political," and it is a political right of people to be enabled by their governors to participate viably in their organizations, institutions, and governments....

It is commonly thought that human relationships among people in military organizations, governments, bureaucracies, businesses, and other such hierarchical organizations are non-political, i.e., not a relationship among equals. They are all considered to be hierarchical and built upon a management style in which there is a superior/subordinate relationship. But this is not fundamentally true (in the spiritual sense of the Declaration of Independence); it only seems true (in the sense of the legal system and the everyday experiences of people).

People normally conduct themselves in their public and private organizational "legal roles" as if the superior/subordinate relationship were really true. Because of this, most human organizations, including those of business, church, and state, upon which the people depend for their very economic, spiritual, and societal survival, often flounder from a lack of overall direction and "leadership." The confusion comes from not knowing fundamentally who is really "in charge." As explained in the previous chapter in the Theory of Authority, the people are in charge....

Fundamentally, all organizations are political, a relationship among equals—including even governmental, military, and police organizations. It is only in the organizational "work-a-day roles" that we each play that "superior/subordinate" relationships appear. But notice that the governor in the relationship does not have the power to prevent a subordinate from leaving if the subordinate is intent on doing so and is willing to disregard any consequences—including death in the case of martyrs....

Citizenship is a job for life. We are all sometimes "unemployed" in our vocational work-a-day world, e.g., during periods of growing up as children, while studying to learn new skills as students, when we lose our "jobs" as individuals and must seek new work, when retired and other such examples. However, as citizens, we can never be "unemployed" in our life work of civilization building. Every citizen in the world is gainfully employed in this task from life to death. That is the administrative reality which leaders and citizens everywhere must realize. Each person simultaneously is a citizen of his or her own country and of the world....

6. THE SELF-FULFILLING PROPHECY

(The Generator of Theories and the Determinant of Individual and Organizational Capacity)

All human beings are prophetic. The way in which an individual (or family, group, organization, institution, community, state, nation, society, or civilization) perceives a situation, perceives "self," or perceives others (the prophecy), will determine its reaction to the situation, "self," or others encountered in its environment. The reactions themselves, in turn, tend to direct events subsequently encountered toward reinforcing the original perception, i.e., they tend to be self-fulfilling.

Perceptions of self are gained from past successes or failures and the "mirror" of the reactions of others. Positive perceptions of self provide the motivation for human beings and organizations to learn and grow in their abilities and capacities.

Desired capacities are best achieved initially by acting as if they were present....

7. THE ADMINISTRATIVE PROCESS—DEFINED

The Administrative Process is: Diagnose the problem, theorize its solution, decide what to do about it, accomplish what was decided, and review what was done. It is an ongoing process.

Most older leaders of today have been taught that the management process is plan, organize, motivate, and control (or a derivative: plan, organize, coordinate, direct, and control). If an individual's concept of being a manager or boss or governor is that one must motivate, direct, or control others, the individual easily moves into an authoritarian management style, the most pervasive style in organizations and society today. This closes doors for two-way communication between leaders and people, feedback from people to people, and the organization begins to "fly blind" with leaders perceptually detached from their constituents. The situation is similar to a ship with defective radar traveling at high speed in dense fog through waters filled with icebergs—its chances of survival are not good.

On the other hand, an organization whose leaders permit their constituencies to participate viably with their ideas and opinions, whenever possible, receives accurate feedback. It is the same ship but with reliable radar. It perceives its environment accurately and can change course frequently to adapt to changes and avoid calamity....

8. THE HELPING PROFESSIONS—DEFINED

[Based on research by Dr. Arthur W. Combs]

Leaders (governors) are a part of the helping professions which include administrators, teachers, counselors, ministers, nurses, parents and such other persons in personal interaction with followers, constituents, students, clients, parishioners, patients, children, citizens and other similar relationships. The characteristics of good and poor helpers are the same regardless of the profession.

Dr. Combs has identified the characteristics of helpers (leaders) to include the following:

POOR LEADERS	GOOD LEADERS
1. External data are important—order, neatness, forms, rules, procedures and so forth.	1. Internal data are important—are sensitive to the beliefs, opinions, attitudes, and values of people.
2. Are concerned about things.	2. Are concerned about people.
3. Feel people are not trustworthy and able.	3. Feel people are trustworthy and able.
4. Violate the dignity and integrity of people.	4. Preserve the dignity and integrity of people.
5. Do not see themselves positive ways.	5. See themselves in positive in ways.
6. Have controlling purposes.	6. Have freeing purposes.

7. Have narrow purposes.	7. Have broad purposes.
8. Are self-concealing.	8. Are self-revealing.

Source: "Human Relationships," address given 1970 by Dr. Arthur W. Combs, DAS Conference, Washington Education Association, Seattle, Washington.

Dr. Combs has stated that in a world where we no longer know the goals, where the goals have to be the development of intelligent persons who are skillful at problem-solving, we need a different kind of psychology. We need a psychology that will help us understand the internal life of human beings. To do this, teachers (leaders) have to turn their attention to values because the beliefs, feelings, attitudes, and understandings which make up the perceptions and prophecies of people will determine the choices they make. Combs believes that teachers (leaders) should help their students (constituents), "explore and discover their own values which is the important question." That is, in the pedagogy of teaching, a teacher should not "teach" values to students but rather should help students explore their own values. The same applies to leaders who should help their constituents explore their own values....

9. THE ZEITGEIST PRINCIPLE

> *(Tsite'-Geist' as in "site" and "guy-st.") THE ZEITGEIST: "Spirit of the time" (Webster)—that is, "The Spirit of Society at a point in time,"—The Supreme Governor.*

To work most effectively, human organizations and institutions (from the smallest—a husband and wife, up to civilization itself—the largest) require a functional feedback communication capability. This is best accomplished in most organizations by a democratic, open, participative, reliable, viable, anonymous, routine, and objective feedback communication system. Most organizations, institutions, and governments in the world today have no such system....

10. THE NATURAL FACTORS OF GOVERNANCE, ADMINISTRATION AND COMMUNICATION

(A New Paradigm Toward Civilization Building.)

When organizations or institutions have a democratic, open, participative, reliable, viable, anonymous, routine, and objective feedback communication system, that enables its members, constituents, or citizens to participate meaningfully, within their time and energy levels with their opinions, in interaction to queries from their leader-representatives, there are three "natural" and favorable administrative dynamics that spontaneously tend to occur:

1. Diagnosis (the first step in the administrative process) of organizational and institutional problems is improved, leading to more effective decision-making in the future.

2. Learning (through the dynamics of the Socratic Method) is improved for individuals participating, the organization, and society, and all move toward being better able to solve system problems in the future.

3. Peace prospects are improved in organizations and institutions because democratic, open, participative, reliable, viable, anonymous, routine, and objective communication processes are therapeutic in nature and tend toward a reduction of tensions and a resolution of conflicts in the future....

CONCLUSION

Values, the prevailing beliefs and opinions of individuals, groups, nations, and of civilization itself, are like switches on a railroad. As a decision-making junction is approached, the cumulative effect of all the values held at that point in time become imperative. The perceptions of individuals, the consciousness of groups, the paradigm, meta-perspective, or Zeitgeist of civilization (which is their "prophecy") will determine the choice made and direction taken at every junction. Sequential value choices over time determine the future for an individual, group, or society for they tend to be self-fulfilling. People and their institutions, therefore, are more the creators of their own destiny than the victims of it.

Values are also a moral force; they tell us right from wrong.

They derive from our experiences and from the very depths of our God spirit. They set the ethos, direction, and mood within which we live and interact with others. And like the tide, they prevail. Values are the source of moral authority for the individual which, in turn, is the only force capable of transcending or changing all legal authority. As we stated before, this is true whenever moral authority confronts legal authority, individually or corporately, publicly or privately. This covers the range from a parent-child relationship to the affairs of the state in its relationship with its citizens. People will make sacrifices and endure great hardships for their values. They will fight for them. They will even die for them. So authority does not lie within some leader. It does not lie within some office, title, task, knowledge, or with property or things. Rather, it's in all of us.

Democratic, open, interaction of ideas within a context of free, respectful, and open discussions is the mortar that binds a creative organization, institution, or society, e.g., an organization, institution, or society which is actively searching for solutions to its problems. Any group, organization, institution, community, society, nation, or civilization which inhibits, innocently or not, the free movement of ideas among its constituents—up, down and across its organizational and societal structures—is depriving itself of its greatest resource, *human thought,* and is in grave danger of being buried in history by the avalanche of the creativity of others!

EPILOGUE....

We have spoken earlier of the ten constituent theories of administrative theory. In this Epilogue we increase the number to twelve: to build a formal bridge from administrative theory to a general theory of civilization. These are placed in the Epilogue because the theories are neither fully developed nor substantiated. They are more our intuitive sense of the direction toward which, we feel, administrative theory is moving.

11. THE UNIFIED SOCIAL THEORY—DEFINED

If a theory used at the micro-level (the relationship among individuals) is accurate for an individual or organization, then it is equally valid at the macro-level....

12. A THEORY OF CIVILIZATION—DEFINED

"Civilization is fundamentally spiritual, not material."[58] *And the spiritual destiny of humankind is unity and love for each other!*

Again, by "civilization building" we mean the dynamic, historical processes of human innovation and social evolution to improve the survivability of the human race and the success of the human species through its enlightened organizations and institutions.

"An Enlightened Organization," argues Jaideep Singh, "is characterized by 'spiritual mission,' 'unified intentionality,' 'egalitarian hierarchy,' 'situational leadership,' 'harmonious teams,' 'relational validation,' 'self-determined self-actualization,' 'entrepreneurial thrust,' 'dynamic equilibrium,' and 'symphonic fusion'—the last attribute implying the rhythmic orchestration of all the above characteristics into the organizational way of life." [59]....

[END OF CONDENSATION]

---

[58] *A.D. Ritchie, CIVILIZATION, SCIENCE, AND RELIGION, 1945, Penguin Books, 245 Fifth Ave., New York, NY, Page 9.*

[59] *ADMINISTRATIVE THEORY, 1984, Ramesh K. Arora, Volume Editor, Indian Institute of public Administration, Indraprastha Estae, Ring Road, New Delhi — 110002. (Page XXII and Page 122 by Jaideep Singh).*

B. A Letter from Russia

March 20, 1998

FROM: Oleg Yashenko, Principal
Secondary School
No 32 Volodarskaya Str., 44 "A"
305000 Kursk, Russia

TO: Richard J. Spady, President,
Forum Foundation
4426 Second Ave. N.E.
Seattle, Washington, USA 98105-6191

To get feedback of any kind is very important for any administrator, especially for a beginner. I learned about the Fast Forum® Opinionnaire® technique from Professor Dr. Tatyana Tsyrlina, and I got excited to use it.

Truthfully, at the beginning I had many doubts, not about the idea and methodology itself, but about the reaction of my students. But everything was successful. I was surprised to learn that the majority of them answered in the affirmative to the first question, "Is such kind of talk of the principal necessary for the students?"

I feel that Fast Forum® strategies are useful for both sides—for the administrator who gets a clearer vision of his/her organization (in my case, of the school and the students) and for the students who get a chance to understand their principal and school programs better. It's amazing how much more stimulating this kind of "talk" was in comparison with traditional forums. I received not only feedback in written form but also from a number of initiatives from the students.

My school is rather small, a little bit more than 600 students and 121 (teenagers) already answered the Opinionnaires®. I am seriously thinking of using them in my work with the teachers too.

Thank you. I feel honored to be the first Russian school principal who used the Fast Forum® technique.

[COMMENT: Actually Mr. Yashenko is the first high school principal in the world to use the Fast Forum® technique; we are honored and thank him for his innovative spirit. My father, grandfather, and grandmother were born in Russia and emigrated from Russia in 1905. (Their ancestors were from Austria and came with Catherine The Great.) It is for these reasons that I have been eager to help Russia in its need to understand Administrative Theory in Volume 1 and Many-to-Many communication here in Volume 2. For a Russian translation of these volumes see "How to Order Books" in Appendix N. RJS]

C. A PSYCHO-SOCIAL EDUCATION PROPOSAL FOR RUSSIA

The Future Molding Game™ and Youth Futures Forum™

Presented to: RUSSIAN ACADEMY OF EDUCATION
Russia's Open University

"New Administrative Theory and Its Meaning for Democracy"
May 30, 1997 Moscow, Russia

RICHARD J. SPADY, President
Forum Foundation Seattle, Washington U.S.A.

In July of 1990 Seattle hosted the Goodwill Games and nearly 1,000 Russians attended and were hosted by our Rotary International District 5030. My club, Bellevue Overlake Rotary, hosted over twenty Russian visitors. My wife and I hosted one guest, Mr. Marat Akylbikoff, from the Soviet Socialist Republic of Kyrgyzstan. The games and exchanges were a wonderful goodwill experience for both guests and hosts. We had an interpreter at the farewell picnic given by our club, and (on a hunch) I gave Marat a copy of our unpublished manuscript on administrative theory. I hoped he would get it to a scholar in Russia who might appreciate it.

It seemed to me that at that time in Russia's history, it was especially important for administrators, both those in and out of government, to be exposed to the new administrative theory which was emerging in the world. With all the rapid changes that were happening politically, economically, organizationally, and socially, Russia needed all the help it could get to lead itself through the labyrinth of solving these kinds of problems. New administrative theory, capable of conceptualizing the reality of their situation, would be an important key to Russia's success in the coming months and years. Whatever their technical environment or problem—be it political, economic, educational, or social—all organizations share the common problems of "administration." Organizations are organized to accomplish a purpose, and by virtue of that fact, they are involved with the administrative process. What are the fundamental dynamics which tend to move all organizations, universally, toward solving their problems and anticipating or adapting to changes that occur in their internal and external environments? That is the question faced by all administrators (including parents, teachers, principals, supervisors, administrators, entrepreneurs, and public officials) in the world. If we can get our theoretical house in order first, i.e., answer the question "WHY," then we can get our technical house in order, i.e., answer the question "HOW." This is a process of civilization building.

Well, sending our unpublished manuscript back to our visitor's country, Kyrgyzstan, was a long shot, but it worked. In the spring of 1991 I received a letter from Dr. Almas Chukin, an Associate Professor of Economics at Kyrgyze State University who read the manuscript. He noted the frontispiece in our manuscript which had two columns. The first was headed "Superficial Administrative Ideas Held By Most Leaders;" the second column was headed "Administrative Reality." He wrote, "Everything in the first column is what the communist philosophy teaches. We need to understand what is in the second column." He invited me to come to his country to speak. My wife and I arrived in Moscow in late September 1991 shortly after the attempted overthrow of Mikhail Gorbachev. We were accompanied by Mr. Leo Pavloff, who was born in Siberia but emigrated as a boy to America after the 1917 revolution in Russia. He served as our personal interpreter. We were met by Dr. Chukin and Marat Akylbikoff, our former house guest. We then toured Moscow with energy and enthusiasm with Dr. Chukin and Marat for a few days. It was all so new to us; it was a special time. We then flew on to Beeshkek, the capitol of his country, Kyrgyzstan, which lies adjacent to southern China, south of Kazakstan, and north of Pakistan. It is a state about equal in size and population to my own state of Washington in the United States. By that time, Dr. Chukin was working with the State Ministry of Economics, and we found ourselves as official visitors of the state. It was a rare and treasured experience.

My colleagues and I had recently written a paper titled "A New View of Authority and the Administrative Process," and I had it translated into Russian for the trip. It was presented at the university and elsewhere because our book was not yet ready for publication. While it was a time of turmoil in the Russian federation at large, we found the people of Kyrgyzstan friendly to their American visitors and very interested in the ideas of democracy! After two weeks in Kyrgyzstan, my wife and I returned on the Trans-Siberian Railroad to visit Moscow again and later St. Petersburg. We passed through Saratov on the Volga River which was especially meaningful for me as my father was born in 1900 in the small neighboring village then known as Norka; he emigrated with my grandparents to America in 1906. So I feel a close kinship with Russia as the land of my forefathers and want to help the country succeed in its transition period to democracy in every way that I can.

In the fall of 1992 I attended a conference on "Moral Education" held at the University of Georgia in Athens, Georgia, USA. It was there that I first met Dr. Tatyana Tsyerlina from Kursk Pedagogical University in Russia and shared with her our recent translated paper. She invited me to attend an educational conference on "Moral Education" that she was organizing in Moscow in April 1993 which I attended. Dr. John Jacobson, computer programmer at the University of Washington and linguist, accompanied me. Dr. Tsyerlina has written several books and attends many international conferences on moral education. It was at a conference in England early in 1996 that she met Dr. Arthur K. Ellis, Director, International Center for Curriculum Studies, Seattle Pacific University and urged us separately to contact each other. We met, and I gave him a copy of our new book that was just published in July 1996 titled *The Search for Enlightened Leadership, Volume 1: Applying New Administrative Theory*. He also attended a workshop on September 21, 1996, in Seattle which my colleague, Dr. Cecil H. Bell, Jr.,[60] and I presented. The moderator was The Rev. Dr. Richard S. Kirby, who occupies the "Stuart C. Dodd Chair in Social Innovation," in the Forum Foundation and is the editor of our book and trilogy.[61]

Dr. Ellis was impressed with the direction of our research in

---

[60] *Dr. Bell is Chair, Department of Management and Organization, School of Business Administration, University of Washington, Seattle, Washington, USA.*

[61] *Dr. Kirby is a theologian, philosopher, and brilliant academic who is also Chair of the World Network of Religious Futurists and director of its Seattle research center. He currently teaches at the University of Washington in the School of Business Administration and at Seattle Pacific University in Education. He has also taught at Pacific Lutheran University in Tacoma and Seattle University (Catholic) in the last year. Dr. Kirby is currently the Executive Director of the new non-profit and tax exempt "Stuart C. Dodd Institute for Social Innovation" currently being formed and centered at the University of Washington and Seattle Pacific University with continued association with the Forum Foundation.*

the Forum Foundation which was co-founded in 1970 as a non-profit, educational research corporation of Washington state by myself, Dr. Bell and others. In his letter of October 1, 1996, he wrote, "I want you to know how much I appreciate the opportunity to have attended your workshop on September 21 at St. Mark's....Having read your book prior to the presentation, I greatly enjoyed your in-person explication of the key ideas found therein. It seems to me, Dick, that your insights to group process have profound implications for the field of education." I feel the same way. I believe the new ideas of administrative theory have extremely important implications for education, governance, "community building," and organizational and institutional peace in the world.

The problem perhaps has been best defined by our former colleague and Forum Foundation board member, Dr. Stuart C. Dodd who wrote:

> As human systems and organizations grow ever larger, more complex, and more impersonal—in our schools, in our communities, in our churches, in our governments, and in our industries and commerce—the individual shrinks toward facelessness, hopelessness, powerlessness, and frustration.[62]

In the early summer of 1996 I received an invitation to join with a professional group of teachers and administrators visiting South Africa for two weeks beginning in late October 1996 under the auspices of the "People to People Citizen Ambassador Program, (Curriculum Instruction Delegation)." The trip gave me, and my wife, an opportunity to visit a truly remarkable and dynamic country at a time in its history when it was (and still is) undergoing historical political changes as it reverses apartheid and moves to implement the broader principles of a truly democratic society. South Africa has high hopes that education will be one of the major institutions to accomplish the task.

The purpose of the Ambassador Program is to build new

---

[62] *Dr. Stuart C. Dodd, Professor-Emeritus of Sociology, University of Washington, and Richard J. Spady, "Citizen Counselor Proposal," The Seattle Times, November 10, 1974 (part of IN-FORUM project co-sponsored by the Church Council of Greater Seattle). Dr. Dodd, an acknowledged pioneer in social science, died in 1975; he did much to focus the research of the Forum Foundation in its early years.*

bridges of understanding with professionals of other countries and to share new ideas. This is difficult to do as the tour format itself is able to provide only cursory opportunities in most cases for professional interaction. Nevertheless, opportunities do exist and impressions are gained from the experiences. In my case, my best opportunity to interact was provided in a spontaneous, four-hour, one-on-one meeting with Dr. John B. Mobbs, Head of Research, Western Cape Education Department in Cape Town which I felt was very fruitful. (I also had an opportunity to gift over 60 copies of our new book during the two week visit.)

Dr. Daniel Tanner, team leader,[63] invited participants to write papers regarding their impressions of the educational situation in South Africa. I submitted my paper on February 1, 1997. Seven papers were submitted overall by the group; they are expected to be published in a special edition in 1997 in *The International Journal of Educational Reform.*

That South Africa paper has been adapted and translated here into Russian for this conference in Moscow today. I appreciate this opportunity, now being given to me by the Russian Academy of Education and Russia's Open University, to submit the first paper earlier today on "Psycho-Social Education" which is centered on the critical education topic of "democracy" facing Russia at this point in its history and suggesting some possible curriculum solutions.

General Considerations

President Yeltsin is the leading political figure in Russia and, as such, is also a leading statesman in the world. Except for Chechnya which was a disaster for everyone concerned[64], Russia has, for the most part, been able to accommodate peaceably the newly independent states and the federation which has emerged in its transition from a centrally controlled dictatorship to democratic institutions following a free market system. From my perspective in America, most communist leaders seemed to have been unable to modify their style of governing from authoritarianism to democracy. Their

[63] *Dr. Tanner is a Professor of Education, Rutgers State University of New Jersey, Department of Educational Theory, Policy, & Administration, Graduate School of Education.*
[64] *See Resurrection by David Remnick, Random House Inc., New York, 1997.*

inability to do so eventually led to the attempted overthrow of the government which undermined General Secretary Gorbachev's broader democratic efforts toward "glasnost" (openness) and "perestroika" (re-structuring). Most communists were unable to bend, accept, and adapt to the storm of political change. Such inflexibility can be disastrous. A case in point is the style of President Slobodan Milosevic of Serbia who used old military solutions which devastated his own country and the Balkans. This is in contrast with the model response set by South African President Mandela's non-violence approach patterned after Ghandi. This means, I believe, that the world's leaders and institutions must continue to nurture and actively support South Africa and Russia in their further social and economic remodeling efforts because the world has too great a stake in the outcome. A successful democratic model, like a picture, is worth a thousand words; it will help illustrate to all people the way toward civilization building and peace on our planet in the future whether the problem is racism or authoritarianism.

The Basic Problem

In my view the basic education and administrative problem in South Africa and Russia (and in the world today) is *communication.* What is missing presently? Feedback! Educational administrators need to utilize new "Many-To-Many" communication technology to communicate better with and among teachers and enable students to communicate with themselves and their parents. President Yeltsin and government ministers initially need to communicate with their government bureaucracies and business, civic, and religious leaders. While there is goodwill on most sides, and people seem to want to do the right thing; the problem is *how* to communicate ideas and opinions more effectively among people in their common search for solutions.

The Russian administrative culture, even more than the larger world itself, is steeped in authoritarianism in which, research shows, there is very little feedback. Research indicates further that, in such a culture, what feedback there is, is highly unreliable. It's similar to two ships traveling at high speed, at night, in dense fog, in heavy seas filled with icebergs. One ship has defective radar—it goes "bing" and gets a reading only once every half hour. The other ship has effective radar—it goes "bing, bing, bing—(oops, iceberg, change course); bing, bing, bing—(oops, iceberg, change course)." Which ship do you think will have the best chance of making port safely? It's the same with the ship of state. It needs to be continually in touch with its component parts of government and with the people who are its constituents on a regular and routine basis.

Most leaders believe that the basic organizing principle of the human race is A over B over C over D, etc. [A>B>C>D...], which is an *Authoritarian Hierarchy* (Authoritarianism and Totalitarianism); it provides no checks and balances in governance and has minimum societal incentives. Our research in the Forum Foundation indicates that the basic organizing principle of the human race actually is A (Administrators) over B (Bureaucrats) over C (Citizens) over A (Administrators) [A>B>C>A...] which is a *Participative Heterarchy* (Freedom and Democracy); it provides checks and balances in governance and has maximum societal incentives.

Toward a Solution

Founded in 1970 and located in Seattle, Washington, the Forum Foundation has conducted educational research in the field of administrative theory. We have identified ten organizational and societal dynamics which (1) tend to move all organizations and societies, universally, toward solving their problems and (2) anticipate or adapt to changes in their internal or external environments. My colleague, Dr. Cecil H. Bell, Jr., and I chose the Eighth General Assembly of the World Future Society[65] as the place to introduce our new book. The book contains our findings of "The Ten Natural Dynamics of Administration and Governance."[66]

Other than those ten dynamics, the essence of over 25 years' research in social science for us is the realization that big meetings at often remote distances are the Achilles' Heel of the democratic process which undergirds society, public and private. People today do not have time to go to big meetings, especially at remote distances. They are too busy earning a living. Besides they remember

[65] *FutureVision: Ideas, Insights And Strategies," July 14-18, 1996, in Washington, D.C.*

[66] *The Basic Attitude, The Theories of Learning, Leadership, Authority, Politics, The Self-fulfilling Prophecy, The Administrative Process (a definition), The Helping Professions (a definition), The Zeitgeist Principle, and The Natural Factors.*

the last time they went; the sheer logistics are such that only a few people can speak, most can only listen. People today are often accused by their leaders of being apathetic in their responsibilities as citizens in their communities, their schools, and their churches. Our research indicates that people are not apathetic. It is just that they have concluded that such big meetings, which are often at remote distances for people, are not worth their time and effort—so they drop out. But that is not apathy, and if the issues are critical enough, they will be there (sometimes marching and protesting) much to the chagrin of leaders who do not understand that sort of behavior.

We in the Forum Foundation have concluded that in order to get at the administrative, educational, organizational, and societal problems better, *leaders must enable their members or constituents to meet in small, four person, "Future Molding Game" groups,* at times and places convenient to themselves during a one or two-month window period in "symbolic dialogue" using an "Opinionnaire®. Instead of a random-sample "Questionnaire" based on statistical and mathematical theory, an "Opinionnaire®" is based on participation theory and administrative theory. While the data is tabulated and reported on a computer, different rules apply!

This process is especially useful for teenage youth as they transition to adulthood. It engages them in critical and civil discussions with each other. They learn (1) to state their own opinions frankly, and (2) to listen respectfully to the opinions of others. These are both essential dynamics and basic citizenship skills required in a democratic society.

But what is gained in understanding through interpersonal communication by being in small discussion groups is simultaneously lost among the overall participants of their opinions as a whole. And the whole is something greater than the mere sum of the parts. To restore this "lost sense of touch," we first developed the Fast Forum® "socialware" program at the University of Washington Academic Computer Center in Seattle in 1970 while I was a graduate student.[67] The technique is a part of "Many-To-Many

[67] *As an administrative theoretician, I knew where to go, but didn't know how to get there; the computer programmer, Dr. John Jacobson, knew how to get there, but didn't know where to go. So together we designed and crafted the first program. The program has been updated several times since then. The last time about three years ago when it was transferred to the Macintosh computer; it is presently being transferred and updated to the PC computer.*

Communication" technology. The technique exists at a degree of complexity below the Delphi Technique and below typical random-sample polling but above letter writing, telephoning, or big meetings. Yet it makes the same contribution to system problems as they do but does it more systematically and economically. Since all data generated is objective, showing percentages of responses to various survey-type questions arranged by demographics of gender, age, geographic, ethnic family, etc., the reports generated never get bigger: they just get better as more people participate. Thus, we can easily compare the opinions of groups of 200 with 2,000, or 20,000. Also, there is no "information overload" for officials, planners, teachers, students, and parents involved as they "talk" together symbolically by gender, age, ethnic family, role and the like. Communication, understanding and goodwill are enhanced. Furthermore, the process is never dependent on the mass media which is free to be involved as much or as little as it wishes.

Psycho-Social Education

Conceptually, the model we propose in this paper of "Psycho-Social Education" recognizes that a head-of-state is the only official elected by all the people to represent their interests and is in the position also of being a "master teacher." It is the prerogative of a head-of-state to articulate and represent what should be done philosophically and politically to enhance the future of the society. Conversely, it is the youth of society who hold the longest stake in that future and should interact in some appropriate manner educationally with the head-of-state. Our new Fast Forum® technique, developed as a part of the Many-To-Many communication "socialware" technology, allows the head-of-state (or ministers or educators or other leaders) to "talk" symbolically to participating youth and parents through brief audio tapes, perhaps quarterly. [We do not recommend use of video tapes at this time; we feel they will introduce extra costs and complexities in the research period which would not be sustainable currently.] Youth openly discuss the ideas in their small, four-person, "Future Molding Game" discussion groups after a two-minute "Day-In-The-Sun" for each student in which others in the group just listen—not interrupt, not comment, not ask questions or do body language, e.g., thumbs up or down.

After their brief, open discussion in the foursome, individuals respond to an "Opinionnaire®" survey using objective yes/no, multiple-choice and value-scale responses. While it resembles a typical "Questionnaire" and random-sample survey based on statistical and mathematical theory, it is instead based on participation and administrative theory. It is called an "Opinionnaire®" to help differentiate the process. The technique uses mass means of communication including audio tapes (when needed), printing, mail, small discussion groups, keying on the computer (when appropriate) or optical scanning, and computer tabulation and manipulation of the data. The process will not break down simply because large numbers of people participate, as is now the case with a cultural reliance on big meetings for people. Usually machine-scannable response sheets are used but they may not be necessary for students who can hand-key their own data on a computer for their own school.

This model meets the criteria of a "psycho-social moratoria" as defined and proposed by Erik Erikson, the internationally renown school psychologist who died recently.

> The need of the adolescent for a psycho-social moratoria (i.e., a public arena where youth can talk openly without fear of reprisal is so great, it is equal to the need of a small child for maternal care. The purpose of psycho-social education as defined by Erikson is to insure the development of healthy citizens who, when they reach the age of legal maturity, are also capable of political maturity.[68]

A child is told by his or her parents, teacher, and culture: "this is a fact." However, when the child reaches adolescence, the youth realizes there is ambiguity and differences of opinion—everything is not clear cut. We all must realize that teenage youth exist at a crucible forming time in the development of the human personality between childhood and adulthood. And if parents and society "don't get it right then"—they may never get it right. During this special formative time, this period of psycho-social moratoria, there is no "right" or "wrong" answer by young people as they reflect

---

[68] *(Robert Pranger, University of Washington political scientist, and author of The Eclipse of Citizenship, 1968).*

on the "facts" they have learned as they search for "meaning." What they need is an educational arena in which to do it.

The process proposed here is a kind of intellectual gaming and for the same reason that we have physical gaming in schools. As the children exercise their bodies, they get stronger physically. Similarly, as youth exercise their reasoning abilities with ideas posed by their head-of-state about real-life problems and their future, and they share their opinions with each other, their parents, and others—they grow stronger intellectually, i.e., they learn through the dynamics of the Socratic Method! And when an individual learns "X" amount, the organization and the society of which he or she is a part learns exactly the same amount and all move toward being able to more easily solve problems in the future.

Fast Forum® reports are all disclaimed and do not purport to represent the views of the parent, sponsoring organizations, or others not participating which frees people to speak openly. They speak only for themselves. The results are, however, 100% valid for the students, parents and citizens who participate. In the final analysis, it allows the parents to say, "Look, son or daughter, even though all other students say this or all other parents say that, I want to call your attention to this fact." They then can offer their own value judgment for their own child which is their parental prerogative—and the process ends right there with remaining questions still unanswered. While the adults participating search for their own "right" answer to the questions posed as mentors, the children participating are not told by anyone ahead of time what the "right" answer is to the ideas and questions posed by President Yeltsin and other government and educational leaders. Since the government leaders have been duly elected and represent all citizens, it is their job, indeed their obligation, to articulate their philosophy and political solutions to problems faced. On the other hand, it is the responsibility of the citizens and children to listen, reflect, and contribute their opinions as to the "right" or "wrong" thing to do. But there are no "right or wrong" answers for children in their search for meaning and in their growth to maturity at this point in their lives between childhood and adulthood. They will begin to discern the morality, the diversity, and the insights of others by gender, age, role, race, geographic and the like as they learn from the process itself using the dynamics of the Socratic Method to gain insights and improve their critical thinking skills.

This educational process will build the essential citizenship and democratic skills of listening, stating one's own opinion, and interacting respectfully in civil discourse with public officials, planners, and others as people pursue their own "happiness" together for a better future. *Governments are not charged with providing their citizens with all the amenities of life they feel they need to make them happy, but governments are charged with enabling their citizens to pursue their own happiness!*

How It Would Work

We believe this educational model has great potential and should be tried. But it needs national political leaders and educational arenas to bring it to life. Russia could well be the first place this occurs because it faces tremendous political, economic, and social pressures at this time of transition. People expect change for the better; things must change for the better. Russia is a great nation, with the largest land mass, and populated by a people used to hardships and striving. The Forum Foundation is willing to assist in consulting and administering, at the national level, an original two-year research program, and to provide the Fast Forum® communication technology. Direct expenses would need to be covered. We believe that President Yeltsin, ideally, or other key officials would meet the criteria of the theory to "talk" to student youth about new ideas under consideration and for students to "talk back" symbolically. Such leaders would make an address approximately three times a year on some philosophical and/or political issue(s) approximately 15 minutes long. Packets would be prepared with materials including an Opinionnaire® and Reproducible Response Sheet for individual students and participating parents to use. Individual teachers could be provided these packets at nominal cost perhaps using distance learning downloaded from satellites and translated into all outlying areas. Students would listen to the tape and talk together and with their parents as noted previously. Detailed reports showing responses by gender, class, regions and ethnic groups could be provided by the foundation. A summary Viewspaper® of results then could be prepared and returned to teachers and parents.

I believe the improved communication in Russia that this process would bring should go far toward solving the monumental educational problems faced to strengthen the democratic processes in the nation. Yet, at the same time, Many-To-Many communication would help to accomplish the transition to democracy among the many large and diverse ethnic groups in Russia. Further, I believe this plan will allow an orderly transition for the benefit of all without having to have "lost generations" during the transition. Instead, the diversity of all will enrich all.

At the same time, other citizens who were interested could participate too, e.g., the elderly, business people, community service people such as Rotary International, people in government, and citizens at large. Costs would be minimal. Most of those persons participating outside the schools would be self funded and thus the project would not require taxes to support. In addition, any citizen interested could go to a library and respond to the "Citizen Councilor"[69] materials and purchase a machine-scannable response sheet from the librarian for about $.50 USD on which to respond. The machine-scannable response sheet does the same thing as a computer; it allows a human being to interface directly with a machine—accurately, swiftly and economically. But while a computer costs hundreds and thousands of dollars, the "socialware" optical scanning sheet costs only $.25 USD per sheet which includes scanning and a few profile reports. *Note:* It is important that the library's participation be "economic," i.e., their cost is 25 cents but they sell to the citizen for 50 cents so they can make a "profit" of 25 cents—which can then be used to pay the labor and other extra costs of the library to support the project. In this way the process is truly self-funding and will not require taxes or resources from educators or government. In addition, the sale of the response sheets takes care of another problem—the potential of "ballot stuffing." If participation by citizens in a library is "free," there is always the likelihood that someone will fill out and deposit many response sheets in some emotional outburst to try to influence and skew the data. But if a person has to pay $.50 USD for each "vote," after ten such ballots the cost of $5.00 USD will be discouraging because the

---

[69] *Councilor: "One appointed or elected to advise a sovereign or chief magistrate." (Webster's New International Dictionary, Second Edition, Unabridged*

impact of ten votes on the total outcome where possibly thousands of others are participating will be of no discernible effect. Furthermore, if the project outside of education is self-funded instead of government funded, then the project will not need the continual approval for financial and budget support of government agencies with their penchant to "control" the process. Democracy and civilization building are better served if the people themselves in effect "own" the communication process by self-funding it and establishing a mass communication system for the benefit of themselves, their governments, and the organizations of which they are a part, e.g., Chambers of Commerce, service organizations like Rotary International, civic organizations, religious organizations and the like.

To get started administratively and get some experience with the process and fine tune it, President Yeltsin could initiate a similar model called the PLAN Forum™ (Planning Long-range Assessment Network). Here he would communicate his philosophy and political ideas similarly to selected government employee groups. They would then meet during a one or two month window period in small groups of 4 persons to hear his audio address, use "Day In The Sun" to openly discuss the ideas, and then individually respond objectively to Yeltsin's questions. Initially the results tabulated can be kept confidential by President Yeltsin (i.e., a "Management Forum" format) as he learns to "talk" symbolically with government bureaucracies. Alternatively, results can be shared openly with everyone (i.e., a "Leadership Forum" format). In all cases the feedback generated by such routines should be of great value and provide key insights to leadership. The feedback might ratify suggestions, suggest other possible solutions to those discussed or disclose that participants feel the need for more information. Either way the symbolic "discussion" should move toward consensus and a clearer "vision" in the bureaucracies which, in turn, should be reflected in more effective government, regulations, and laws and with more "authority" flowing to government leaders at all levels from the people. This will make governing easier and more effective with happier people and happier leaders.

Most of the knowledge of the world is in books and computer databases. But most of the wisdom in the world is in the minds of people walking the earth, and we have to learn how to reach it. I believe that libraries in the world should store both knowledge and wisdom, and that citizens of Russia should be enabled to participate in community and civilization building together by contributing their opinions in response to President Yeltsin's and other government leader's vision of a common quest in:

> RUSSIA—"An Inspirational Nation in Pursuit of Happiness!"

> The discussion of ideas within a constructive, open, democratic context is the *mortar* which binds a "creative" organization or society, i.e., an organization or society which is actively searching for solutions to its problems. Any group, organization, institution, community, society, or world ideology which inhibits (innocently or not) the free flow of ideas among its constituents—up, down, and across its organizational and societal structures, is depriving itself of its greatest asset—*human thought*—and is in grave danger of being buried in history by the avalanche of the creativity of others.

D. FORUM FOUNDATION COUNCILOR™ REPRODUCIBLE RESPONSE SHEET

COUNCILOR™ REPRODUCIBLE RESPONSE SHEET

(A *FAST FORUM*® GROUPWARE PRODUCT)*

INSTRUCTIONS: 1. Please indicate your personal and organizational categories as requested.
2. Please respond to each statement or question, as follows:

* *Councilor is defined by Webster as: "an official advisor to a sovereign or chief magistrate."*

FILL IN (Y) (Yes) if you can identify with the statement or question without reservation -- a clear Yes.
(N) (No) if you cannot identify with the statement or question, also without reservation -- a clear No.
● (The One Best Choice) if the statement or question is multiple choice.
(OBJ) (Object) if you believe that the statement or question is misleading or inappropriate in some manner.

MAKE NO MARK IF YOU ABSTAIN TO A QUESTION OR STATEMENT, i.e., if you are undecided or feel unable to respond at this time. For example, if you feel you need more information before answering, you should abstain.

YOUR PERSONAL AND ORGANIZATIONAL CATEGORIES:

1 SEX	① MALE ② FEMALE	6	⓪ ① ② ③ ④ ⑤ ⑥ ⑦ ⑧ ⑨	11	⓪ ① ② ③ ④ ⑤ ⑥ ⑦ ⑧ ⑨
2 AGE	① 10-19 ② 20-29 ③ 30-39 ④ 40-49 ⑤ 50-59 ⑥ 60-69 ⑦ 70-79 ⑧ 80+	7	⓪ ① ② ③ ④ ⑤ ⑥ ⑦ ⑧ ⑨	12	⓪ ① ② ③ ④ ⑤ ⑥ ⑦ ⑧ ⑨
3	⓪ ① ② ③ ④ ⑤ ⑥ ⑦ ⑧ ⑨	8	⓪ ① ② ③ ④ ⑤ ⑥ ⑦ ⑧ ⑨	13	⓪ ① ② ③ ④ ⑤ ⑥ ⑦ ⑧ ⑨
4	⓪ ① ② ③ ④ ⑤ ⑥ ⑦ ⑧ ⑨	9	⓪ ① ② ③ ④ ⑤ ⑥ ⑦ ⑧ ⑨	14	⓪ ① ② ③ ④ ⑤ ⑥ ⑦ ⑧ ⑨
5	⓪ ① ② ③ ④ ⑤ ⑥ ⑦ ⑧ ⑨	10	⓪ ① ② ③ ④ ⑤ ⑥ ⑦ ⑧ ⑨	15	⓪ ① ② ③ ④ ⑤ ⑥ ⑦ ⑧ ⑨

YOUR OPINION OF EACH QUESTION OR STATEMENT:

	1 A	2 B	3 C	4 D	5 E	6
1–50 (each item)	Y	N	○	○	○	OBJ

YOUR COMMENTS: If you have any comments or suggestions, please outline your key points and explain your position below or continue on reverse side. Please print or write clearly. *Thank You!*

General Area of Comment: ______

OPTIONAL: Name ______ Day Phone ( ) ______ Time Zone ______ Date ______

Outline of Key Points: 1. ______ 2. ______ 3. ______

Detailed Explanation: ______

FORUM FOUNDATION *COUNCILOR*™ RESPONSE SHEET*

(A *FAST FORUM*® MACHINE-SCANNABLE SOCIALWARE PRODUCT)

E-Mail: fastforum@aol.com SIDE A WWW: http://weber.u.washington.edu/~forum

Mark Reflex® by NCS MM217043-1 654321 HH04 Printed in U.S.A.

INSTRUCTIONS:
1. Make a dark mark, using only a regular No. 2 pencil.
2. Do not use ink pens.
3. Make a dark mark that fills the bubble completely. (RIGHT ● WRONG ⊘⊗◒⊙)
4. Cleanly erase any mark you wish to change.
5. Do not fold or write comments on this sheet; write all comments on a separate sheet.
6. It's IMPORTANT that you indicate your personal and organizational categories as requested.
7. Please respond to each statement or question, as follows:

FILL IN: (Y) (Yes) if you can identify with the statement or question without reservation – a clear Yes.

(N) (No) if you cannot identify with the statement or question, also without reservation – a clear No.

● (The One Best Choice) if the statement or question is multiple choice.

(OBJ) (Object) if you believe that the statement or question is misleading or inappropriate in some manner.

MAKE NO MARK IF YOU ABSTAIN TO A QUESTION OR STATEMENT, i.e., if you are undecided or feel unable to respond at this time. For example, if you feel you need more information before answering, you should abstain.

YOUR PERSONAL AND ORGANIZATIONAL CATEGORIES:

1 SEX	MALE (M) FEMALE (F)	6	0 1 2 3 4 5 6 7 8 9	11	0 1 2 3 4 5 6 7 8 9
2 AGE	10 20 30 40 50 60 70 80+ / 1 2 3 4 5 6 7 8 / 19 29 39 49 59 69 79	7	0 1 2 3 4 5 6 7 8 9	12	0 1 2 3 4 5 6 7 8 9
3	0 1 2 3 4 5 6 7 8 9	8	0 1 2 3 4 5 6 7 8 9	13	0 1 2 3 4 5 6 7 8 9
4	0 1 2 3 4 5 6 7 8 9	9	0 1 2 3 4 5 6 7 8 9	14	0 1 2 3 4 5 6 7 8 9
5	0 1 2 3 4 5 6 7 8 9	10	0 1 2 3 4 5 6 7 8 9	15	0 1 2 3 4 5 6 7 8 9

YOUR OPINION OF EACH QUESTION OR STATEMENT:

1 2 3 4 5 6 / A B C D E	1 2 3 4 5 6 / A B C D E	1 2 3 4 5 6 / A B C D E	1 2 3 4 5 6 / A B C D E	1 2 3 4 5 6 / A B C D E
1 (Y)(N)○○○(OBJ)	11 (Y)(N)○○○(OBJ)	21 (Y)(N)○○○(OBJ)	31 (Y)(N)○○○(OBJ)	41 (Y)(N)○○○(OBJ)
2 (Y)(N)○○○(OBJ)	12 (Y)(N)○○○(OBJ)	22 (Y)(N)○○○(OBJ)	32 (Y)(N)○○○(OBJ)	42 (Y)(N)○○○(OBJ)
3 (Y)(N)○○○(OBJ)	13 (Y)(N)○○○(OBJ)	23 (Y)(N)○○○(OBJ)	33 (Y)(N)○○○(OBJ)	43 (Y)(N)○○○(OBJ)
4 (Y)(N)○○○(OBJ)	14 (Y)(N)○○○(OBJ)	24 (Y)(N)○○○(OBJ)	34 (Y)(N)○○○(OBJ)	44 (Y)(N)○○○(OBJ)
5 (Y)(N)○○○(OBJ)	15 (Y)(N)○○○(OBJ)	25 (Y)(N)○○○(OBJ)	35 (Y)(N)○○○(OBJ)	45 (Y)(N)○○○(OBJ)
6 (Y)(N)○○○(OBJ)	16 (Y)(N)○○○(OBJ)	26 (Y)(N)○○○(OBJ)	36 (Y)(N)○○○(OBJ)	46 (Y)(N)○○○(OBJ)
7 (Y)(N)○○○(OBJ)	17 (Y)(N)○○○(OBJ)	27 (Y)(N)○○○(OBJ)	37 (Y)(N)○○○(OBJ)	47 (Y)(N)○○○(OBJ)
8 (Y)(N)○○○(OBJ)	18 (Y)(N)○○○(OBJ)	28 (Y)(N)○○○(OBJ)	38 (Y)(N)○○○(OBJ)	48 (Y)(N)○○○(OBJ)
9 (Y)(N)○○○(OBJ)	19 (Y)(N)○○○(OBJ)	29 (Y)(N)○○○(OBJ)	39 (Y)(N)○○○(OBJ)	49 (Y)(N)○○○(OBJ)
10 (Y)(N)○○○(OBJ)	20 (Y)(N)○○○(OBJ)	30 (Y)(N)○○○(OBJ)	40 (Y)(N)○○○(OBJ)	50 (Y)(N)○○○(OBJ)

YOUR COMMENTS: If you have any comments or suggestions, please use a separate sheet, or the comments page of the Opinionnaire® and return it to your convener or mail directly to the Forum Foundation. Please print or write clearly. *Thank You!*

***"Councilor" is defined by Webster as "an official advisor to a sovereign or chief magistrate."**

E. THE COMMUNITY FORUM™

Founded in 1970
Non-Profit

December 24, 1997

Mayor-Elect Paul Schell
City of Seattle, Municipal Building
600 4th Ave.
12th Floor
Seattle, WA 98104

Re: Community Building and Affordable Housing Proposal

Dear Mayor Schell:

Congratulations on your election and forthcoming installation as Mayor of Seattle. We are all fortunate to be part of such a vibrant and beautiful city. It has accomplished much and by many standards is ahead of most cities, but it faces major problems in transportation, affordable housing, and community building. I have a workable suggestion to help solve these specific problems.

I am enclosing a copy of a new proposal, just submitted November 14, 1997 for your information. It is, "Psycho-Social Education, The Future Molding Game, and United Methodist Youth." This is a proposal to the White House for consideration as a nationally designated "Millennium Community Project." This paper proposes a "symbolic dialogue" between the President of the United States and United Methodist Youth. It is a model that can be easily adapted by yourself with Seattle citizens, businesses, schools, and neighborhoods. [Please note the sample Viewspaper®, Reproducible Response Sheet, and machine-scannable sheet attached.]

I am a Seattle businessman and co-founded the Forum Foundation and serve as president. The foundation has been doing research in administrative theory since 1970. It started for me when I was a graduate student at the University of Washington beginning in 1968 concentrating in Administrative Theory and Organizational Behavior. In an advanced course in Management Theory in 1970, the professor assigned us a term paper with the words, "Just take anything in management theory and make it sound rational." I thought it was a fun assignment. I came up with eight theories at the time that "tended to move all organizations universally toward solving their problems and anticipating or adapting to changes in their internal or external environment."

Seattle Office
4426 Second Avenue N.E. • Seattle, WA 98105-6191 • Fax (206) 633-3561 • Phone (206) 634-0420
http://weber.u.washington.edu/~forum

Forum Foundation Re: Affordable Housing Proposal December 24, 1997 Page 2

Today that term paper has been expanded and documented into a book, *The Search for Enlightened Leadership, Volume 1: Applying New Administrative Theory*, 1996, (a personal copy is enclosed). The book is now being used as an undergraduate textbook at the University of Washington School of Business Administration in two classes of "Business and Environment" taught by Dr. Richard S. Kirby. The first classes of students this year have been enthusiastic; I am grateful. We are learning.

I would like to meet with you to discuss an idea that I believe has merit to provide Seattle with both a significant affordable housing project and to mesh better its transportation needs into the future. While I am not currently active in the field, in my younger years I did work in land development and had a real estate brokers license for many years. So I do have some academic and professional background in building construction and land planning. These issues are extremely important as well as very political which equates, for me, to "communication" as being the "natural factor" involved (see page 91 in the book).

I am hoping that your schedule will allow you some time to look over these materials during the holidays before your rigorous routine as Mayor of Seattle may well preclude such study. I believe the ideas in the book may be very useful to you in the future. I am leaving on a business trip to Amsterdam on January 1st and will return January 16th. I would like to meet with you personally and with Gary Lawrence, Richard Kirby, Jim, and others nearly anytime after January 26 if possible. I hope your interest and schedule will permit. An appointment can be made by your staff by calling my son, Jim Spady, at his office: 206-634-0589. Thank you for your consideration.

"Merry Christmas" to you, and I hope you, and Seattle, have the Happiest of New Years!

Sincerely,

Richard J. Spady, President

Enclosures: As shown and "Example Sheet with Sample Questions and Formats"

cc w/o Enclosures:
J. Gary Lawrence, Director, Center for Sustainable Communities, UofW
Dr. Richard S. Kirby, Executive Director,
Stuart C. Dodd Institute for Social Innovation
Directors, Forum Foundation

Founded in 1970
Non-Profit

PROPOSAL: March 21, 1998

To: The Honorable Paul Schell, Mayor of Seattle and Community Conference on Affordable Housing, Seattle Center

From: Dick Spady, President

Seattle is constrained physically from growing in all directions except one, and that is up. We need higher-density housing close to the downtown core of Seattle to mitigate transportation and that can provide housing for all income groups but predominantly low-cost, affordable housing which is needed most.

We need to look at our problems from the perspective of a new communication paradigm which is emerging. That is, we need to look at the problem of affordable housing, not as a political zoning problem, but as an economic opportunity based on the self-interests of the citizens involved. I believe there is a probability for success when city planners, in acts of statesmanship, propose suitable projects for consideration of citizens for implementation through specific Local-Improvement-District or Economic-Opportunity-Zone efforts essentially self-funded by market forces.

At the heart of the matter is finding a new way for public officials and planners to communicate informally with citizens in large or small groups, routinely, without using big public meetings. I propose that a symbolic dialogue using new "Many-to-Many Communication" and the Fast Forum® technique be established. Blocks, neighborhoods, regions, or groups can be easily queried in a symbolic dialogue of officials with citizens. The benefits are (1) better diagnostic data to assist officials in their decision-making, (2) increased learning among citizens and the community at large for better decisions in the future, and (3) societal peace. Viable processes, which encourage and enable citizens to contribute their thinking to the solution of those problems which interest and concern themselves are therapeutic, reduce tensions, and lead to peace.

If you are interested, I would appreciate an opportunity to meet with you or others to show you more materials and answer your questions. Best wishes for success!

Distribution: *The Search for* ENLIGHTENED LEADERSHIP,
Volume 1: Applying New Administrative Theory (1996)
Volume 2: Many-to-Many Communication (outline, May 1998)
Forum Foundation *Councilor* Response Sheet (Replica of Form K, 1998)

Seattle Office
4426 Second Avenue N.E. • Seattle, WA 98105-6191 • Fax (206) 633-3561 • Phone (206) 634-0420
http://weber.u.washington.edu/~forum

Founded in 1970
Non-Profit

MEMO: March 23, 1998

To: The Honorable Paul Schell, Mayor of Seattle
600—4th Ave., 12th Floor
Seattle, WA 98104

From: Dick Spady, President

Re: Affordable Housing

Ref: My ltr of December 24, 1997/ Book, Vol. 1, *The Search for* ENLIGHTENED LEADERSHIP. My ltr/packet of March 21, 1998, Seattle Center, (Hand Delivered to Ms. Alex Field)

Congratulations on a highly successful Affordable Housing Conference last Saturday at the Seattle Center Northwest Rooms. The Rainier Room was filled to capacity, perhaps 500 citizen activists; everyone seems to have thoroughly enjoyed it.

You have just successfully taken the first step in establishing an ongoing network with Seattle citizens which we call "Mainstreaming." It is one of the four foundations of the Fast Forum® technique developed by the Forum Foundation. Mainstreaming is a concept in administrative theory that states: "Unless the people who are asked to participate with their time and energy perceive that what they are being asked to do is mainstream, and a part of the decision-making processes of the organization or society of which they are a part, they are not likely to participate." This theory recognizes that active "citizen participation" in a community is more a function of leadership style than it is a function of apathy of the people. Our research indicates that citizens are not apathetic, it is more that they have concluded that going to traditional big public hearings at often remote distances is not worth their time and effort—they are too busy earning a living. You, as a new Mayor, can now make significant changes in the way citizens relate with you, the City Council, city planners, the county, HUD, and Chambers of Commerce in planning the future for this great city. It is imperative that you continue this great wave of goodwill which you have unleashed with the issue of "Affordable Housing." It can be a breakthrough in leadership for Seattle!

I recommend you now take the following steps:

(1) Thank every citizen by letter who attended yesterday.
(2) Invite those who attended to become a convener of a group of between four and twelve persons who are willing to meet quarterly, but not more than monthly, in a continuing "symbolic dialogue" with you and your staff. As the elected Mayor you represent the interests of all Seattle citizens, and it is your prerogative and responsibility to articulate your views on affordable housing and other civic affairs to the citizens. Equally, it is the responsibility of every Seattle citizen to listen to you, talk among themselves, and respond to your questions in an objective format as you did last Saturday. Most citizens will not be able to do this, but that is not what is important. What is important is that the viable opportunity to participate is made available to all citizens (John W. Gardner).

Seattle Office
4426 Second Avenue N.E. • Seattle, WA 98105-6191 • Fax (206) 633-3561 • Phone (206) 634-0420
http://weber.u.washington.edu/~forum

The Fast Forum® technique we have developed meets this criteria. People are enabled to meet in small groups in their homes or businesses during a 30 or 45 day window period. They will listen to an audio tape about the issue under discussion then each person gets a two-minute "Day-In-the-Sun" to tell what he or she feels about the issue. The role of the other citizens is to listen—not interrupt, not comment, not ask questions, not do body English (thumbs up or down), rather, just listen. We don't have enough programs in our society where we listen to each other. This is one of those precious times. After their "Day-In-the-Sun," citizens talk back and forth in their group asking each other questions and responding but always with the "Basic Attitude" in mind. No one has to agree with what another person says, but everyone should always be treated with respect and consideration—**in order to best protect one's own freedom to speak!** Before leaving, citizens will take a few minutes to respond to a survey. The cost of the overall process should be minimal and could even be self-funded, without taxes, if needed.

The data can be either keyed (if there are not over about 1,000 people) or tabulated by an optical scanner—accurately, swiftly, and economically. Detailed profile reports can then be generated by any attributes you wish, for example, renter/owners, neighborhoods, regions, gender, age, [Live and Work in Seattle/ Live in Seattle and Work Outside Seattle, Work in Seattle and Live Outside of Seattle, Live/Work Outside of Seattle but Often Visit Seattle for Business and Cultural Reasons, Other], Ethnic Family (i.e., African-American, Asian-American, Caucasian American, Hispanic/Latino American, Mixed Heritage American, Native American, Pacific-Islander American and the like). Finally, a summary Viewspaper® of highlights can be prepared (ranging from 1 sheet to elaborate presentations). In any event, our experience indicates it all will work and costs are minimal.

Since 1970 the Forum Foundation has been doing educational research in the field of administrative theory. We have identified ten dynamics of administration which tend to move organizations, universally, toward solving their problems and anticipating or adapting to changes in their internal or external environments. (I hope you will be able to look over our book: *The Search for* ENLIGHTENED LEADERSHIP, *Volume 1: Applying New Administrative Theory* (1996) given to you earlier. It is now being used as a textbook for undergraduate students in business at the UofW. The book was co-authored with Dr. Cecil H. Bell, Jr., who is on the faculty of the University of Washington and most recently Chair of the Dept. of Management and Organization, School of Business Administration. Dr. Bell was a co-founder and is vice president of the Forum Foundation. He is currently on sabbatical as a co-author to write *Organization Development* which is now in its sixth edition, Prentice-Hall publishers.

The Forum Foundation would be honored to provide consultation and Fast Forum® computer tabulation services for you and the city without cost as part of your and our own research program. Please let me know if I might meet with you or members of your staff to answer your questions and share other materials. Thank you. Again, congratulations on a great conference.

cc: Mr. Tom Boyers, Deputy Mayor; Ms. Alex Field, Assistant to the Mayor

MEMO: May 7, 1998

To: The Honorable Paul Schell, Mayor of Seattle
600—4th Ave., 12th Floor
Seattle, WA 98104

Re: *Volume 2: Many-To-Many Communication*

From: Dick Spady, President

Ref: My ltr of December 24, 1997/ Book, *The Search for ENLIGHTENED LEADERSHIP. Volume 1: Applying New Administrative Theory*
My ltr/packet of March 21, 1998, Seattle Center, (Hand Delivered to Ms. Alex Field)
My ltr of March 23, 1998, Affordable Housing

Enclosed is an extract of the "Community Forum" model which is a part of the manuscript of *The Search for Enlightened Leadership, Volume 2: Many-To-Many Communication* which was turned over to the printer just two weeks ago. We expect the book to be available for distribution in June to the Pacific Northwest Annual Conference of The United Methodist Church which will meet at the University of Puget Sound. The book will be available through the University Bookstore in Seattle. An outline of the book is enclosed.

Dr. Richard S. Kirby, Executive Director, Stuart C. Dodd Institute for Social Innovation, is on the faculty of the University of Washington. He teaches "Organization and Environment" to undergraduates in the School of Business Administration and is using Volume 1 now as a textbook. He has written a "Teacher's Guide;" students like the book. He, my son, John, and I have been invited to lecture at Kursk State Pedagogical University in Russia this September. So from a term paper in 1970 to textbooks in 1996 and 1998, we are making progress.

As a theoretician in administrative theory and social science, I continually try to design and articulate social models that are helpful in the functioning of organizations and society. Enclosed is a letter sent to Dr. John Hope Franklin, Chair, President Clinton's Initiative on Race, which will be included in the manuscript. I have also inserted into the book the three letters addressed to you which are listed above.

I believe that Volume 2, *Many-To-Many Communication,* will be a real breakthrough in social science providing workable democratic governance models for governments, schools, and churches. I hope you will take the time, personally, to look the proposal over and judge for yourself. With contributions and in-kind services by the Forum Foundation and little effort and cost to the city, you could be the first mayor to establish a viable *"Citizen Councilor"* participation program. You have the opportunity now to make a significant contribution to the noblest experiment in governance—democracy! The process will take nothing away from the elected or appointed leaders in the city, political or private. Indeed "authority" will begin to flow from the people to you and other leaders making the process of governance easier and more enjoyable for all.

I hope that we can meet sometime soon to discuss the potentials that are available to Seattle.

Enclosures: as shown

Seattle Office
4426 Second Avenue N.E. • Seattle, WA 98105-6191 • Fax (206) 633-3561 • Phone (206) 634-0420
http://weber.u.washington.edu/~forum

F. EXAMPLE OF VIEWSPAPER®—AUTHORITY

WHAT UNITED METHODISTS BELIEVE

Viewspaper®

Volume 1, Number 1 (October 11, 1992) (updated 10/23/92)

Topic #1: Authority in the Church

On October 11 and 18, 1992, United Methodists from eight churches in Washington State, Ohio and South Dakota met for the first time to participate in a new developmental project called **"What United Methodists Believe."** The purpose is to take a first step toward developing a new communication process, based on new participation and administrative theories, and thereby enable large numbers of people to communicate with each other over large distances. We are trying to replace our cultural over-dependence on big meetings at often remote distances. Such meetings do not work well; indeed, they are the "Achilles' Heel" of the democratic process which undergirds our society, public and private. **Although 109 people participated in this new process, most participated through small discussion groups of 8 to 10 persons who listened to a cassette tape presenting The Social Setting by The Rev. Dr. William B. Cate, Theological Reflections by The Rev. Dr. Wiilliam D. Ellington, and A Layman's Perspective by Mr. Don Duncan.** Each participant was then invited to present his or her views in a two minute **"Day In The Sun" process** while others listened without interruption, comment, or question. Following an open discussion in the small groups, participants then responded to an *Opinionnaire* composed of questions on this topic. **This *Viewspaper* summarizes the objective opinions of everyone who participated and completed an *Opinionnaire*.** A more detailed profile report (analyzing the participants' opinions by gender) was mailed to your church for review by your small discussion groups and for posting on your bulletin board for further reference by the congregation at large.

-- Dick Spady, President, Forum Foundation, Project Sponsor

WHAT UNITED METHODISTS BELIEVE
Viewspaper #1: Authority in the Church, Page 1

SUMMARY OF OPINIONS

1. Before you learned of this series, had you known of the Social Principles of The United Methodist Church?
Yes 52% No 44% Abstain 4% Object 0%

2. Before this series, had you read or studied from the Social Principles?
Yes 27% **No 68%** Abstain 6% Object 0%

3. In general do you affirm the Social Principles of The UMC?
Yes 70% No 2% Abstain 28% Object 1%

4. Do you feel in good conscience that to affirm the Social Principles it would have to be changed in some manner?
Yes 18% No 38% **Abstain 43%** Object 1%

5. Before you learned of this series, had you known of The Book of Resolutions of The United Methodist Church?
Yes 41% **No 53%** Abstain 6% Object 0%

6. Before this series, had you read or studied from The Book of Resolutions?
Yes 15% **No 80%** Abstain 6% Object 0%

7. As a Protestant, do you believe in the doctrine of the infallibility of the church?
Yes 8% **No 64%** Abstain 27% Object 1%

8. Paragraph 610 of The Book of Discipline states that only the General Conference has the authority to speak officially for The United Methodist Church. Would it also be true to state that, in turn, the General Conference of The UMC does not have the authority to speak on behalf of any individual United Methodist? Accordingly, as we all search together for greater theological understanding, each such person is free to dissent from any or all provisions of The Book of Resolutions and still not be ostracized from the church. Do you believe this theology is true?
Yes 71% No 6% Abstain 20% Object 4%

WHAT UNITED METHODISTS BELIEVE
Viewspaper #1: Authority in the Church, Page 2

COMMENTS & ANSWERS

Many useful and interesting written comments were contributed by the participants. We have included a few of the comments in this *Viewspaper*. Thanks to everyone who submitted a comment!

"I was raised a Presbyterian but became a United Methodist because I believe the UM emphasis on an interplay between scripture, tradition, reason and experience most accurately describes the way God actually works in our lives. I also like the way UM requires each individual to be accountable for his/her development and not just accept a "handed down faith."

" Paragraph 75 VI World Community C) War and Peace (1992 Social Principles). I cannot support this position. With radical world elements I believe the threat of force is necessary to protect Life and Liberty."

"Though I didn't object to being a part of this process, I wonder how a visitor to this morning's service may have felt. Their ability not to participate is reduced some in the service."

Editor's Reply: St. Peter's UMC is the only congregation in this series that is participating through a worship format--all other churches use Sunday adult/youth discussion groups. This was because our pastor, Rev. Iwamoto, has been on the General Board of Church and Society the past 8 years and Vice Chair the past 4 years. We wanted to learn from his theological insights and experiences. Your point, however, is a good one. We will add the demographic "Am not a Member" as soon as possible to allow comparisons and encourage all to participate. The worship experience will then become *evangelistic* allowing dynamic interaction with our visitors theologically.

A CLOSER LOOK AT THE PARTICIPANTS

The first 11 questions of *Opinionnaire* #1 were demo - graphic questions. We use these to better understand the answers. In this case, the "typical" participant is between 40 and 49 years old, female, Caucasian, lives in the Pacific time zone, has been a member of the United Methodist Church for over 20 years, but has never been a church officer or committee chair.

Why Talk About "What United Methodists Believe"?

In our tradition as Protestants, we do not believe in the infallibility of the church. We are taught that our responsibility is directly to God through Christ and there is no institution or person between us. Accordingly, I believe that The Social Principles and The Book of Resolutions are the greatest treasures of our church after the Bible. However, we treat the Book of Resolutions as a "finished document." It is not. But it is a "great beginning document" if we can learn to use it. Perhaps this series is a start. Thank you for participating in Building the Kingdom of God!

--Dick Spady, Lay Speaker, St. Peter's UMC, Editor.

DISCLAIMER CLAUSE: The purpose of this report is to communicate ideas, issues, and problems among people as a platform for future, meaningful discussions of concerns. Participants are assisted in becoming aware of their own beliefs as well as of those intellectual and moral beliefs of others at a point in time--the "Zeitgeist," or "Spirit of the Time." The views and opinions expressed herein are those of the individuals who participated and do not necessarily represent the official views of the parent group or sponsoring organization. Nor will the views expressed necessarily represent those of the same participants at a later period of time; as humans we each have the ability to receive new information, consider it, and change.

-- FORUM FOUNDATION.

G. EXAMPLE OF VIEWSPAPER®—EVALUATION

WHAT UNITED METHODISTS BELIEVE

Viewspaper®

Volume 2, Number 9 (March 13, 1994)

Topic #9: Evaluation

[United Methodist *Councilor* Network Proposal]

On March 13, 1994 United Methodists from churches around the country met to participate in a discussion of the last topic, Evaluation, in our project on **"What United Methodists Believe."** The purpose is to take a first step toward developing a new communication process, based on new participation and administrative theories, and thereby enable large numbers of people to communicate with each other over large distances. 380 people participated in small, four-person, "Future Molding Game" groups. They listened to a cassette tape regarding a UM *Councilor* Network proposal. Each participant was then invited to present his or her views in a two minute "Day-In-The Sun" process while others listened without interruption, comment, or question. Following an open discussion in their groups, participants then responded to an *Opinionnaire* composed of questions on their topic. This *Viewspaper* partially summarizes the objective opinions of everyone who participated and completed an *Opinionnaire*.

A full, detailed, profile report (analyzing the participants' opinions by jurisdiction) was mailed to your church for later review by your discussion groups and/or for posting on your church bulletin board for further reference by the congregation at large. All profiles of gender, age, role, ethnic family etc. were sent to the General Board of Church and Society and UMCom for their information and reference.

Thank you all for participating in this national research project. It has been a first and, I believe, an important learning experience for us all.

Dick Spady, President, Forum Foundation, Co-sponsor

WHAT UNITED METHODISTS BELIEVE
***Viewspaper* #9 Evaluation, Page 1**

PARTIAL SUMMARY OF OPINIONS

[Editor: The Polarization Rating is the % of 380 participants answering only yes or no. The Consensus Rating is the % positive of those polarized. So 42 out of 100 answered "Yes" in this first question--the balance "No."]

1. At the start of this series were you familiar with the UMC Social Principles? [Rounding can affect totals + or - 1%.]
Yes (40%) No(56%) Abstain (3%) Object (2%); **PC Rating (96%-- 42)**

2, Do you feel that you are familiar with the UMC Social Principles now?
Yes (78%) No(14%) Abstain (6%) Object (2%); **PC Rating (92%--85)**

3. At the start of this series were you familiar with UMC Book of Resolutions?
Yes (27%) No(69%) Abstain (3%) Object (1%); **PC Rating (96%--28)**

4. Do you feel that you are familiar with the UMC Book of Resolutions now?
Yes (71%) No(18%) Abstain (8%) Object (3%); **PC Rating (89%--80)**

6. Each week in the Viewspaper® the editor wrote, "We are taught that our responsibility is directly to God through Christ and there is no institution or person between us." Do you believe this theology is true?
Yes (88%) No(6%) Abstain (5%) Object (1%); **PC Rating (94%--94)**

7. Do you believe in the infallibility of the church?
Yes (9%) No(81%) Abstain (9%) Object (2%); **PC Rating (90%--10)**

8. Each week in the Viewspaper® the editor wrote, "Accordingly, I believe that the Social Principles and The Book of Resolutions are the greatest treasures of our church after the Bible." Do you share this enthusiasm?
Yes (22%) No(60%) Abstain (12%) Object (6%); **PC Rating (82%--26)**

9. Each week in the Viewspaper® the editor wrote, "However, we treat The Book of Resolutions as a 'finished document.' It is not. But it is a 'great beginning document' if we can learn to use it." Do you share this belief?
Yes (77%) No(9%) Abstain (10%) Object (3%); **PC Rating (86%-- 90)**

21. It was recommended to the General Board of Church and Society that they basically replicate this series on What United Methodists Believe

WHAT UNITED METHODISTS BELIEVE
Viewspaper #9: Evaluation Page 2

beginning in January, 1995 "to help introduce the Social Principles and Book of Resolutions to other church groups interested and further evolve in our efforts to learn how better to communicate and create a new social context." Do you agree?
Yes (60%) No(23%) Abstain (11%) Object (6%); **PC Rating (83%– 72)**

22. It was recommended to the General Board of Church and Society that they "establish a United Methodist *Councilor* Network as a two-year, *national research program* to provide member and constituent responses to the General Board of Church and Society and thus the General Conference concerning social issues." Do you agree?
Yes (64%) No(19%) Abstain (11%) Object (6%); **PC Rating (83%--78)**

23. Would you be supportive of an additional paragraph similar to the following in italics to further clarify authority in our church?
3. We acknowledge from our Protestant tradition that we do not believe in the infallibility of the church. Accordingly, the General Conf., in its turn, does not have the authority to speak for any individual United Methodist. We believe that our individual responsibility is directly to God through Christ and there is no other institution or person between us. Thus, any individual United Methodist is free to dissent in accordance with the Holy Spirit within himself or herself from passages in the Social Principles and The Book of Resolutions without being ostracized from the church.
Yes (72%) No(6%) Abstain (18%) Object (4%); **PC Rating (78%–93)**

COMMENTS & ANSWERS

Thanks to all who submitted comments.

"It has been an interesting and meaningful project for us to participate in this, and the one thing that is sure is that more local members know about 'United Methodists Social Principles' and 'The Book of Resolutions' than before."

"Having served the Church as layman and minister, I found this project very interesting and helpful. I feel we have the machinery to make the UMC the outstanding denomination in the world. This will be a good start in dealing with the 'grassroots.' "

"With regard to the Councilor Network, what assurance is there that the responses will be heeded?" [Editor: None, the General Conference will still retain all its prerogatives. The first step in solving a problem, however, is to be aware of it; with better diagnosis, better solutions should follow.]

A CLOSER LOOK AT THE PARTICIPANTS

The first 15 questions of *Opinionnaire* #9 were demo - graphic questions. We use these to better understand the answers. In this case, the "typical" participant is between 40 and 49 years old (28%); female (52%); Caucasian (92%); lives in the Central time zone (44%); has been a member of the United Methodist Church for over 20 years (59%); are Ordained Ministry (3%), Local Church Laity (54%), Officers (15%), or a member of local Church, District, Conf., or General Boards of Church and Society (19%), and Unidentified (8%).

Why Talk About "What United Methodists Believe"?

In our tradition as Protestants, we do not believe in the infallibility of the church. We are taught that our responsibility is directly to God through Christ and there is no institution or person between us. Accordingly, I believe that the Social Principles and The Book of Resolutions are the greatest treasures of our church after the Bible. However, we treat The Book of Resolutions as a "finished document." It is not. But it is a "great beginning document" if we can learn to use it. Perhaps this series is a start. Thank you for participating toward building the Kingdom of God!

Dick Spady, Lay Speaker, St. Peter's UMC, Seattle District, Editor

DISCLAIMER CLAUSE: The purpose of this report is to communicate ideas, issues, and problems among people as a platform for future, meaningful discussions of concerns. Participants are assisted in becoming aware of their own beliefs as well as of those intellectual and moral beliefs of others at a point in time--the "Zeitgeist," or "Spirit of the Time." The views and opinions expressed herein are those of the individuals who participated and do not necessarily represent the official views of the parent group or sponsoring organization. Nor will the views expressed necessarily represent those of the same participants at a later period of time; as humans we each have the ability to receive new information, consider it, and change.

-- FORUM FOUNDATION.

H. Examples of "Everywoman's Delegation" Northwest, Women's International Conf., Beijing, China; Economic Development Opinionnaire, Report, and Viewspaper® Page One

EVERYWOMAN'S DELEGATION

Viewspaper ®

Volume 1, Number 1 (November 1995)

United Nations Fourth World Women's Conference

Our intention in using an Opinionnaire® at Beijing, China was to demonstrate its potential to examine commonalty and differences in values among women and men worldwide through a democratic process.

This Viewspaper is a partial summarization of the opinions of those who completed the Opinionnaire. The statements in the Opinionnaire were created based on the Twelve Critical concerns of women: poverty, education, health, violence against women, effects of armed conflict, economic structures and policies, inequality of men and women in decision-making, gender equality, women's human rights, media, environment and the girl child. Full, detailed, profile reports are available. They will be posted through February 1996 by the Forum Foundation, Project Sponsor, on its World Wide Web homepage: http://weber.u.washington.edu/~forum with some limited copies available on request by U.S. Mail.

A CLOSER LOOK AT THE PARTICIPANTS:

The first 7 questions of the *Opinionnaire* were demographics. These are used to analyze the responses to the statements. With **1,102 respondents** , 82% were female, 10% male, and 8% not identified. The "typical" participant was 36-49 years old; Caucasian 31%, Asian 27%, Latina 13%, African 9%; Resided in North America 37%, Asia 23%, Europe 14%, Africa 6%, South America 5%. Professionally 26% were educators, 11% were administrators, 11% were students, 7% were in medicine, 6% were legal, 6% were political, and 5% from media. Vocationally 19% were social workers and educationally 46% had 17+ years, 27% 13-16 years, 11% 0-12 years with 16% not identified. The Opinionnaire was responded to in <u>four</u> languages: English 74%, Spanish 12%, Chinese 10%, and French 4%. This was a first for us.

***Viewspaper* #1: Fourth World Women's Conference: Page 1**

PARTIAL SUMMARY OF OPINIONS

<u>EQUALITY</u>

1. Women's control over their reproductive choices should be viewed as a human right.

Agree	Neutral	Disagree	Abstain	Object
86%	4%	7%	2%	1%

[The strongest agreement, over 90%, came from the mixed ethnic group and those from India.]

2. There is discrimination and prejudice against women entering public life in my community.

Agree	Neutral	Disagree	Abstain	Object
63%	10%	23%	4%	1%

[Asians were divided equally between Agree and Disagree.]

3. Discrimination against lesbians is a violation of human rights.,

Agree	Neutral	Disagree	Abstain	Object
70%	13%	8%	9%	1%

<u>ECONOMICS</u>

4. Free market capitalism depends on the domestication of women, exploitation of a low-paid labor base made up of minorities and women as well as unlimited access to National resources.

Agree	Neutral	Disagree	Abstain	Object
61%	11%	17%	10%	2%

[Factory and agricultural workers registered over 79% in agreement.]

5. Establish an international tribunal where indigenous women may testify and present crimes against them and/or violation of collective rights.

	Agree	Neutral	Disagree	Abstain	Object	Profession
	80%	8%	9%	3%	0%	Religious
	82%	7%	5%	7%	0%	Legal
	82%	5%	4%	10%	0%	Political
						Other
1102	73%	10%	7%	9%	1%	Total

6. Free trade zones expand employment opportunities for women.

Agree	Neutral	Disagree	Abstain	Object
46%	18%	21%	14%	2%

***Viewspaper* #1: Women's Fourth World Conference: Page 2**

7. Conclude by the end of the year 2000 a negotiated binding schedule for the phased elimination of nuclear weapons within a time frame, and with provisions for effective verification and enforcement.

Agree	Neutral	Disagree	Abstain	Object
85%	5%	1%	8%	0%

COMMENTS & ANSWERS

1. **It is self-defeating to achieve equality in a dysfunctional institution with negative values of racism, sexism, elitism and militarism.**
[56% agreed, 11% abstained, and 3% objected; some comments were: "Too complicated, poorly worded." "Isn't it better to work in a dysfunctional situation equally than not equally?" "Insert words 'try to' before achieve."]

2. There was criticism of the Professional and Vocational demographics. The categories were not specific enough. Women wanted more exact identification of the work they do. [Editor: We provided 10 categories this time but could expand to 99 in the future if felt necessary.]"

3. "It is imperative to include **African-American** in your ethnic family." [Editor: We can run a compound search of "North America" (Region) and "African" (Ethnic) and come close to this data. The reports available are almost infinite.]

4. "This questionnaire (Opinionnaire) is loaded and misleading--also geared towards industrialized countries, middle-class women. I find it difficult to answer." [Editor: If questions are too difficult, just abstain or object; we will see it. It is hard to think in these new ways, and we are all learning Thanks for your comment.]

5. **Letters to Hillary.** "This conference is a disaster, total chaos...Waiting for an hour and a half ...to see Hillary. No transportation."
"Hillary, I am sure by now you are aware of the chaos in getting into the hall to hear you. Add this to the complaints about the conference. The Japanese press was particularly bad about pushing and getting in front of everyone..."
"The handling of the meeting is atrocious. The organizing committee didn't use inspiration to create a unified conference. Hillary should never have been late."

6. "Great experience wasn't it. Thanks for your survey work."

Viewspaper **#1: Women's Fourth World Conference: Page 3**

Everywoman's Delegation Mission Statement

The Everywoman's Delegation is a coalition of grassroots women who are uncompromisingly committed to a vision of universal peace, justice and human rights for all people. We recognize that the realization of this vision is inexorably and intimately linked to the full social, economic, and political participation of every woman in every family, in every community, and in every nation. We pledge to dedicate ourselves and our work to the United Nations Fourth World Conference Twelve Areas of Critical Concern and to the implementation of the Forward Looking Strategies for the global enhancement of women. In so doing, we uphold our steadfast commitment to achieve equality, development and peace for every woman worldwide so that posterity may know genuine peace, justice and freedom.

DISCLAIMER CLAUSE: The purpose of this report is to communicate ideas, issues, and problems among people as a platform for future, meaningful discussions of concerns. Participants are assisted in becoming aware of their own beliefs as well as of those intellectual and moral beliefs of others at a point in time--the "Zeitgeist," or "Spirit of the Time." The views and opinions expressed herein are those of the individuals who participated and do not necessarily represent the official views of the parent group or sponsoring organization. Nor will the views expressed necessarily represent those of the same participants at a later period of time; as humans we each have the ability to receive new information, consider it, and change.
-- THE FORUM FOUNDATION.

The design and tabulation of this survey is being accomplished with the generous assistance of the Forum Foundation, a non-profit, educational and research foundation located at 4426 Second Ave NE; Seattle WA 98105-6191 USA. •Fax(206)633-3561 •Phone (206)634-0420. ***"Opinionnaire"*** and ***"Viewspaper"*** and ***"Fast Forum"*** are registered trademarks of the Forum Foundation. Used by permission.

Note: See the full reports at:
http://weber.u.washington.edu/~forum

Viewspaper **#1: Fourth World Women's Conference: Page 4**

I. WASHINGTON STATE SENATE RESOLUTION 1993-8636

SENATE RESOLUTION
1993-8636

By Senators Pelz and Moyer

WHEREAS, The Forum Foundation is a nonprofit, research corporation of Washington State organized in 1970 to improve the functioning of organizations and society; and

WHEREAS, Founders Richard J. Spady, President of The Forum Foundation, and Dr. Cecil H. Bell, Jr., of the University of Washington Graduate School of Business Administration and Vice-President of The Forum Foundation have worked tirelessly to promote new theories and technologies of innovative and effective communication strategies; and

WHEREAS, These new theories of administration and communication have been developed in Washington State to strengthen the effectiveness of new citizen involvement and education applications with the assistance of the late Dr. Stuart C. Dodd, professor-emeritus of sociology at the University of Washington; and

WHEREAS, A new communication technology called the "Fast Forum" technique, developed at the University of Washington Academic Computing Services beginning in 1970 and continuing there today, has emerged from these theories; and

WHEREAS, This communication technology facilitates the exchange of ideas among people in large and diverse groups, improves citizen participation, and has been used successfully by the municipalities of Redmond and Kent, and the Republic of Kryrgyzstan of the Commonwealth of Independent States; and

WHEREAS, The application of this communication technology to enhance citizenship education and critical-thinking curriculum materials for secondary schools in our state and elsewhere holds great promise;

NOW, THEREFORE, BE IT RESOLVED, By the Senate of the state of Washington, that the members of The Forum Foundation be recognized for their excellent work and research to improve communication in organizations and society, and that copies of this resolution be immediately transmitted by the Secretary of the Senate to the Governor, the Department of Community Development, the Superintendent of Public Instruction, Richard J. Spady, and Dr. Cecil H. Bell, Jr. to encourage the further innovative research of The Forum Foundation in citizenship education programs for communities and educational programs in schools.

I, Marty Brown, Secretary of the Senate,
do hereby certify that this is a true and
correct copy of Senate Resolution 1993-8636,
adopted by the Senate April 13, 1993.

Marty Brown

MARTY BROWN
Secretary of the Senate

J. FORUM FOUNDATION FACT SHEET

FORUM FOUNDATION
Founded in 1970; Non-Profit
Enhancing Communication in Organizations and Society
April 12, 1998 (Easter)

Web Address: http://weber.u.washington.edu/~forum
KEYWORDS: SOCIAL SCIENCE, FUTURES RESEARCH, ADMINISTRATIVE THEORY, CIVILIZATION BUILDING, SOCIAL INNOVATION, LEADERSHIP, CITIZEN PARTICIPATION, MANY-TO-MANY COMMUNICATION, ZEITGEIST COMMUNICATION, FAST FORUM®, OPINIONNAIRE®, VIEWSPAPER®, PLAN FORUM®, QUEST FORUM™, CENSUS FORUM™, DODD, SPADY, BELL, ELLINGTON, CATE, KIRBY, BEDELL, FRIEDLANDER.

PURPOSE: Conducts futures research in the field of Administrative Theory and Many-To-Many Communication technology to discover those dynamics which tend to move organizations and institutions, universally, toward solving their problems and anticipating or adapting to changes in their internal or external environment.

PRINCIPALS AND ASSOCIATES:

- RICHARD J. SPADY, President and co-founder; also CEO Dick's Drive-In Restaurants, Seattle.
- JAMES R. SPADY, Executive Vice President; also CFO Dick's Drive-In Restaurants, Seattle.
- DR. CECIL H. BELL, JR., Vice President and co-founder; Associate Professor and recent Chair, Dept. of Management and Organization, School of Business Administration, University of Washington; Co-author, Organization Development, 6th Ed., 1998, Prentice-Hall publisher.
- REV. DR. WILLIAM D. ELLINGTON, PH.D., Theology, co-founder and board member, retired minister UMC, Associate Ecclesiastical Professor for United Methodist Ministries, Fuller School of Theology.

- Rev Dr. William B. Cate, Ph.D., Social Ethics, President-Emeritus, Church Council of Greater Seattle, and Ms. Jan Cate, MA, Values Education, Board Members.

- Rev. Dr. Richard S. Kirby Ph.D., Theology, Executive Director, Stuart C. Dodd Institute for Social Innovation; Faculty, University of Washington, School of Business Administration; Chair, World Network of Religious Futurists.

- Rev. Dr. Kenneth L. Bedell, Ph.D., Sociology, President, Ecumenical Programs In Communications, Inc. (EPIC Inc.); Vice President Research, Forum Foundation

- Dr. Bernard Z. Friedlander, Ph.D., Psychology, Professor-Emeritus of Psychology, University of Hartford and Visiting Scholar, Department of Psychology, University of Washington.

Writings:

- "A New View of Authority and the Administrative Process—(Revisited 1980)"
- *The Search For ENLIGHTENED LEADERSHIP*, a trilogy, *The Civilization of Tomorrow*
  Volume 1: *Applying New Administrative Theory* (1996)
  Volume 2: *Many-To-Many Communication* (June 1998)
  Volume 3: *The Civilization of Tomorrow* (Est. 2000)

Concept: The basic organizing principle of the human race in the present and historic past has been the Authoritarian Hierarchy, A>B>C>D..., (authoritarianism and dictatorships)—it provides no checks or balances in governance and minimum societal incentives. Research indicates that the basic organizing principle of the human race actually is the Participative Heterarchy, A>B>C>A, (i.e., **A**dministrators over **B**ureaucrats over **C**itizens over **A**dministrators, freedom and democracy)—it provides checks and balances in governance and maximum societal incentives in civilization building!

Services: The foundation is primarily in a research mode and not a service delivery mode. It is interested in applying the Fast Forum® groupware technique using an "Opinionnaire®" and "Viewspaper®" to assist leaders to "talk" symbolically with constituents and for them to "talk" back. This assists in (1) diagnosing system problems as a first step in solving them, (2) learning through the dynamics of the Socratic Method by individuals and organizations participating, and (3) moving organizations and individuals participating toward organizational and societal peace. Some limited grants are available to support services to organizations interested in participating in the research. States, cities, schools, and organizations interested are invited to apply.

BRIEF HISTORY

Between 1965 and 1968 the Seattle District Board of Laity of The Methodist Church first experimented with traditional forums. Big meetings at often remote distances using Robert's Rules of Order to pass resolutions was not working well. These were often emotional and frustrating experiences for both people and leaders.

From this effort emerged the prototype of what today is known as the "Fast Forum" technique. There are no motions, no amendments, no win-lose situations, no controversy, no arguments, no talking at the point of decision-making as all talking precedes decision-making—thus there is no emotionalism or heat. Instead, there is just light, that is, swift, silent, rational, synaptic mind-to-mind, response to some idea posed in writing for objective response such as yes, no, abstain, multiple-choice, or value scales. Hence the name, Fast Forum®.

Today the question the foundation is asking is, "What is the role of a citizen, that is, what is the unique contribution of citizenship that leader-representatives and experts cannot do, no matter how great their knowledge nor how good their intentions?" A member of a religious or church group is a citizen of the group, a member of a union or association is a citizen of that group, a member of Rotary International or The Women's International League for Peace and Freedom is a citizen of those groups, and so forth and, of course, a member of society is a citizen of the society. What is the *unique* contribution of citizenship in all those contexts? We in the Forum Foundation believe there are three unique contributions of a citizen. First, to contribute one's opinion, second, to respond to the opinions of one's peers, and third, to respond to the queries of leader-representatives to the solution of those problems which interest and concern oneself. This is a process of *civilization building.*

The Fast Forum® technique, as a new Many-To-Many communication technology using mass means of communication, does not use random-sample, objective questionnaires based on statistical and mathematical theory. Instead it uses objective "Opinionnaires" based on participation and administrative theory. An Opinionnaire® looks much like a typical survey questionnaire, but it is not; different rules apply. We in the foundation are working with scholars to define them. Because we properly disclaim the responses on reports from all participants, the results are 100% valid for those persons participating; they are just as valid as letters and telephone calls and testimony given at public hearings. Thus reports accurately project individual opinions to the questions asked which is every person's right. It's as if those persons participating were meeting at one place in a forum to voice their opinion but instead of meeting physically together, which is not possible, they are meeting symbolically together at a point in time through computer tabulation. Usually this is done in small groups of 4-12 persons meeting at a time and place convenient for themselves such as in their own homes or workplaces. These are places where people already are; they don't have to go someplace to meetings which are often at remote distances for people.

Their conveners receive audio or video tapes from leaders by regular mail, approximately quarterly, but not more than monthly on issues of concern. People review the tape, engage in a structured "study circle" format using a process called "Day-In-the-Sun" to assure each person has an opportunity to speak while others listen. Following this there is open discussion. But before the group leaves, each person responds to an objective Opinionnaire to questions posed for response by Yes, No, Abstain, multiple-choice, or value scale questions. Responses are marked onto Forum Foundation "Councilor" Response Sheets which are machine-scannable. This sheet does the same thing as a computer but for just a fraction of the cost—it allows a human being to interface directly with a machine, accurately, swiftly, and economically. These are returned by mail to the foundation for optical scanning and processing.

In this way hundreds or even thousands of people can "meet" symbolically to try to discover their Zeitgeist, that is, their "Spirit of the Time," (which is their degree of consensus on topics being discussed). The Zeitgeist, the prevailing ideas of a group, institution, or society, is actually the *Supreme Governor;* in a democracy it is that from which is derived not only our laws but our constitutions as well. Thus citizens can participate fully in the "Administrative Process" functions of Diagnosing, Theorizing, and Reviewing. Yet the process takes nothing away from those who are legitimate leaders, either elected or appointed, who still retain all their prerogatives in the "Administrative Process" of Deciding and Accomplishing. Again, this is a democratic process of community and civilization building as leaders and citizens search together for a better future. The process is therapeutic and leads to a reduction in organizational and societal tensions and leads toward peace—and thus toward "happiness." *And this is a fundamental reason for forming all governments, public and private, "For Life, Liberty, and the Pursuit of Happiness!"* Governments are not charged with providing their citizens with all the amenities of life they feel they need to make them happy. But governments are charged with enabling their citizens to pursue their own happiness. Any organization, institution, government, or civilization which inhibits, innocently or not, the free movement of ideas and opinions about those ideas—up, down, and across its organizational and societal structures—is depriving itself of its greatest resource—*human thought*—and is in grave danger of being buried in history by the avalanche of the creativity of others.

K. STUART C. DODD INSTITUTE FOR SOCIAL INNOVATION FACT SHEET

ADDRESS: 4427 Thackeray Place NE;
Seattle, WA 98105-6124
PHONE: (206) 545-0547 Tel;
FAX: (206) 633-3561;
E-MAIL: DrRSKirby@aol.com

Incorporated on May 9, 1997. 501(c)(3) application approved on September 9, 1997.

Purpose:

SCDI/SI encourages scholarly, interdisciplinary research in the archives of Stuart C. Dodd (1900-1975), Professor Emeritus of Social Science at the University of Washington. Scholars pursue the intellectual, moral and civic legacies of Dr. Dodd in the fields of sociology, business administration, education, urban planning, sustainable communities, cosmology, statistics and mathematics. Topics of particular interest include organization development, administrative theory, many-to-many communications and value reporting.

Brief History:

Dr. Dodd published over two hundred scholarly works in his career and is recognized as one of the pioneers in his field. After earning his B.S. (1922), M.A. (1924) and Ph.D. (1926) at Princeton University, Dr. Dodd served as a professor of sociology at American University in Lebanon for twenty years. During World War II, Dr. Dodd served as a Lieutenant Colonel with the American Army in Italy. After the war, he was offered and accepted a position at the University of Washington as a Walker-Ames Professor of Sociology. There he stayed for almost thirty years, and for 14 years was the director of the Washington State Public Opinion Laboratory. During this time, Dr. Dodd was the leading authority on random-sample polling in the Northwest. Among his many accomplishments, Dr. Dodd was the only pollster to predict that President Truman would defeat Governor Dewey in the 1948 election and was later called before Congress to explain what happened. Dr. Dodd's work at the University of Washington continued until his death in 1975.

Principals

REV. DR. RICHARD S. KIRBY, SCDI/SI Executive Director; member of the part-time faculty of the University of Washington's School of Business Administration; former Director of Administration, International Mensa (the high I.Q. society); Chief Executive Officer of the World Network of Religious Futurists; and co-author: The Temples of Tomorrow: World Religions and the Future, Grey Seal, publisher, 1993.

DR. CECIL H. BELL, JR., SCDI/SI Director; former Chair, Department of Management and Organization, School of Business Administration, University of Washington; and co-author: *Organization Development*, 6th Ed., 1998, Prentice-Hall publisher.

JAMES R. SPADY, SCDI/SI Director; SCDI/SI President; Seattle attorney; and businessman.

L. BIBLIOGRAPHY

Arora, Ramesh (Ed.) *Administrative Theory.* New Delhi: Indian Institute Public Administration, 1984

Baker, Richard John Stenson *Administrative Theory and Public Administration.,* London: Hutchinson and Co. Ltd., 1972

Campbell, Roald Fay (Ed.) *Administrative Theory as a Guide to Action.* Midwest Administration Center, University of Chicago, 1960

Ferencz, Benjamin B., *Planethood,* 1988, Coos Bay, Oregon: Vision Books

Griffith, Francis J. *Administrative Theory in Education: Text and Readings.* Midland, Mich.: Pendell, 1979

Griffiths, Daniel Edward *Administrative Theory.* New York: Appleton-Century-Crofts, 1959

Halpin, Andrew W. (Andrew Williams) (Ed.) *Administrative Theory in Education.* Chicago: Midwest Administration Center, University of Chicago, 1958

Interdisciplinary Seminar on Administrative Theory (1961, University of Texas) *Papers Presented at an Interdisciplinary Seminar on Administrative Theory, March 20-21, 1961 at the University of Texas.* Austin: University of Texas, 1961

Kuhn, Robert Lawrence (Ed.) *Generating Creativity and Innovation in Large Bureaucracies.* Westport, Conn.: Quorum Books, 1993

Self, Peter *Administrative Theories and Politics: An Enquiry into the Structure and Processes of Modern Government.* London: Allen & Unwin, 1977

Spady, Richard J. *The Christian Forum or (Fast Forum) Why and What It Is!.* Seattle, Washington, 1969.

Wenk, Edward Jr. *Making Waves,* Urbana and Chicago, University of Illinois Press, 1995.

M. COPYRIGHT INFORMATION

N. INSTRUCTIONS TO ORDER BOOKS

THE SEARCH FOR ENLIGHTENED LEADERSHIP
A TRILOGY: THE CIVILIZATION OF TOMORROW
Volume 1: Applying New Administrative Theory (1996)
ISBN: 1-881908-14-3
Volume 2: Many-To-Many Communication (1998)
ISBN: 1-881908-19-4
Volume 3: The Civilization of Tomorrow (Estimated 2000)

THE SEARCH FOR ENLIGHTENED LEADERSHIP, Volume One: Applying New Administrative Theory and this book *Volume Two: Many-To-Many Communication* are each available for $**19.95** from the **University Bookstore**, 4326 University Way NE, Seattle, WA 98105-1009 in Seattle, Washington. Shipping and handling costs are included for shipments in the United States. (All prices are subject to change without notice.)

Phone: **1-800-335-READ** to order from anywhere in the United States. They will accept VISA, MASTER, and American Express credit cards. For further information call the University Bookstore: (206) 634-3400, General Office; (206) 545-0945.

These books are also available in the Russian translation. For information in the United States contact the Forum Foundation as shown below:

Forum Foundation
4426 Second Ave., N.E.
Seattle, WA 98105-6191 (USA)
Tel: **(206) 634-0420**; or fax **(206) 633-3561** or **<fastforum@aol.com>** via e-mail.

See <http://**weber.u.washington.edu/~forum**>

RICHARD J. SPADY

Richard J. Spady

Dick was born and reared in Portland, Oregon. He served in WWII as a Navy enlisted man and afterwards attended Oregon State University graduating with honors with a Bachelor of Science in Business and Technology in 1950. He then served as an officer in the Air Force during the Korean War and was active in the reserves until 1977. A Seattle businessman since 1954, he cofounded Dick's Drive-In Restaurants and today serves as president of this historic and successful Seattle fast-food chain. From 1965-1968 Dick served as Seattle District lay leader of The Methodist Church. It was here he first began his research. He then attended the University of Washington Graduate School of Business from 1968 to 1970 concentrating in the field of Administrative Theory and Organizational Behavior. It was here as a student that he first developed his administrative theories and designed and developed the "Fast Forum®" computer groupware program. From 1971-1990 he served on the volunteer staff of the Church Council of Greater Seattle with the portfolio of "Futures Research" (not forecasting but the search for ways to influence the sociological and technological future). Thus the religious community of Seattle provided the arena of people and organizations to conduct the research undergirding this book. He has been a Rotarian with an active classification of "Futures Research" since 1980 and was the recipient of the "Earl Award" as "Religious Futurist of the Year 1993" from the World Network of Religious Futurists. He has long been active in community and church affairs and has been an active member of the nonprofit, scientific-educational World Future Society since 1973. Dick and his wife, Ina Lou, have five children now grown.

CECIL H. BELL, JR.

Cecil H. Bell, Jr.

Cecil was born in Nashville, Tennessee and reared in Richland, Washington. He attended University of Puget Sound in Tacoma, Washington where he received a B.A. degree in Biology. He went on to Boston University completing a Masters in Psychology and Ph.D. in Social Psychology and Personality Theory in 1970. He is co-author (with Wendell French) of *Organizational Development*, 6th ed. (Prentice-Hall, 1998) and co-editor (with Wendell French and Robert Zawacki) of *Organization Development: Theory, Practice, and Research* (Irwin, Inc., 4th ed., 1994). Cecil is currently Associate Professor of Management and Organization and most recently Chair of the Management and Organization Department in the School of Business Administration at the University of Washington in Seattle.

P. ENDORSEMENTS

"In *The Search For ENLIGHTENED LEADERSHIP, Volume 2: Many-To-Many Communication* Richard Spady moves his trilogy on enlightened leadership from the theoretic into the more practical aspects of leadership in creating a democratic, healthy society. He has developed new tools that will help leaders everywhere to work democratically and successfully toward societal change. It is a must reading for those in both church and state who hope to be successful, democratic leaders in our modern world."

—REV. DR. WILLIAM B. CATE
President-Emeritus (1970-1990)
Church Council of Greater Seattle

"Congratulations on your paper in Moscow....I am in awe of your sense of commitment and mission in sharing this wonderful way of receiving feedback....The importance of hearing all sides and listening to each other—it's such a vital message."

—REV. JOE A. HARDING
Director of Vision 2000
General Board of Discipleship (1996)
The United Methodist Church

"Over the last year, Dick Spady has really captivated me with his ideas. He has forced me to re-think this business of leadership. He and his colleague, Cecil Bell, have developed civilization-building tools which every leader or would-be leader needs to study, learn and use."

—MR. TIMOTHY E. MOSS, DIRECTOR
Lay Leadership Development
General Board of Discipleship
The United Methodist Church

Sharing and Becoming, A Theological Poem (See Frontispiece 2)

—REV. DR. WILLIAM D. ELLINGTON, PH.D., Theology
Forum Foundation, Co-founder and Board Member
Assoc. Ecclesiastical Professor for United Methodist Ministries,
Fuller School of Theology

Q. PETITION TO PACIFIC NORTHWEST ANNUAL CONFERENCE

Petition to PNW Annual Conference
The United Methodist Church

April 15, 1998

To: Rev. Dan Smith, Director, Conference Council
2112 Third Ave., Suite 300
Seattle, WA 88121-2333

From: Dick Spady, Lay Speaker, St. Peter's UMC, Bellevue, WA

Explanatory Statement:

At the time Rev. Joe Harding was District Supt. of the Seattle District, the District Board of Laity conducted a series of forums to try to improve the overall processes of communication in the church. Attending big meetings with 200 or 300 people using Robert's Rules of Order to pass resolutions was not working well. It was often a frustrating experience for both leaders and people. From this research emerged the prototype of what today is known as the "Fast Forum" technique. There are no Robert's Rules of Order, no motions, no amendments, no win-lose situations, no controversy, no talking at the point of decision-making so there is no heat. Instead there is swift, silent, synaptic mind-to-mind response, to questions posed in **writing** for objective response—yes, no, abstain; multiple-choice; or value scale responses, hence the name "Fast Forum."

In 1970 the Forum Foundation was organized as a non-profit educational research corporation of Washington state. It was founded by United Methodists including the Rev. William D. Ellington, Ph.D., Theology and Dick Spady, Seattle District Lay Leader, 1965-68. They are still active and serve on the board together with the Rev. Dr. William B. Cate (Social Ethics), President-Emeritus of The Church Council of Greater Seattle and Ms. Jan Cate.

A contract was then made with the University of Washington Academic Computer Center to write a computer program known today as "groupware" or "socialware" which facilitates communication among large numbers of people. The research continued through the Church Council of Greater Seattle where Dick served on the volunteer staff (futures research) from 1971-90. He served as agent for UMCom in the early 1980s in the first formation of the "Circuit Writer" electronic network nationally using the computer services available at The University of Washington.

Dick Spady was invited to conduct two workshops at the United Methodist Men's Congress '97 held at Purdue University July 11-13, 1997 on his book *The Search for Enlightened Leadership, Volume 1: Applying New Administrative Theory* (1996). The workshops were well attended and received. While there he presented a new paper titled "The Spiritual Forum Network, *United Methodist Councilor Network* Proposal." This was a proposal to form a national network among interested churches

Petition to PNW Annual Conference April 15, 1998

in systematically studying the UM Book of Resolutions using the Fast Forum technique. It was endorsed by Joe Harding, Bill Ellington, and Bill and Jan Cate. Dick was then invited to meet in October, 1997 in Nashville with leadership teams from both the UM Commission on United Methodist Men and the Global Board of Discipleship to discuss the proposal. A suggestion was made to try this new communication technique at the annual conference level to gain additional research experience before moving to the national level. This petition will effect that suggestion.

Next to the Bible and the Hymnal many people consider the UM Book of Resolutions to be the greatest written treasure of our church. Unfortunately, it may also be the greatest secret. Research has indicated that a majority of United Methodists do not know about the Book of Resolutions and the "Social Principles" from which it is derived. The current 1996 B/R contains 294 resolutions which have been painstakingly crafted to provide a moral sense of direction to (1) individual parishioners, (2) churches, and (3) our society in the areas of the Natural World, Nurturing Community, Social Community, Economic Community, Political Community , and World Community. It was approved by the 1996 General Conference and contains "the official expressions of The United Methodist Church." One-hundred twenty-five (43%) of the resolutions were just passed in 1996. This means that unless we study the B/R systematically, we will not know of the changes since 1992 that have been made to UM theology as it is being applied to the world in which we live.

The Forum Foundation has volunteered to provide the leadership and computer technology using the "Fast Forum" technique to study the Book of Resolutions, without cost to local churches participating, for a two-year research project in the PNW Conference. The project will not require any additional budgeted costs from the PNW Conference or from local churches. The project will have no costs to participants if they have a local church "communicator" who can tabulate responses following simple instructions and send them via e-mail and Internet to the foundation. If there is no communicator available, "Councilor" machine-scannable response sheets can be provided to participants at 25 cents. These can tabulate responses accurately, swiftly, and economically regardless of the number of participants.

The proposal is to study all new resolutions passed in 1996 beginning from the start of the list. Study groups from local churches interested can meet weekly, bi-montly, or monthly to study 1, 2, or 4 resolutions. Participants will be asked only two questions regarding each resolution: First, How appropriate is this resolution? Second, As it is now written, can you ratify this resolution or not? All responses will be e-mailed on Internet or by U.S. Mail by the end of each month to the foundation for tabulation. A "Viewspaper" will then be returned to participating church groups showing the highlights of responses by gender, age, and districts (and possibly by conferences if other conferences participate in the research too which is a possibility).

Petition to PNW Annual Conference April 15, 1998

Be it Resolved:

That the PNW Conference and the Forum Foundation conduct a two-year research program in a study of the 1996 Book of Resolutions beginning in the fall of 1998 with response information and scheduling of studies in advance through the coordinated mailing.

Dick Spady

Rev. William B. Cate (s)

Ms. Jan Cate (s)

(See Explanatory Statement for More Information)

"As human systems and organizations grow ever larger, more complex, and more impersonal in our schools, in our communities, in our churches, in our governments, and in our industries and commerce—the individual shrinks toward facelessness, hopelessness, powerlessness, and frustration."

—DR. STUART C. DODD, Director, Forum Foundation, "Citizen Counselor Proposal" Seattle Times, November 10, 1974.

"Science is the world of what is. Ethics is the world of what ought to be....(There are those who are) in love with the aristocracy of the intellect. And that is a belief which can only destroy the civilization that we know. If we are anything, we must be a democracy of the intellect. We must not perish by the distance between people and government, between people and power."

—DR. JACOB BRONOWSKI, *The Ascent of Man*, p. 435, (1973) Book and TV series.

Freedom of speech, assembly, and petition are hollow rights if, as a practical matter, people feel unable to be heard! Humankind can measure the world of what ought to be and can be the cartographers of human purpose!

RICHARD J. SPADY and CECIL H. BELL, JR.
